DUST AND DREAMS

A Window on The United Arab Emirates

Robin Trounson

A Bright Pen Book

Text Copyright © Robin Trounson 2011

Cover design by Robin Trounson and James Fitt ©

All rights reserved. No part of this publication may be reproduced, stored in a retrieval system, or transmitted in any form or by any means, electronic, mechanical, photocopy, recording or otherwise, without prior written permission of the copyright owner. Nor can it be circulated in any form of binding or cover other than that in which it is published and without similar condition including this condition being imposed on a subsequent purchaser.

British Library Cataloguing Publication Data.
A catalogue record for this book is available from the British Library

ISBN 978-0-7552-1391-7

Authors OnLine Ltd
19 The Cinques
Gamlingay, Sandy
Bedfordshire SG19 3NU
England

This book is also available in e-book format, details of which are available at www.authorsonline.co.uk

Dedicated to Bill O'Connor
1955 – 2010

*My thanks go to all
the team for their friendship and support:
particularly to Mr Baz and Mr John with whom
I embarked upon the adventure; to Mr Gareth
for his companionship on the road; and
to Abu Marcus for his help
and encouragement.*

CONTENTS

NOTE xiv

ACKNOWLEDGEMENT xv

GLOSSARY OF MORE COMMONLY USED ARABIC WORDS... xvi

INTRODUCTION..1

PROLOGUE...5

1. ARABIAN MAGIC...7
Abu Dhabi, 7 October 2008

2. FOOTPRINTS IN THE SAND...8
Abu Dhabi, 13 October 2008

3. OPPORTUNITY KNOCKS..10
Abu Dhabi, 16 October 2008

4. BALM FOR THE SOLE...13
Abu Dhabi, 18 October 2008

5. A TALE OF TWO CITIES...14
Abu Dhabi, 22 October 2008

6. FORBIDDEN LOVE..17
Abu Dhabi, 23 October 2008

7. FLAT HUNTING..19
Abu Dhabi, 26 October 2008

8. FALSE START 20
   Abu Dhabi, 27 October 2008

9. SIGN OF THE TIMES 22
   Abu Dhabi, 28 October 2008

10. THE THIN END OF THE WEDGE 23
   Abu Dhabi, 29 October 2008

11. ALL'S WELL THAT ENDS WELL 24
   Abu Dhabi, 30 October 2008

12. DESPERATE REMEDIES 26
   Abu Dhabi, 2 November 2008

13. FRONT PAGE NEWS 28
   Abu Dhabi, 4 November 2008

14. OLYMPIAN TASK 30
   Abu Dhabi, 7 November 2008

15. THE EMIRATES DIAMOND 31
   Abu Dhabi, 9 November 2008

16. URBAN WARRIOR 32
   Abu Dhabi, 11 November 2008

17. HOMELESS 34
   Abu Dhabi, 12 November 2008

18. SHIFTING SANDS 36
   al Ain, 13 November 2008

19. A FAMILY AFFAIR 38
   al Ain, 16 November 2008

20. THE DUBAI SMILE 38
   Dubai, 17 November 2008

21. THE SPIRIT OF DUBAI 40
Dubai, 21 November 2008

22. LEAPING HORSES 41
al Ain, 22 November 2008

23. REFLECTIONS ON PROGRESS 42
al Ain, 23 November 2008

24. WORKERS OF CHOICE 44
Abu Dhabi, 24 November 2008

25. SLEEPLESS 45
Abu Dhabi, 2 December 2008

26. ZAYED AND THE DREAM 46
Abu Dhabi, 3 December 2008

27. FINAL FRONTIER 48
Abu Dhabi, 13 December 2008

28. A GOODBYE KISS 49
Abu Dhabi, 16 December 2008

29. WORLD IN A SPIN 51
Abu Dhabi, 19 December 2008

30. GOD'S GIFT 52
Abu Dhabi, 23 December 2008

31. GIFTS AND GOODWILL 55
Abu Dhabi, 25 December 2008

32. BEAUTY AND THE BEAST 56
Madinat Zayed, 28 December 2008

33. PUPPET SHOW 58
Abu Dhabi, 1 January 2009

34. HAMMER BLOWS 60
   Abu Dhabi, 9 January 2009

35. VAULTING AMBITION 62
   Abu Dhabi, 16 January 2009

36. GREEN DESERT 64
   Abu Dhabi, 23 January 2009

37. THE AUDACITY OF HOPE 66
   Abu Dhabi, 26 January 2009

38. LEAKING PIPES AND EXPLODING SOCKETS 67
   Abu Dhabi, 6 February 2009

39. SCHADENFREUDE 69
   Abu Dhabi, 7 February 2009

40. MARCH OF TIME 70
   Abu Dhabi, 12 February 2009

41. DOCTOR WHO AND THE SHAMAL 72
   Abu Dhabi, 14 February 2009

42. THE ROAD TO UNION 73
   Semeih, 20 February 2009

43. SHOW OF FORCE 76
   Abu Dhabi, 27 February 2009

44. THE LURE OF THE EAST 77
   Sharjah, 6 March 2009

45. WHEEL OF CHANGE 79
   Abu Dhabi, 12 March 2009

46. THE FIRST DROPS OF RAIN 80
   Abu Dhabi, 27 March 2009

47. OPULENCE AND BLING 82
  Dubai, 3 April 2009

48. ECHOES 83
  Abu Dhabi, 9 April 2009

49. PRIDE AND PREJUDICE 86
  Dubai, 14 April 2009

50. A ONE-ARMED BANDIT 88
  Abu Dhabi, 17 April 2009

51. TALE OF THE UNEXPECTED 89
  Abu Dhabi, 19 April 2009

52. THE ARABIAN OSTRICH 90
  Abu Dhabi, 30 April 2009

53. PICTURES AT AN EXHIBITION 92
  al Ain, 23 May 2009

54. THE DEVIL'S GAP 94
  Ras al Khaimah, 29 May 2009

55. ECLIPSE 95
  Sharjah, 6 June 2009

56. RECRIMINATIONS 98
  Abu Dhabi, 16 June 2009

57. LEAP OF FAITH 99
  Abu Dhabi, 30 June 2009

58. WHAT'S IN A NAME? 101
  Abu Dhabi, 4 July 2009

59. OPEN SECRET 103
  Abu Dhabi, 9 July 2009

60. ABANDON SHIP **105**
   Dubai, 11 July 2009

61. GOAL DIFFERENCE **107**
   Abu Dhabi, 19 July 2009

62. FRUIT PICKING **108**
   Abu Dhabi, 20 July 2009

63. TREE OF LIFE **109**
   Abu Dhabi, 25 July 2009

64. DWELLING IN THE PAST **111**
   Abu Dhabi, 6 August 2009

65. BLANK CANVAS **115**
   Abu Dhabi, 21 August 2009

66. NIGHT OF THE CRESCENT MOON **118**
   Abu Dhabi, 19 September 2009

67. THE RAINBOW SHEIKH **119**
   Shanayl, 26 September 2009

68. THE FALCON AND THE FALCONER **121**
   Abu Dhabi, 2 October 2009

69. LIFE ON MARS **125**
   Abu Dhabi, 6 October 2009

70. GRAND PRIX FEVER **127**
   Abu Dhabi, 16 October 2009

71. THE PEARL FISHERS **128**
   Ras al Khaimah, 23 October 2009

72. COUNTDOWN **131**
   Abu Dhabi, 1 November 2009

73. FIELD OF DREAMS **134**
   Abu Dhabi, 10 November 2009

74. THE DOWNSIDE **136**
   Abu Dhabi, 21 November 2009

75. THE FRUIT BEARING TREE **138**
   Dubai, 11 December 2009

76. IT'S BEGINNING TO LOOK A LOT LIKE CHRISTMAS **142**
   al Ain, 19 December 2009

77. RUBBLE AND DUST **143**
   Fujairah, 25-29 December 2009

78. GOING ROUND THE BEND **146**
   Oman, 30-31 December 2009

79. AN UNEXPECTED TWIST **150**
   Dubai, 9 January 2010

80. THE VIEW FROM SHEBA'S PALACE **152**
   Ras al Khaimah, 15 January 2010

81. DISORIENTATION **155**
   Abu Dhabi, 23 January 2010

82. THE ENVY OF ICARUS **159**
   al Ain, 29 January 2010

83. ON THE ROAD **161**
   Sila, 5 February 2010

84. WAITING FOR GODOT **164**
   Abu Dhabi, 11 February 2010

85. SINDBAD AND THE MOUNTAIN OF COPPER **165**
   Oman, 20-25 February 2010

86. THE MERCY 169
   Abu Dhabi, 5 March 2010

87. GODS, GRAVES AND SCHOLARS 171
   Umm al Quwain, 14 March 2010

88. PRE-NUPTIAL DISAGREEMENT 174
   Dubai, 29 March 2010

89. A STORY OF THE WIND 176
   Abu Dhabi, 3 April 2010

90. TOURIST TRAP 177
   Dubai, 5 April 2010

91. BIRDS OF LIGHT 180
   Abu Dhabi, 8 April 2010

92. COLD COMFORT 182
   Ajman, 10 April 2010

93. THE TERMINAL 186
   Abu Dhabi, 24 April 2010

94. HOSTAGES TO FORTUNE 188
   Abu Dhabi, 1 May 2010

95. THE SHEIKH'S NEW CAR 191
   Abu Dhabi, 6 June 2010

96. THE WRITING ON THE WALL 193
   Ras al Khaimah, 11 June 2010

97. ELEPHANTS BREATHING FIRE 196
   Sharjah, 26 June 2010

98. WISHING ON A STAR 198
   Abu Dhabi, 30 June, 2010

99. THE MOUNTAIN 200
   al Ain, 9 July 2010

100. AN ARAB TRAGEDY 203
   Ras al Khaimah, 17 July 2010

101. CAT AND MOUSE 206
   Abu Dhabi, 20 July 2010

102. IN THE HEAT OF THE NIGHT 207
   Sharjah, 23 July 2010

103. THE DOGS OF WAR 209
   Abu Dhabi, 27 July 2010

104. STITCHES IN TIME 210
   Abu Dhabi, 1 August 2010

105. HARRY POTTER AND THE GARDEN OF PARADISE 213
   Yemen, 6-9 August 2010

106. A PIECE OF THEATRE 218
   Abu Dhabi, 30 August 2010

107. JOURNEY'S ECHO 220
   Abu Dhabi, 1 September 2010

108. THE SLEEPER IN THE SAND 221
   Fujairah, 8 September 2010

109. REPUTATIONS 223
   Abu Dhabi, 11 September 2010

110. A CLOUD ON THE HORIZON 225
   Abu Dhabi, 17 September 2010

111. THE EIGHTH EMIRATE 227
   Abu Dhabi, 18 September 2010

112. THE TEST OF TIME 230
   Abu Dhabi, 29 September 2010

113. SNOW UPON THE DESERT'S DUSKY FACE 232
   Ras al Khaimah, 30 September, 2010

114. IN THE FOOTSTEPS OF IBN BATTUTA 234
   Dubai, 1 October 2010

115. THE LOST WORLD 237
   Oman, 8 October 2010

116. A BURJ-EYE VIEW 240
   Dubai, 22 October 2010

117. THE END OF THE ROAD 243
   Liwa, 27 October 2010

EPILOGUE 248

BIBLIOGRAPHY 251

INDEX 255

NOTE

There is no single system for the transliteration of Arab names and Arabic words into English. So we have Muhammad/Mohammad/Mohammed/Mohamed; Zayed/Zayid; Saeed/Said; Rub' al Khali/Rub al Khali; Ed Dur/al Dur; Sana'a/San'a/Sana; Qur'an/Quran/Koran; shaikh/sheikh/sheyhk; etc. While guided by the principles of convention and consistency, my only rule has been to respect the form in quoted sources.

Where the word *Al* appears in connection with a family or tribal name it is capitalised (e.g. Al Nahyan, Al Maktoum). When used as the definite article it is not (e.g. al Ain, Ras al Khaimah).

Each of the seven emirates in the UAE shares the same name as its own main city. So Abu Dhabi can refer to the city of Abu Dhabi and the wider emirate. The same goes for Ajman, Dubai, Fujairah, Ras al Khaimah, Sharjah and Umm al Quwain. Where necessary I have tried to make the distinction clear.

Translations from the pre-Islamic Golden Odes are taken from *The Seven Golden Odes of Pagan Arabia, known also as The Moallakat (1903)*, by Anne Blunt and Wilfrid Scawen Blunt.

During the period covered (October 2008 - October 2010) the currency exchange rate in the UAE varied from over seven to under five dirhams per pound. For simplicity I have used a single rate of Dh6 to the £. Conversions are approximate.

ACKNOWLEDGEMENT

Extracts from Wilfred Thesiger's *Arabian Sands* are taken from the Penguin Classics 2007 edition with the kind permission of Penguin UK.

GLOSSARY OF MORE COMMONLY USED ARABIC WORDS

Abaya: long, loose outer garment worn by women
Aflaj (sing. Falaj): traditional irrigation system of subterranean water channels
Salaam alaykum: Peace be unto you
Barasti: a house built of palm fronds.
Ghazu: a raid
Ghutra: cloth head covering worn by men
Inshallah: If God wills it
Kandoura: long-sleeved, ankle-length shirt worn by men
Majlis: an audience, meeting or meeting place
Sabkah: desert salt flats
Sheyla: headscarf worn by women

Proverbs are the lamp of speech
  - Arabic proverb

INTRODUCTION

In the old airport museum in Sharjah there are some photographs of British RAF servicemen at leisure. For the most part they spent their spare time swimming and sailing, reading books and newspapers, and writing long letters home. Substitute driving for sailing and email for letter-writing and their list of pastimes is not far removed from my own in Abu Dhabi half a century or so later.

When I arrived in the United Arab Emirates I knew little about the country beyond Sheikh Mohammed of Dubai's global reputation for horse-racing and Abu Dhabi's new fondness for English premiership football. But a two-year contract of employment as an advisor to Abu Dhabi Police left ample time to explore. So I would read and travel and relate my impressions in long emails home. This diary-cum-travelogue is the fruit of my experience.

Like many a visitor I was immediately struck by the scale and pace of change in the emirates. Within living memory there were few permanent buildings, no schools or surgeries, let alone universities or hospitals, and not a yard of tarmac road: now the country boasts the tallest building in the world and is fast developing the infrastructure to become a global hub for knowledge, culture, sport and tourism. Yet there is a parallel dimension in which change is not rapid but slow. Islam has long been the bedrock beneath Arabia's shifting sands and Arabic – the language of God in the Quran – the music of its soul. Today, for all their urban sophistication, the descendants of the Bedouin still live by a desert creed, cling to customs fashioned by their remote ancestors, and embellish speech with proverbs rooted in Arab and Islamic tradition. Skyscrapers may fill the eye – but modern life constantly reverberates with echoes of the past.

My story begins in *Shawwal* (the month in which camels are traditionally got in calf) in the year 1429 – that is to say, October 2008 in the Western calendar. Muslims count the passing years from the time an Arab merchant and his followers fled persecution in the city of Mecca and travelled some

250 miles north to a small oasis settlement that came to be known as Madinat al Nabi – the City of the Prophet – or simply Medina. The year of their *hijra* (migration) – AD622 – marks the start of the Islamic era. It happened at a moment of all too familiar disunity in the Arab world when modernity rubbed against tradition. Since time immemorial the tribes of Arabia had sustained themselves with collective values which emphasised compassion and common good. In the new mercantile societies of the cities individuals competed for wealth and ideals of social justice became lost in a growing gap between rich and poor. Muhammad preached *Islam* (surrender) to Al-Lah (God) and social justice to one other.

Within a year of the Prophet's death Islam had been consolidated across all Arabia, providing his followers (Muslims) with a code for living in which day to day practicalities from birth to burial were integrated with divine submission – so creating harmony and unity in God. For preservation and support people collaborated in tribes, sub-divided into clans with nominal ancestral links. Members had a right to protection and a duty to serve. To insult or injure one was to insult or injure a whole tribe and would incur collective revenge. Similarly dishonour by one brought shame on all and could lead to an individual being cast out: reputation was life itself. Each tribe had its own territory, albeit boundaries were blurred, within which members pursued a settled or nomadic existence. But tribal tradition tended to be anarchic and conflict between tribes was endemic.

On the coast of the lower Gulf, under the maritime protection of the British government in India from 1820, people lived by fishing, pearling and trade. In the desert, where the Bedouin cultivated dates and reared sheep, goats and camels, there was no such protection and blood-feuds and grab-raids (*ghazus*) were part and parcel of tribal life. God determined fate but governance was entrusted to sheikhs for whom plots, murder and insurgency were occupational hazards. At a domestic level a man would have a *majlis* in which to receive male visitors while the women of the family lived in a segregated area called a *harim*. Society was patriarchal and roles were strictly delineated. Much of the work was done by slaves.

So might life in the Trucial States (i.e. those emirates which had treaties of maritime protection with Britain) have continued but for oil. As early as 1922 the Trucial rulers promised not to grant oil concessions to any company not appointed by the British government. For the coastal-based sheikhs, who mostly welcomed the idea of opening their hinterlands to foreign prospectors, it marked the start of a more assertive relationship with the independent tribes of the interior. For the British it marked a shift of policy; hitherto they had largely confined their attention to economic interests and peace-keeping at sea. After oil was discovered in commercial quantities in Bahrain in 1932 the search moved along the coast. Deals were done inviting foreign companies upon the land – the first to grant a concession was Dubai in 1937; Sharjah signed in the same year and Abu Dhabi in 1939; agreements with Ras al Khaimah, Umm al Quwain, Ajman and Fujairah were delayed until after the Second World War – and borders were fixed (albeit not without dispute), so transforming ill-defined tribal territories into discrete sovereign states.

For the sheikhs, whose incomes had been greatly diminished by the collapse of the pearl market following the Wall Street crash of 1929 and subsequent development of cultured pearls in Japan, oil royalties could hardly have come at a better time. And there remained, of course, the possibility of far greater riches. But first they had to endure more than two decades of false starts and frustrated hopes.

In the northern emirates hardly any oil was found but Abu Dhabi started exporting from an offshore field in 1962 and exports from Dubai began seven years later. In the interim benevolent sheikhs restored ancient *aflaj* (man-made irrigation channels) and built the first hospitals and schools. Over time red hot cauterising irons were banished by modern medicine and classes were no longer held under the shade of a tree. Camels were slowly superseded by motor vehicles; even before tarmac roads were laid journeys which had taken a week by camel could be accomplished by car or truck in a single day. And gradually hair tents and *barasti* (palm-frond) huts were replaced by concrete houses with electricity and plumbing.

Oil alone, however, would have brought limited benefit. In Abu Dhabi Sheikh Shakhbut hoarded banknotes rather than spend until they were consumed by infestation. Only when his brother assumed power in 1966 did the people of Abu Dhabi begin to enjoy the fruits of oil.

'I want five years' development to be achieved in one year,' said Sheikh Zayed – so dictating a pace of change that has continued largely unabated ever since.

In Sharjah the old RAF station has long been lost among the concrete towers of the modern city centre. Every day thousands of motorists commute along the runway from which British aircraft were deployed on secret missions over Cold War Europe, while on the beach where airmen and maintenance crews once resorted to swim there's a new maritime museum and aquarium. The turning-point came in 1971 when the British government withdrew its military forces from the Persian Gulf. The rulers of Sharjah and six other abandoned emirates put differences behind them and united under the leadership and oil wealth of Sheikh Zayed

'to promote a better life, more enduring stability and a higher international status for the Emirates and their people ... desiring also to lay the foundation for federal rule in the coming years on a sound basis ... and progressing by steps towards a comprehensive, representative, democratic regime in an Islamic and Arab society free from fear and anxiety.'

Dust is already settling on the window I opened. In Abu Dhabi work never stops to realise President Khalifa bin Zayed's dream of 'a great world metropolis' and, despite the downturn, key projects continue elsewhere. As the UAE prepares to celebrate its 40th anniversary, however, it generates the largest environmental footprint in the world, people gorge themselves on fast food and diabetes is rife, expats drive the economy, unemployment among young nationals is rising, and democracy gets barely a nod. There are also questions about inadequate public utilities, economic imbalance and the long term viability of the union. With wealth concentrated in Abu Dhabi and trade and business centred on Dubai, the other five lag ever further behind.

But any threat to political stability only serves to increase the prospect of a more integrated model of development in the future. Given the country's extraordinary capacity for construction, modernising national infrastructure will be the easy part. Persuading people to take a more responsible attitude towards health, education, work and the environment will likely prove more challenging.

PROLOGUE
Northern Arabia, May 1877

Promises made in the night be not binding by daylight
- Arabic proverb

In the parched wilderness a lone Englishman travelling with a caravan of Bedouin finds his old camel too feeble to carry him any further. It is early summer, the air is dry and suffocating: the very Earth appears to faint. Water, food and grazing are scarce and during the day the temperature rises to over 40C. 'We seemed to breathe flames,' he said.

Sand and gravel give way to black mountains of basaltic lava. As they begin to climb steep cragged paths the Bedouin dismount and lead their labouring animals on foot. The traveller alights too, but, overcome by hunger, thirst and the scorching sun, he is as jaded as his toothless mount. 'A long dying without death,' is how he remembered it. So he rides upon a hired camel and is openly derided by the babbling daughter of its owner. 'Heathen! Christian! Jew!' she chides – every step of the way.

As the sun sets, the Bedouin strike camp. Fires are lit, coffee pots put to boil and beans to roast. Twenty-four hours have passed since our weary traveller last had food and rest. But moonlight redeems and moods mellow. To silence the girl's torments the traveller makes a play for her hand in marriage, and intoxicated with coffee and tobacco the Bedouin agree to hire him the camel to continue the ascent next morning. Yet sleep comes uneasily. In the darkness he overhears one Arab suggest to another that they kill him for his baggage. And come morning the Bedouin quote a proverb to renege on their night-time agreement to lend him the camel.

The story comes from Charles Montagu Doughty's nineteenth century travelogue, *Travels in Arabia Deserta*, which was commended by T. E. Lawrence as 'the first and indispensable work upon the Arabs of the desert.' The world Doughty describes is stuck in Time: the people are unchanging, the landscape eternal. The life he shares with the Bedouin – 'with their tents, their camels, and their flocks' – comes straight from the pages of the

Old Testament. As befits one who travels to seek knowledge, he expresses neither anger nor resentment towards his companions for their broken promise. Resigned to perpetual hardship, abuse and deceit, Doughty merely speculates that the proverb invoked may be so old as to have pre-Islamic origins, belonging to a time when desert-dwellers drank wine at night and made rash promises when drunk which they would afterwards disavow in the cold light of morning.

All of which is a far cry from modern industrialised Arabia epitomised by the tall towers, luxury tourist resorts and theme parks of the UAE – or maybe not …

1. ARABIAN MAGIC
Abu Dhabi, 7 October 2008

As 'tis prepared with art, so one should drink it with art
- Arabic proverb

Falling stock markets in the Gulf states dominate today's newspaper headlines, suggesting that while I can leave the gloomy weather behind there's no escaping the financial crisis which is undermining the economies of Europe, America and Asia.

I have arrived in Abu Dhabi with two other former UK police officers. Others have been here for several years and more are on their way. We are joining a mission to improve the performance of the emirate's police force: to draw on our experience to advise and coach its officers and, in the language of the legendary Colonel Lawrence, 'batter and twist them into something they, of their own accord, would not have been.' Yet he who supported the Arabs in their revolt against the Turks counselled against others setting out 'to prostitute themselves and their talents in serving another race.' Disillusioned and ashamed by what he considered to be a betrayal of his ideal to forge a new Arab nation, Lawrence wrote of being caught in a void between 'two customs, two educations, two environments,' and being left with a feeling of 'contempt, not for other men, but for all they do.'

Knowing little about what's expected of us apart from our themes, we are not burdened by missionary zeal. My role will be to advise on performance management: a Western world of targets and key indicators pressed upon the force by a modernising government. As to what the job entails, only time will tell. Meanwhile a meeting with the team leader this morning may give something of a clue – but first comes a ritual rooted in the Bedouin code of hospitality.

Traditionally the guarantee of coffee, food and a bed for the night in the scattered communities of the desert ensured the health, safety and protection of travellers. In today's air-conditioned government offices tradition persists. Only after coffee is served can business begin. Each of us is handed a small bowl no bigger than an egg cup in which spiced coffee is then poured from a tall long-spouted pot called a *della*. The coffee is cardamom flavoured, pale and bitter; sweet, sticky dates prove the perfect complement. We sip under a watchful gaze and the moment the first cup is drained more coffee is poured. To interrupt the pattern the cup should be held out and wiggled between thumb and forefinger. I have heard that a third cup confers a blessing and drink one more.

'Where no coffee is,' wrote Charles Doughty, 'There is not merry company.'

In his desert travels he was often greeted by the rhythmical ring of roasted beans being pounded in a mortar; the same welcoming sound was remarked upon by the Gulf diplomat Edward Henderson over half a century later. But there was an occasion when Doughty came upon 'an uncheerful village' which had run out of coffee.

'Their coffee hearths now cold,' he observed, 'Every man sat drooping and dull.'

'This was the life of the old nomads in the days before coffee,' explained his Arab companion.

Not so now. This morning the chattering laughter of officers in police headquarters drowns any rhythmical ring and belies the economic gloom.

Such is the magic of Arabian coffee – or oil, perhaps?

2. FOOTPRINTS IN THE SAND
Abu Dhabi, 13 October 2008

Any water in the desert will do
- Arabic proverb

Legend has it that a gazelle guided the first Bedouin settlers to where the city of Abu Dhabi now stands.

A party of tribesmen from the oasis of Liwa – some 230 kilometres (144 miles) south-west of the modern capital – was hunting near the coast one day when they spotted some hoof prints in the sand. So they followed the tracks to the edge of a shallow channel of water. Beyond lay an island shrouded in mist where they resumed the trail. This must have gone on for some time because they had travelled almost the entire length of the island before the mist lifted to reveal a gazelle drinking at a brackish spring. When they reported back to their leader, Sheikh Diyab bin Isa Al Nahyan, he ordered that the water should be harnessed and that the place should be called Abu Dhabi, which literally means father of the gazelle. In another account the island is dubbed Umm Dhabi, or mother of the gazelle.

There are other versions, too, but central to each is the discovery of a source of drinkable water and the leading role of the Al Nahyan family. Fresh water allowed settlement and the Al Nahyans, who rule Abu Dhabi to this day, saw the opportunity of supplementing date farming and camel husbandry in the desert with seasonal exploitation of the rich pearl banks in the Gulf.

So it was in 1761 that a well was dug on the island and a watchtower built to protect it. As families migrated from the interior a village grew and in 1795 Sheikh Diyab's son, Sheikh Shakhbut, incorporated the watchtower into a small fort which became his principal residence and seat of government for the federation of tribes known as the Bani Yas. The rest, as they say, is history.

The much renovated and extended descendant of Shakhbut's original fort – Qasr al Hosn – remains as a rare relic of Abu Dhabi's pre-industrial age, set in a large square dwarfed on all sides by towering office blocks, apartments and shops and encircled by traffic-choked streets. But the Emiratis' love of hunting is as keen as ever. This week I joined thousands of visitors at an International Hunting and Equestrian Exhibition hosted by Abu Dhabi's National Exhibitions Company (ADNEC) where there were enough rifles, shotguns, knives and cross-bows – many elaborately engraved and embellished with silver and gold – to equip an army. There were also beauty competitions for Saluki hunting dogs and purebred Arabian horses, while an auction of falcons prompted a winning bid of Dh100,000 (£16,666) for a single bird.

In the mythological accounts of the founding of the city, it's not clear what happened to the gazelle. But the fate of its descendants, which have only recently been granted protection, suggests a likely end: for the native gazelle, once abundant across the deserts of Arabia, now only survives in the wild in isolated groups: its numbers severely depleted by modern hunting with rifles and four-wheel-drive vehicles; and the whole species brought to the brink of extinction by human exploitation of its natural habitat.

Happily the indigenous sand gazelle and similarly endangered Arabian oryx now thrive in private nature reserves on the mainland and islands of Abu Dhabi and in the public wildlife park in al Ain.

3. OPPORTUNITY KNOCKS
Abu Dhabi, 16 October 2008

Poverty in one's homeland is estrangement; wealth in exile is a homeland
- Arabic proverb

Emiratis are a minority in their own country. Traditionally they prefer others to do the work, which is why some 80% of the resident population and 88% of the workforce are expatriates.

For centuries the inhabitants of the lower Gulf bought slaves to do their labour. The practice was condoned by the Quran and continued unimpeded until the importation of slaves by sea was outlawed by the British in 1847. Even then many Africans continued to arrive overland via traders in Oman, and in the 1920s civil war and famine in Central Asian Baluchistan led to an exodus of Baluchis in search of work, many of whom found themselves kidnapped and enslaved in the emirates. A Baluchi slave in the royal household was complicit in the attempted murder of the ruling sheikh of Abu Dhabi in 1928. When visiting a village near al Ain in late 1948 Sir Wilfred Thesiger secured the release of a young Arab who had been kidnapped after being shipwrecked in the Gulf and was then awaiting collection by a slave dealer from Saudi Arabia. A few days later, when travelling near Liwa, he came across the tracks of a caravan of forty-eight slaves belonging to the same dealer returning home where American oil money was driving up demand. Not until 1963 was slavery abolished.

Today slaves have been replaced by expats. Many administrative and management jobs in the public sector are carried out by non-Gulf Arabs. Americans and Europeans tend to be employed in advisory and specialist posts, while Indians, Pakistanis, Bangladeshis, Sri Lankans, Filipinos and other Asian nationals labour in the construction, hospitality and service industries. In all there are said to be expatriate workers from over two hundred countries, most lured by the prospect of earning more money here than would be possible at home.

At the top of the tree there are not only lucrative tax-free salaries but a quota of paid return flights home, free healthcare, free schooling, subsidised accommodation and abundant holidays. Sun, sea and shopping malls provide a host of options for exercise, rest and play, while the location of the country allows easy access to the rest of the Arab world, Europe, India and Asia. Although money must enter the reckoning, the attraction for higher earners is as likely to be experience, opportunity and lifestyle.

At my hotel I ask an Indian employee of a French oil pipeline company what brought him here.

"Greater exposure to the world," he says.

There's a pause …

"But the money's useful too," he adds.

But the benefits don't come without sacrifice. An Italian sighs as he enters the hotel lift one morning and I glance to see if he's ok.

"I'm thinking of my family," he explains, and his eyes well with tears.

A Filipino concierge, poorly educated and without professional qualifications, tells me he is paid as much here as a schoolteacher in the Philippines. So they labour on building sites, sweep the streets (a futile exercise, because for every speck of dust removed two others quickly return), gather stinking refuse, water gardens, weed flowerbeds, serve petrol, wash cars, launder clothes, cut hair, drive taxis, work in shops, bars, hotels, cafes and restaurants, clean homes and look after children – all to support their families back home.

'The United Arab Emirates is a land of opportunity,' says the Minister of Economy, 'People come here to realise their dreams.'

But dreams can turn sour. A thirty year old Nepalese man called Keshab, who is employed as a porter at Abu Dhabi airport, was recently profiled in a newspaper article. He has been here for a year, works 12-hour shifts six days a week and earns Dh700 (£116) a month, of which he sends Dh500 (£83) to his wife and four year old daughter in Nepal. He telephones home about once a month (more if tips permit) and will not be eligible for his first paid visit home for another year. In the meantime he shares a bedroom and small kitchen with eighteen other workers. He says he doesn't mind the hard work or cramped living conditions but worries that he barely earns enough to support his family.

My thoughts return to Keshab this morning as I'm driven to a government building to sign a contract and so join the ranks of expatriates. Early fog has given way to scorching sun and in the short walk from the car my forehead quickly grows damp.

If he's lucky Keshab will be working inside today: loading and unloading bags in the X-ray department or helping passengers with their luggage. If not he'll be working outside on trolley collection and will not be allowed indoors all day.

Slaves were often well treated, as prescribed by the Quran, and some rose to high positions. In the late 1860s two half-brothers, one the son of a slave, were joint rulers of Sharjah. An African slave named Bakhit bin Saeed was appointed wali (administrator) of Dibba by the ruler of Sharjah in the 1920s. Another called Barut governed Sharjah's enclave of Kalba for several decades. Thesiger encountered a slave with similar responsibility in Saudi Arabia and tells with graphic detail of another dressed in an expensive robe whom he observed in the role of executioner.

4. BALM FOR THE SOLE
Abu Dhabi, 18 October 2008

Tolerance is generosity. Tolerance is a sign of faith.
- the Prophet Muhammad

If I was to be asked to give just one reason for visiting Abu Dhabi I would have no hesitation in nominating the Sheikh Zayed bin Sultan Al Nahyan Mosque.

Forget tall towers, turquoise seas and marble shopping malls. By all means come and bask in the sun or watch it set over the Arabian Gulf. Explore the desert by four-wheel-drive and ride a camel if you wish. But all such attractions can be enjoyed elsewhere.

For an experience truly unique you must visit the Sheikh Zayed Mosque – even though the finishing touches have yet to be completed. And if this sounds unduly promotional, I make no apology but simply say come soon before it gets too popular.

If it's statistics you want – its basic dimensions, the number of columns and arches and domes, the height of its minarets, its capacity and the cost of construction – turn to the internet. Better still – come and measure and count for yourself. Rest assured: it is elegant and imposing, rich and sumptuous, a feast for the eyes and balm for the soles of bare feet.

To give you an idea of its size, the main prayer hall contains the largest hand-woven carpet in the world. I'm told that when it was delivered it weighed about 46 tons. Now it would weigh just 39 tons – the difference being the offcuts removed to accommodate the many columns.

For architectural symmetry and beauty of design it invites comparison with India's Taj Mahal. For ornament and decoration it draws from the same Islamic motifs. But for concept and symbolism Shah Jehan's memorial to his beloved wife Mumtaz Mahal pales beside Sheikh Zayed's founding vision for dialogue between different religions, civilisations and cultures.

Although the late sheikh happens to be buried here, Abu Dhabi's Grand Mosque is no mere mausoleum. It was built for the living, for those of the country's official religion and for those of other faiths, too. For it was Sheikh Zayed's wish that contrary to local custom non-Muslims should be allowed entry to encourage cross-cultural understanding and to reflect the true spirit of Islam as a religion of tolerance, peace and education.

'Islam is a civilising religion that gives man dignity,' he said, 'A Muslim is he who does not inflict evil on others. Islam is the religion of tolerance and forgiveness, of dialogue and understanding, and not of war.'

While the iconic towers of Abu Dhabi may catch the eye and sunshine gladden the heart, the Sheikh Zayed Mosque promotes a universal vision that appeals not simply to the spirit but also to the imagination.

Abu Dhabi's Grand Mosque is said to be the size of five football pitches and capable of accommodating 40,960 worshippers. It has eighty-two 24 carat gold-topped domes of Moroccan design, under the largest of which hangs the biggest chandelier in the world (15 metres high, 10 metres in diameter, and weighing 9 tons); four minarets, each about 107 metres tall, also burnished with gold; over a thousand marble-clad columns inlaid with lapis lazuli, red agate, amethyst, abalone shell and mother of pearl; eighty hand-crafted ceramic wall tiles and 7,874 square metres of tiled pools; twenty-eight types of marble, mainly from Greece, Macedonia, Italy, India, and China; and that enormous carpet – crafted by 1,200 pairs of hands in small villages in Iran, brought to Abu Dhabi in pieces, and re-stitched in situ by the same hands.

5. A TALE OF TWO CITIES
Abu Dhabi, 22 October 2008

A single source of income is bad
- Arabic proverb

"Abu Dhabi?" said my father quizzically when I told him of plans to work in the Gulf, "I thought that was a made-up name."

But almost the very next day it became a household name in the UK when a group of Abu Dhabi businessmen announced plans to buy a controlling interest in Manchester City Football Club. It was the latest in a flurry of investments by Abu Dhabi in sport, film and culture. All of which begs the question, 'What's going on?'

The answer lies in government plans for diversifying the economy. When oil was first discovered here in 1958 there was little more than an old fort, a scattering of *barasti* houses and a small souk. Since then revenue from oil and gas has transformed Abu Dhabi into one of the richest cities in the world. Oil exports last year generated over $260 billion. And with some 8% of the world's known oil and over 3% of natural gas, the emirate has enough reserves to last for another ninety years. But while hydrocarbon energy remains the cornerstone of the economy, the revenue it generates is increasingly being invested in new sectors of productivity.

'We must not rely on oil alone as the main source of our national income,' said the late Sheikh Zayed, 'We have to diversify the sources of our revenue and construct economic projects that will ensure a free, stable and dignified life for the people.'

Construction continues 24 hours a day. Over breakfast at my hotel one morning a civil engineer from the UK who specialises in building foundations for tower blocks told me that over a third of the world's tower cranes are currently based in the UAE. Cheap energy already fuels thriving domestic aluminium, petrochemical and fertiliser industries. Now there are plans to open two steel manufacturing plants. Meanwhile property development drives the retail and service sectors. Attracted by the tax-free economy, lifestyle and investment opportunities, the population of Abu Dhabi has risen sharply and is expected to double in the next ten years.

But tourism is still in its infancy – which is where Manchester City fits in. It's part of an overseas investment strategy. The acquisition of an English premiership football club is calculated to raise Abu Dhabi's profile and so help attract three times as many visitors – 7.9 million a year by 2030 – and more foreign investment. And there will be plenty for the anticipated waves of tourists to see if models, pictures and plans at the Emirates Palace are anything to go by.

Government-owned, this luxury Moorish-style hotel is Abu Dhabi's shop window to the world. Set beside the sea, above green gardens with fountains, cascades and avenues of palms, visitors are transported to ancient Cordoba. In vast halls of marble and gold hang over a thousand crystal chandeliers, while under its great dome all the shades of the desert are reflected in countless hues of bronze. And if staring open-mouthed should bring on a thirst, a cappuccino can be had – sprinkled with tiny flecks of gold.

The Emirates Palace is currently hosting exhibitions about major developments for tourism on Yas Island and neighbouring Saadiyat Island. In November next year the Yas Marina Circuit will host the Etihad Airways Abu Dhabi Grand Prix, the final race of the season.

> We will Welcome the World

is the banner headline, and a glossy brochure promises 'the most beautiful, innovative and luxurious motor sport circuit ever built' – which, judging by the table top model and computer-generated images, I can well believe. And after the Grand Prix puts Yas Island on the world map of major sporting arenas, a cluster of galleries, museums and theatres on Saadiyat Island is set to transform Abu Dhabi into a city of culture. The Guggenheim Abu Dhabi – the largest Guggenheim in the world – will be dedicated to modern and contemporary art, while the Louvre Abu Dhabi will house classical pieces and temporary international exhibitions. There will also be a performing arts centre, and national and maritime museums to celebrate the UAE's own culture and heritage. In each case the unique architecture and design of the building is likely to prove as big a draw as anything it contains. The models alone are breath-taking.

Nor is Yas simply about the Grand Prix or Saadiyat merely about culture. At the Ferrari World theme park a 65 metre-high 'G Force Tower' will allow two people to race against each other at speeds similar to those achieved on the racing circuit next door. And in a water park, as adventurous tourists test their nerve on the 'Giant Maelstrom' and 'Hurricane Ride,' the more timid will be able to relax in the 'Bubba Tub' or 'Lazy River.' Meanwhile on Saadiyat Island, should tourists want a break from visiting galleries, museums and theatres, there will be hotels, cafes and restaurants, beaches, marinas and a golf course.

In 1877 Charles Doughty was asked by Mohammed ibn Rashid, the Emir of Hail and most powerful of all the Bedouin sheikhs of Arabia, whether the fame of his dominion had reached as far as Europe. Hail was then a major watering hole on the pilgrim trail to Mecca and Emir Mohammed was piqued to hear Doughty say that few people at home had heard of his desert kingdom.

'It is time to shut the doors,' he said, drawing the audience to a close.

To escape obscurity Abu Dhabi is opening its doors and just as the dusty travellers who walked the buried streets of Babylon must have stood and gazed in wonder, so visitors here will stand transfixed long after the oil runs out – and never again shall anyone say, 'Abu Dhabi? I thought that was a made-up name.'

In 2011 Abu Dhabi's Etihad Airways signed a 10-year extension to their sponsorship of Manchester City Football Club. The original deal, signed in 2009, provided for shirt sponsorship and was worth $3.7 million a year. The new contract extends beyond shirts to ground naming rights, which is how Eastlands came to be called the Etihad Stadium. The parties involved were reluctant to disclose the cost but Abu Dhabi's National newspaper reckoned it was up to three times the previous English premiership record set when Dubai's Emirates Airlines signed a 15-year deal with Arsenal in 2004 worth Dh589 million (£98.2m). Abu Dhabi was probably delighted to score one over its neighbour. 'The Blues' too – until fans of their more famous Manchester rival pointed out that Etihad is Arabic for 'United.'

6. FORBIDDEN LOVE
Abu Dhabi, 23 October 2008

Esteem finds love but love doesn't always find esteem
- Arabic proverb

The late Sheikh Zayed bin Sultan Al Nahyan, ruler of Abu Dhabi and first President of the UAE, is still much revered.

He was one of the two architects of union in 1971/72 and is popularly regarded as the Father of the Nation. It's said that during a health scare in 1999 when medical tests confined him to hospital he received a 'Get Well

Soon' and 'Thank You' letter signed by a million and a half UAE citizens.

The much loved sheikh still keeps a paternal eye over the emirate. His portrait hangs in the lobby of my hotel in the middle of a triptych of large gold-framed photographs. Looking aside with one eye-brow raised, he looks suitably removed from the ordinary comings and goings below. On one side he is flanked by his eldest son Sheikh Khalifa, the current ruler of Abu Dhabi and UAE President, who looks away. On the other side is another son, Sheikh Mohammed, the Crown Prince of Abu Dhabi, who stares one straight in the eye. It's a pattern repeated across the capital on public billboards, in government offices, shopping malls and even small shops.

Sheikh Khalifa and the Crown Prince are also frequently depicted with Sheikh Mohammed bin Rashid Al Maktoum, ruler of Dubai and Vice-President of the UAE, whose fame extends far beyond the Gulf to racecourses in Europe, America, Australia and Japan. For the people of the emirates their ubiquitous images are welcome symbols of the ideal tribal leader described in the pre-Islamic ode of Lebid ibn Rabia:

> *A just judge, a tribe-sheykh, wise, fair-worded, bountiful,*
> *sweet of face to all men, feared by the warriors.*

But some citizens are taking their love too far. Police in Abu Dhabi and Dubai have announced a crackdown on motorists who display photographs of the sheikhs on their car windows and number plates.

'Their love for the rulers should be in their hearts,' warns a senior police spokesman.

A fine of Dh200 (£33) and one penalty point await any transgressors.

7. FLAT HUNTING
Abu Dhabi, 26 October 2008

The pleasure of food and drink lasts an hour,
of sleep a day, of women a month, but of a building a lifetime
- Arabic proverb

'Sun Tower: Where The World Revolves Around You.'

I am reading from a brochure for a new apartment block being built on Reem Island, some 300 metres off the coast of Abu Dhabi island.

The Sun Tower will be next to the Sky Tower, which according to the author of the brochure is the most prestigious address in town. While second best would not be to everyone's satisfaction, prospective purchasers of apartments in the Sun Tower will probably be encouraged by news that it will share a fitness and leisure centre with its superior neighbour, and a shopping mall, cafe and restaurants.

With its elliptical shape lending 'a futuristic perspective,' the Sun Tower is described as a '65-storey architectural masterpiece ... home to elegant residential spaces with captivating views of the Gulf and Abu Dhabi skyline ... luxurious yet affordable ... for those who like to make a statement in life.' What's more, it's handy for both the city centre, five minutes' drive, and the airport, half an hour away: perfectly positioned, boasts the brochure, for 'upper crust living.' Close by stand another half-dozen incomplete structures and I have heard it said that when development is complete Reem Island will have more towers than Manhattan.

Despite the recent boom in construction, finding reasonable, affordable accommodation in the capital is all but impossible.

"A nightmare," is how one colleague described it, and everyone else who has shared their experience has spoken of difficulties, stress and expense.

"So far I've looked at twenty-eight properties and have yet to find somewhere suitable" said a Sudanese sales consultant who has recently switched jobs from Dubai to Abu Dhabi, "Annual rent for a one-bedroom flat in a villa is Dh110, 000 (£18,333)."

And she works for a real estate company – selling apartments on Reem Island.

I was warned of the problem before I ever left the UK so you can imagine my relief when I learnt on arrival that Abu Dhabi Police has decided to provide a block of apartments to accommodate any new expatriate advisers.

A couple of days ago I ventured to the suburbs to take a look at it. Like the Sun Tower it is not yet finished, but that's about all they have in common. The police tower is not nearly as tall. Nor is it likely to be as elegant, although it's hard to tell with scaffolding front and back. And by no stretch of the imagination, despite four rows of palm trees to shield it from the road, could the views be described as captivating.

But I have to admit that, with an eight-lane highway and bus stops out in front, a school and construction site close behind, shops and offices below, and flanked as it is by almost two dozen similar residential towers, each having at street level its own permutation of laundries, banks, tailors and car repairers, grocers, barbers, bakers, cafes and restaurants, I may well get that Sun Tower feeling – that the world is revolving around me.

8. FALSE START
Abu Dhabi, 27 October 2008

Haste is of the devil
- Arabic proverb

"You're not required tomorrow," said our liaison officer yesterday, "So you can have a lie-in."

Work has got off to a false start. Last week I had an afternoon meeting and a day's training. This week – so far, nothing. Little can be done until we have residency visas and contracts of employment.

"They'll be sitting on someone's desk," we are told, "And if that person is away nothing will be done until they return."

Delayed by the upward referral of his request to excavate in southern Arabia in the 1950s, the American archaeologist Wendell Phillips observed that making people wait is 'a favourite pastime in all the Arab world.'

So I spend my days exploring the high-rise streets and palm-lined avenues of the city, grid by grid on foot and by free public bus, invariably stopping for coffee and a scan of the newspapers along the way, perhaps calling into the Cultural Foundation to visit the library or listen to an impromptu recital by the resident Ukrainian pianist.

This morning I forgo the opportunity for a lie-in and take a bus to the start of the UAE Desert Challenge, the final leg of the World Cross-Country Rally Championship, which begins this morning not in the desert but at the Emirates Palace.

In the grounds of the hotel riders, drivers and navigators are making the final adjustments to motorcycles, quad bikes and modified four-wheel-drive vehicles. Among them is the prime minister of the Russian republic of Tatarstan at the wheel of a giant truck. Twenty vehicles took part in the inaugural event in 1991. This year there are a 115 and each is equipped with a satellite navigation system to guide it across the trackless sands of the infamous Rub al Khali (literally Quarter of Emptiness), which is just as well because one of the drivers takes a wrong turn on the way to the starting gate and has to reverse and start over again.

The signal for drivers to get ready for the off comes when the band of Abu Dhabi Police strikes up with *Ishy Bilady* – 'Long Live my Nation' – after which the first one is flagged away. As there's a minute's pause between competitors the start is somewhat staggered, so the band continues with an international programme of light entertainment while each vehicle in turn is waved on its way. And though the sound of bagpipes playing 'The Skye Boat Song' might in some circumstances prompt a nostalgic longing for home, recent news of storms in the UK keeps any such feelings at bay.

And what of tomorrow?

"You're not required tomorrow," says our liaison officer, "We're still waiting for visas."

A lie-in may be in store.

9. SIGN OF THE TIMES
Abu Dhabi, 28 October 2008

If thou seest a wall inclining, run from under it
- Arabic proverb

Abu Dhabi National Exhibitions Company (ADNEC) is asking the *Guinness Book of Records* to recognise a new tower in the city as the most inclined in the world.

Pisa's famous cathedral bell tower leans less than 4 degrees while Abu Dhabi's 35-storey Capital Gate is being built to incline 18 degrees. The current world record apparently belongs to a fifteenth century church steeple in Germany which leans a mere 5.19 degrees.

Located beside ADNEC's grandstand on the main highway from the airport into the city, Capital Gate is being built by RMJM, the architects and engineers behind the Scottish Parliament building in the UK, using cutting edge construction techniques. When complete it will be 160 metres high and the focal point of a 23-tower commercial and residential development.

Meanwhile, in other news today under the headline 'Quake-proof Buildings are a Must for the UAE,' we are reminded that the UAE sits uncomfortably close to an earthquake zone.

'Taking precaution by building the right infrastructure to face natural calamities is important,' said a spokesman at this week's National Security Summit in Abu Dhabi, 'It will save money and avoid tragic events.'

ADNEC's chief executive is quoted as saying, 'Capital Gate will be a building that the world will talk about.'

A fitting symbol, perhaps, for precarious times.

Capital Gate has now been formally recognised by the Guinness Book of Records as the 'World's Furthest Leaning Manmade Tower' – much to the delight of ADNEC's chairman, who said: 'Capital Gate is a landmark development for Abu Dhabi and with this recognition the tower takes its place among the world's great buildings. It is a signature building which speaks to the foresight of the emirate.' Scheduled for completion in 2011, it will contain offices and a 5-star Hyatt Hotel.

10. THE THIN END OF THE WEDGE
Abu Dhabi, 29 October 2008

Money is the dust in the mansion of the world
- Arabic proverb

As motorists in the UK enjoy the benefit of cheaper fuel as the price of crude comes down, there are concerns in the UAE about the impact of falling oil revenue.

There's some relief in newspapers here that the Organisation of Petroleum Exporting Countries (OPEC), of which the UAE is a member, has moved quickly to try and halt the fall in the price of crude oil by agreeing to cut production. But the prospect of reduced demand in many of the world's leading economies is giving rise to speculation that further cuts will be required, and that any moves by OPEC alone will be compromised if non-OPEC producers seek to bolster falling revenue by increasing production.

Fluctuations in the price of crude are nothing new and publicly the government is maintaining a brave face. But the speed and magnitude of the market collapse – from $147 a barrel as recently as July to less than $64 today – and the potential impact of the global credit crunch on foreign investment in the Gulf are causing concern. There are also fears of 'corrections' in the property market, which has enjoyed a huge boom of late, and talk among the expatriate community suggests that cracks in the economy have already started to appear in Dubai.

Meanwhile the International Monetary Fund (IMF) is encouraging the government to introduce a tax on domestic services and consumption to provide a steadier, more reliable stream of revenue for sustaining long term development. A rate of 5% has been mooted and a starting date of four years' time. While this may not seem very much compared to paying Value Added Tax (VAT) at 17.5% in the UK, the very idea has come as a shock in this largely tax-free environment. Historically public services and social development have been funded by oil revenue. There's no personal income tax and businesses enjoy a liberal regime.

The prospect of VAT comes on top of high inflation and escalating rents and is starting to cause quite a rumpus in the press.

'The thin end of the wedge,' is how I saw it described in a letter to one newspaper, 'Today VAT … tomorrow, income tax?'

Doom-mongers are predicting that it will deter tourists, put off foreign investors and undermine the country's longer term prosperity: none of which is likely to arouse much sympathy from hard-pressed motorists and tax-payers in the UK.

While the VAT rate in the UK has increased to 20%, it has yet to be introduced in the UAE. Demand in Asia and war in Libya has bolstered the price of crude and the cost of fuel in the UK keeps on rising.

11. ALL'S WELL THAT ENDS WELL
Abu Dhabi, 30 October 2008

Every knot has someone to undo it
- Arabic proverb

I am on a bus exploring the city when a telephone call summons me back to the Sands Hotel.

"Start packing," says our liaison officer, "You have to be out by two o'clock."

"Where are we going?"

"I don't know yet," he says.

Hotel accommodation is at a premium. There are currently some 13,000 hotel rooms in the capital and given how difficult it is for expats to find private apartments many are in permanent occupation. To make matters worse any spare rooms are quickly taken up whenever there's a special event – and the forthcoming International Petroleum Exhibition and Conference, dull as it may sound, promises to be very popular this year.

A little over an hour later I am dropped off with two colleagues at the Capital Hotel, only to find we are not expected – which is a shame given its seafront location. A frantic telephone call recalls our driver, by this time departed, and then it's off to the Regency, where we are politely refused admission.

"Without a passport you will be without a hotel," says the manager.

The problem is our passports are with the Immigration Department while residency visas are processed and the photocopies we proffer will not do.

But there's a concept here called *wasta* – from the Arabic word *wasatah*, which means 'middle' – by which seemingly impossible things get done when someone with influence intercedes. So it happens that someone with *wasta* has a word with the hotel manager and we find ourselves being shown to our rooms.

If you were to suggest that all this haste and confusion could have been avoided with a little forward thinking, I could not possibly comment: for in Arab culture to criticise is to risk insult or offence. In any case, I have a room with a view over the sea so am perfectly happy with the way things work out.

By 2010 there were said to be 17,500 hotel rooms in Abu Dhabi and another 5,000 in the pipeline. This number is set to rise to 74,000 by 2030 when the emirate hopes to attract 7.9 million visitors a year, a threefold increase on current rates.

12. DESPERATE REMEDIES
Abu Dhabi, 2 November 2008

Only the tent pitched by your own hands will stand
- Arabic proverb

Half-way up a staircase in Abu Dhabi's Cultural Foundation, facing across a short landing, are two black and white photographs. Both record an aerial view of the old fort, Qasr al Hosn, about half a century ago. While the perspectives are different, the features are essentially the same: clusters of small *barasti* houses between the fortress and the sea and acre upon acre of sand.

To gaze upon these images is to wonder at the speed with which the city has grown and to marvel that the very spot where they hang appears in each photograph as mere desert.

The Cultural Foundation stands beside the fort, two equally grounded neighbours in the heart of the high-rise city centre, surrounded by tall buildings and encircled by busy roads. Here courtyards with fountains and colonnaded walks provide a welcome escape from the relentless heat and traffic, while a cafe, library, theatre and exhibitions offer refreshment for body and mind.

'Our grandfathers and ancestors have left a wealth of cultural heritage we are proud of,' said the late ruler and first President of the UAE, 'We shall conserve it and build on it, as it is the soul of this land and its future generations.'

So the fort is set to become a museum, and the Cultural Foundation, as well as hosting temporary exhibitions of Middle Eastern art, has on permanent display a replica Bedouin tent and modern examples of traditional household utensils, textiles, basket-weaving, crafts and embroidery.

While preserving, proclaiming and celebrating the past, however, Sheikh Zayed also preached a vision of change.

'Future generations will be living in a world that is very different from that to which we are accustomed,' he said 'It is essential that we prepare ourselves and our children for that new world.'

For evidence of transformation one simply has to compare the two photographs from fifty years ago with the modern metropolitan sprawl which continues to spread and rise every minute of every day – all fruit of the discovery of oil. But to sustain development Sheikh Zayed recognised that money alone would not be enough.

'The government's first priority is the development of its people,' he said, 'Financial capability is useless without the presence of local able professionals capable of constructing the nation.'

And this is where his vision wears thin. Although Emiratis swell the ranks of government services to the point of saturation, they are barely represented in the private sector which has more than half of all employment opportunities. While lack of qualifications and cultural difficulties (particularly longer working hours) are cited as the main reasons for under-representation, pay expectations and willingness to work are also issues. Consequently there's a growing problem of unemployment and dependency among young nationals, perhaps not helped by a generous benefits system of grants, loans and free and heavily-subsidised services including education, housing and healthcare.

Towards the end of his life Sheikh Zayed is said to have been shocked at the growing idleness and dependency of many young nationals. Investment in better teaching and vocational training may improve employment prospects in the long term. In the meantime a desperate government has resorted to a discredited policy of 'Emiratisation' which requires certain private sector banking and insurance companies to reserve a specific quota of posts for Emiratis. It has also passed legislation to provide a special pension fund for nationals employed in the private sector and to limit their working hours.

Today is the fourth anniversary of the much loved Zayed's death and in the newspapers there's a mood of introspection. Reflecting on his legacy and the country's prospects for the future, they flaunt statistics showing increased national wealth and productivity as proof of his achievement. But I can't help but think he would judge his own performance by the willingness and capability of the UAE's own people to contribute to the economy of their country.

In July 2011 the Arab News reported that Abu Dhabi was cutting expatriate jobs in the public sector to reduce costs and promote employment opportunities for its own citizens. Experts suggested that it was prompted by fears that unemployment among young Emiratis might lead to similar unrest as that seen in other parts of the Arab world. Nationally the unemployment rate among Emiratis is 10%. In Abu Dhabi it is 14%. Earlier in the year the Minister of Labour said that up to 20,000 private sector jobs a year were needed over the next decade to meet demand from Emirati school-leavers. Currently only 7% of jobs in the private sector are carried out by Emiratis.

13. FRONT PAGE NEWS
Abu Dhabi, 4 November 2008

*Meet a person with an open hand
and they'll meet you with an open heart*
- Arabic proverb

A copy of the broadsheet *Gulf News* lies folded on a table in the cafe of Abu Dhabi's Cultural Foundation displaying an eye-catching headline in bold letters:

DATE WITH HISTORY

Beside it is a small photograph of Sheikh Khalifa, ruler of Abu Dhabi and President of the UAE, with Gordon Brown, Prime Minister of the UK.

A remarkable turnaround, I reflect, as I go to pick it up. Five days ago the local media were questioning the wisdom of Mr Brown's intended trip to Saudi Arabia, Qatar and the UAE this week after comments he made about OPEC's recent decision to cut oil production to stabilise the market. 'Scandalous,' is how he is said to have described it.

But now, reporting on yesterday's visit to Abu Dhabi, there's praise for the British Prime Minister. 'A fund of good sense,' is one editorial headline I spotted earlier this morning: a reference to Mr Brown's suggestion that the countries of the Gulf should be allowed a role in the governance of the IMF in return for contributing to its economic relief fund.

Two hundred years ago the British were very wary of the Gulf states. After attacks on British East India Company shipping they dubbed the area 'the Pirate Coast' and retaliated with a devastating show of force in 1819 before forcing a series of exclusive treaties of protection on each of the coastal sheikhs (hence the UAE's former name, the Trucial States) as a means of exercising control in the Gulf. It was blunt diplomacy that preserved the independence of the emirates and provided Britain with a strategic power-base in the region until 1971.

Mr Brown has had to tread more carefully. He comes cap in hand recognising that the world's economic axis has shifted and that the wealthy Gulf states should have a more influential role in international financial regulation. And given that the British delegation has managed to persuade Qatar and Abu Dhabi to commit multi-million pound investments in low carbon technology (mostly in the UK) one could be forgiven for thinking, as a glance at the front page of the *Gulf News* would suggest, that Mr Brown's visit has taken on something of an historic dimension – particularly after a report published by the World Wide Fund for Nature this week said that the UAE has the highest per capita environmental footprint in the world, largely due to carbon dioxide emissions.

On unfolding the paper, however, I see large portraits of US presidential candidates Obama and McCain beneath the DATE WITH HISTORY headline and observe a thin line separating their side of the page from the photograph of Sheikh Khalifa and Mr Brown.

History, of course, will judge itself – but inviting the oil-rich countries of the Gulf to participate in the IMF and persuading them to invest in the development of low carbon alternatives may prove historic steps towards a more sustainable economic future.

In the UAE exception is taken to the term piracy to describe the nineteenth century confrontations between local tribes and British shipping; Sheikh Sultan bin Mohammed Al Qasimi of Sharjah has written a book about it – The Myth of Arab Piracy in the Gulf – based on his Ph. D thesis at Exeter University. For centuries tribes lived by raiding the caravans of rival tribes. There was even a name for such raids: ghazu. Attacks in the Gulf were simply maritime ghazus. British East India Company ships sailing between Bombay and Basra would call regularly at ports on the coast of Persia. But

Anglo-Persian co-operation restricted Arab trade, so tribesmen from the shores of the lower Gulf would raid British merchantmen and seize their cargos – just as tribes on land would plunder their enemies' caravans and carry off their camels.

The suggestion that Britain preserved the independence of the emirates may also be contentious. It came from Lord Curzon, the Viceroy of India, in a formal address to a gathering of the Trucial sheikhs in Sharjah in 1903. But history supports his claim. The emirates were always fighting each other and Britain's presence protected the weaker ones and helped to maintain the overall status quo. Further more, without British protection – or rather, intervention – Saudi Arabia would surely have succeeded in its attempt to seize a large chunk of Abu Dhabi fifty years later.

14. OLYMPIAN TASK
Abu Dhabi, 7 November 2008

What is learned in youth is engraved in stone
- Arabic proverb

The Ministry of Education has announced that standards of food and nutrition in schools in the UAE are to be linked to academic accreditation.

This follows research which found that over 70% of the country's schoolchildren go without breakfast before leaving home and that many school menus tend to offer chips, high sugared drinks and chocolate rather than nutritionally rich foods such as milk, dates, fruit and vegetables. New regulations are currently being applied in four schools with a view to extending them throughout the UAE and linking them to academic accreditation. Chips, fizzy drinks and chocolate will be strictly prohibited.

'A change in our mindset about nutrition is needed,' said one of the researchers, adding that children should also be encouraged to take part in family activities and exercise.

Today's Olympic Run in Dubai is therefore well-timed. Sanctioned by the International Olympic Committee to celebrate Olympic Day, over 4,000 people are expected to take part. And each contestant has been promised a goody-bag to take home – courtesy of McDonald's, official sponsor of the event.

15. THE EMIRATES DIAMOND
Abu Dhabi, 9 November 2008

If your luck becomes a stone, carry it with you
- Arabic proverb

A very large rough diamond was unveiled at the first Middle East-China Diamond and Jewellery Summit in Dubai yesterday and is expected to be 'snapped up' by a local buyer.

Named *Light of Letseng* after the South African mine in which it was discovered, the 478-carat white stone, which is over five centimetres long, is the twentieth largest diamond in the world. As traditional markets shrink in the cash-strapped West, local diamond dealers hope to capitalise on emerging demand in the Middle East and China. A spokesman at this week's trade fair in Dubai says that diamonds are fast becoming the luxury of choice in the countries of the Gulf and it's estimated that this giant specimen will make more than £6 million when offered for sale.

Another rare stone is also making headlines this morning. Scientists believe that *peridotite*, which has been found in the mountains in the east of the emirates and over the border in Oman, could help to reduce greenhouse gas emissions. It is being tested as a 'carbon capture' material by researchers at Columbia University who explain that contact between carbon dioxide and peridotite causes a chemical reaction which converts them into harmless minerals such as calcite.

'We're talking about billions of tons of carbon dioxide a year,' said one of the research team, adding that as much as 10% of the world's production could be safely eliminated by trapping gas in this way.

While peridotite does not quite have the ring of a diamond, it may prove no less precious.

The Light of Letseng made $18.4 million at auction in Antwerp the following month – making it the most valuable rough diamond ever sold.

16. URBAN WARRIOR
Abu Dhabi, 11 November 2008

*Treat your horse as if it were your friend;
ride your horse as if it were your enemy*
- Arabic proverb

Just as his Bedouin ancestors loved their horses, so modern Emirati man loves his car – or cars, because more likely than not he will own several.

One of the earliest references to the Bedouin's equestrian passion comes in Lebid ibn Rabia's *Golden Ode*, a pre-Islamic poem composed about AD600 though not committed to writing for several more centuries. The poet describes a series of reflections evoked by a chance happening upon an abandoned campsite – 'tent floors smooth, forsaken, bare of all that dwelt in them' – such as he would have seen on his desert journeys in pagan Arabia. Among the images he conjures is that of himself as a hunter warrior, the guardian of his people, mounted on a favourite mare.

*Swift was she, an ostrich; galloped she how wrathfully,
from her sides the sweat streamed, lightening the ribs of her;
Strained on her her saddle; dripped with wet the neck of her,
the white foam-flakes wreathing, edging the girth of her;
Thrusteth her neck forward, shaketh her reins galloping;
flieth as the doves fly bound for the water-springs.*

Anyone who has seen a racehorse reaching for the finish line will be able to testify to the quality of his portrayal. One can imagine the poem being spoken or sung at the end of the day when nomadic tribesmen gathered around campfires after sunset. While all male adults were hunters and warriors, a gift for poetry was rare and poets were highly esteemed. Their purpose was not so much to entertain as to preserve the history of the tribe, honour its chiefs, defend its reputation and perpetuate its fame. The story goes that Lebid's skill came to notice when he was 'still almost a boy' and avenged his tribe in verse during an audience with a king after it was insulted by the poet of a rival tribe.

The image of the warrior on his horse remains deeply ingrained in modern Emirati society, and it is surely no coincidence that one of the most popular photographs of the Founding Father of the UAE sees him mounted on a grey mare, in concept not unlike Van Dyck's famous equestrian portrait of King Charles 1st – but in Sheikh Zayed's case with a falcon perched on his wrist.

With urbanisation, however, the car has become a substitute. Just as his ancient ancestors sought beauty, speed and endurance on four legs, modern Emirati man is drawn to sleek, powerful sports cars and monstrous four-wheel-drive vehicles. And he drives them as Lebid rode his mare. So should you be unlucky enough to find yourself behind the wheel of a car in Abu Dhabi you will see the urban warrior's vehicle approaching fast in your rear-view mirror, headlights flashing, horn blasting, brakes screeching – regardless of whether or not you have any room for safe manoeuvre. You will not actually see the warrior himself because all his windows will have dark tinted glass, but you will know him from his expensive, top of the range status symbol and the throaty roar it leaves in its wake.

If further evidence is required of the feeling our urban warrior has for his mechanical steed it comes in a custom of our times. On special occasions people will bring a tray of confectionary to work to share with colleagues. Yesterday I was offered a marzipan-filled date, today a gold-wrapped chocolate: one to celebrate a marriage, the other to mark the birth of a child. But it came as no surprise to hear that one young Emirati recently passed a small mountain of sweets round the office – to celebrate the purchase of a new car.

17. HOMELESS
Abu Dhabi, 12 November 2008

When God shuts one door, He opens another
- Arabic proverb

Our departure from the Regency Hotel is even more chaotic than our arrival thirteen days ago – because this time we have no place to go.

We are told that the hotel has no rooms available for tonight. So after check-out time passes at noon we sit in the lobby with our suitcases: reading newspapers, awaiting instructions.

After an hour without word the three of us go over the road to a cafe. Another hour passes. Still we hear nothing. So, about two o'clock, we ring our liaison officer.

"Your stay at the Regency has been extended one night," we are told.

But the Regency has no knowledge of this – and anyway, it remains fully booked.

For a change of scene we try another cafe. A cup of coffee, pot of tea and several telephone calls later we are instructed to retrace our steps.

"Your stay at the Regency has been extended one night," we are told.

But again the Regency has no knowledge of this – and anyway, it still remains fully booked.

Meanwhile, of his own volition, the manager of the Regency has kindly telephoned five or six hotels on our behalf, albeit to no avail, and is still waiting to hear from one.

"Perhaps we'll end up in al Ain," we muse, referring to the emirate's second city, an hour and half's drive across the desert.

"Fully booked," replies the manager, "Sharjah, perhaps."

"Too far!" cries one, "It's three hours away."

The fact that Sharjah happens to be a 'dry' state where alcohol is prohibited may explain the vehemence of his protest.

At a quarter past four, following a further flurry of telephone calls, we receive fresh instructions.

"You're booked into the al Raha Beach for tonight."

Hurrah! The al Raha Beach is one of the capital's flagship hotels. Spirits instantly lift. Almost simultaneously the manager of the Regency reappears.

"I have found rooms at the Sands Hotel," he says triumphantly, referring to the rather more modest, albeit comfortable, establishment where we spent our first couple of weeks.

After all the effort he has made on our behalf you might think it churlish that we should turn down the offer of the rooms he has found for us – but we are already half-way out of the door looking for a taxi.

Let the al Raha Beach brochure explain: the al Raha Beach is 'a world where elegance, luxury and sophistication is combined with a touch of Arabian hospitality … set in beautiful landscaped gardens and located in Abu Dhabi's premier al Raha Corniche the hotel overlooks white sandy beaches and offers magnificent views of the Arabian Gulf … the perfect haven for a getaway.'

As to what will happen tomorrow, we have no idea; nor, having fallen on our feet, do we care.

18. SHIFTING SANDS
al Ain, 13 November 2008

Don't look too far ahead, lest you trip up
- Arabic proverb

"You're staying at the al Raha Beach Hotel for the next few days. Then you're off to the Intercontinental in al Ain."

Such is the gist of the telephone message we receive before breakfast this morning.

"Start packing. You're off to the Intercontinental Hotel in al Ain today."

Such is the gist of the telephone message we receive *after* breakfast this morning.

Abu Dhabi's second city lies some 160 kilometres (100 miles) away and the prospect of a change of scene lifts my spirits, especially as the journey will take us across what the nineteenth century adventurer Richard Burton called 'the glorious Desert.'

'What can be more exciting? What more sublime?' he wrote, 'Man's heart bounds in his breast at the thought of measuring his puny force with Nature's might, and of emerging triumphant from the trial. This explains the Arab's proverb, Voyaging is a Victory.'

The ride from Abu Dhabi to al Ain took Sir Percy Cox (then British Political Agent and Honorary Consul in Muscat, afterwards Political Resident in the Gulf) 'fully forty hours of actual travelling' by camel in 1902. By air-conditioned minibus it takes us little more than an hour and a half. But so much for seeing the desert: the multi-lane highway is lined throughout with trees planted, so I've heard, on the instructions of Sheikh Zayed, who had no wish to gaze upon a wilderness while travelling between his home city and the capital. So scrub, sand and drifting dunes lie half-hidden behind a curtain of dusty palms, small farms and date plantations which continue all the way to the oasis of Buraimi and the 'Garden City' of al Ain. Only towards the end is there any hint of Burton's glorious landscape 'of drifted sand-heaps, upon which each puff of wind leaves its trace in solid waves,' when hills of red sand appear over the top of the roadside trees.

Our search for accommodation has brought us to the far reaches of the emirate, to the very border between the UAE and the Sultanate of Oman. The fence separating the two splits Buraimi, which has long been amicably shared between the two countries, and runs within a quarter of a mile of our hotel. From the balcony of my room I can see far into Oman to the distant Hajar mountains, and much closer, straddling the border, to the Jebel Hafeet (or Hafit) which towers over 3,000 feet above a flat plain in which the low rooftops and minarets of the city are almost lost in the dense foliage of trees.

Buraimi's economy is based on agriculture, its date groves fed since time immemorial by underground water from the foot of the mountains. But for centuries it also thrived on slave-trafficking and trade. Five ancient caravan routes converged here, linking the lower Gulf coast and Nejd ('highland') of Saudi Arabia with the interior and coast of Oman. In the nineteenth century Buraimi's strategic commercial location made it a magnet for tribesmen and tax-collectors from the Arabian Nejd seeking to extend the influence of the strict Islamic sect of Mohammed bin Abdul Al Wahhab over the Bedouin. Wahhabi incursions frequently exploited local tensions to challenge the authority of Abu Dhabi and Oman over the tribes of the oasis, and rival claims by the House of Saud (which championed the Wahhabi cause) led to several clashes, the last of which flared as recently as the 1950s.

Today, however, all is tranquil in the oasis and al Ain – the largest of its settlements – provides a refreshing retreat from the hustle, bustle and humidity of the capital. But for how long? Two weeks we were assured before leaving the al Raha Beach Hotel. Only five days insists our host at the Intercontinental – before checking again and saying four.

In the heart of the desert one must grow accustomed to shifting sands.

19. A FAMILY AFFAIR
al Ain, 16 November 2008

Your family may chew you, but they will not swallow you
- Arabic proverb

Celebrated as an owner and breeder of some of the world's most successful racehorses, Sheikh Mohammed bin Rashid Al Maktoum, ruler of Dubai and Vice-President and Prime Minister of the UAE, is acclaimed as a jockey in several of the Gulf newspapers this morning.

Yesterday His Highness and seventy-four other riders from five different countries competed in the gruelling 120 kilometre (75 miles) international endurance horserace in the Wadi Rum desert in Jordan. Sheikh Mohammed finished first in a time of 4 hours, 59 minutes and 55 seconds. In second place, just one second behind, came his son, Sheikh Hamdan, the Crown Prince of Dubai, while a younger son, Sheikh Majid, finished in third place, another second behind his brother.

To mark his achievement Sheikh Mohammed was presented with a golden sword by a member of the Jordanian royal family – who also happens to be his sister-in-law.

If only there were bookmakers here to take bets on such events.

20. THE DUBAI SMILE
Dubai, 17 November 2008

What camel ever saw its own hump?
- Arabic proverb

There's a big smile on the front page of the *Khaleej Times* this morning – reference to an artist's impression of the new, twelve-lane road bridge intended to ease traffic congestion in Dubai.

The Smile, which takes its name from the inverted arch that dominates the design, will be the seventh crossing over the sea inlet which bisects the city.

Planners say it will be able to carry some 24,000 vehicles an hour, although the artist chooses to show no more than twenty in his idealised snapshot depiction. The cost will be in the region of Dh810 million (£135m).

The new bridge is part of a strategy to ensure Dubai's traffic infrastructure keeps pace with urban development.

'Not before time,' motorists will say.

Only a week or so ago there was gridlock in the city on all approaches to the newly-opened 'world's largest shopping mall' and rarely does a day go by without accidents, traffic jams and bottlenecks featuring in radio bulletins, newspaper headlines and letters.

Turn to today's business section, however, and the mood is rather more downbeat.

'Gulf Shares Plunge' is the headline.

Only last week authorities here reviewed spending plans in the light of the global credit crunch, diminishing oil returns and signs of a serious slump in the property market. But despite the gloom the government is maintaining a brave face.

'We can confidently say that the Arab world has largely not been affected by the crisis,' insists the Minister of Economy.

But stock market falls reflect a massive withdrawal of foreign capital, which must be worrying when development plans in Dubai are to a large extent predicated on credit and overseas demand for real estate and tourism.

Behind the Smile there may yet be tears.

21. THE SPIRIT OF DUBAI
Dubai, 21 November 2008

Fire today, ashes tomorrow
- Arabic proverb

Reading about last night's party to celebrate the official opening of Atlantis, The Palm in Dubai, I am reminded of the story, in all likelihood apocryphal, that the Emperor Nero fiddled and sang songs about the destruction of Troy while watching Rome burn in a great fire in AD64.

As the rest of the world tightens its belt, some $20 million were lavished on gourmet food, champagne and exclusive entertainment for more than two thousand private guests headed by the royal family of Dubai and including many celebrities from the worlds of business, politics, sport, stage and screen. Kylie Minogue topped the bill and the entire 43 kilometre shoreline of the palm-shaped island on which the hotel stands was illuminated by the world's biggest firework display.

More than a million fireworks were discharged in less than ten minutes from more than seven hundred locations, the highest rising about 300 metres before bursting into a floral display the size of two football pitches – visible, rumour has it, from the space station orbiting the Earth.

Yet only recently it was reported that 800 employees had been laid off from the Palm's sister resort in the Bahamas where bookings have taken a dive.

'The spirit of Dubai lives on,' declares one editorial this morning, which may come to mean much the same as fiddling while Rome burns.

22. LEAPING HORSES
al Ain, 22 November 2008

The path of destiny has many crossroads
- Arabic proverb

On the A181 between Durham and Wheatley Hill, at the point where it meets the road to Trimdon Station, there is a roundabout on which stands a life-size model of a pit pony harnessed to a coal wagon.

I am reminded of this scene from home each time I enter or leave al Ain: because on the outskirts of the city, on the main road to and from Abu Dhabi, there is a roundabout surmounted by four leaping horses.

Wheatley Hill's pit pony recalls the mining heritage of England's northern coalfield, the dim depths of the coal seams, the labour and sacrifice of generations of local families, a vanished world remembered in monuments, headstones and sepia photographs. Al Ain's leaping horses are similarly symbolic. They recall the equestrian heritage of the Arabs – but they also suggest a dynamic future. Unlike the little pit pony they are larger-than-life, not bound by the Earth but poised to leap into the sky, an appropriate image for an oasis settlement that constantly seeks to challenge the natural environment.

'With God's blessing and our determination we have succeeded in transforming this desert into a green land,' said Sheikh Zayed.

But the exploitation of finite resources, whether in County Durham or the UAE, points to the same end and environmentalists are concerned about the impact of modern development on the water table in Arabia's vast subterranean system of aquifers. Once plentiful, fresh water supplies are diminishing and there is increasing reliance on desalination plants.

As al Ain extends its green tentacles into the desert, roads and roundabouts proliferate. And it's not enough that they should be functional: they have to be decorative, too. So roads are tree-lined and traffic islands embellished with huge Arabian coffee pots, cups and incense jars, rocks, boulders and palm trees, an abundance of fountains, cascades and waterfalls, and, near the wildlife park, a zebra, giraffe, lion, oryx and gazelle.

"I'll show you my favourite roundabout," says a seasoned colleague as we travel along a wide, green boulevard after a morning spent dune-bashing and visiting camel farms in the desert.

It sounds like a desperate chat-up line, and perhaps only in al Ain could such an offer be made in all sincerity – leastways until the water runs dry and the sands blow in.

Alas, Wheatley Hill's little pit pony has departed – or rather, disintegrated: the victim of vandals or a traffic collision. Sadly, too, my seasoned colleague, who died in 2010.

23. REFLECTIONS ON PROGRESS
al Ain, 23 November 2008

Grapes are eaten one by one
- Arabic proverb

The Palace Museum in al Ain has a treasure far richer than can be measured in material terms.

For all the beauty of its oasis backdrop, quaint turreted towers, shaded walks and pleasant courtyard gardens, the private rooms are small, austere and sparsely furnished. Swords, curved daggers and old British rifles hang on the walls. Ragged rugs and date palm matting cover the floors. There are few ornaments, no books or papers. But for the red, green, blue and gold of the cushioned seats there would be little to colour the scene. Only the public chambers, two spacious *majlis* rooms where audiences would be held, are remotely sumptuous. Life at the palace was little removed from that of the desert-dweller, albeit within sand-coloured walls, and in the garden a large Bedouin tent, carpeted and cushioned, evokes the sentiment expressed by the seventh century poetess, Maysun, who left her Bedouin roots in the desert for a luxurious life as wife of the Caliph in Damascus:

> *A tent with rustling breezes cool*
> *Delights me more than palaces high*
> *And more the cloak of simple wool*

Than robes in which I learned to sigh.

The treasure is one of association, for the palace was built for Sheikh Zayed, who was governor of the city before he became the ruler of Abu Dhabi in 1966. In Bedouin culture loyalty to family, respect for tribal leaders and preservation of honour and reputation count for much more than material wealth. As one-time residence of the Father of the Nation the precincts of the palace verge on the sacred. Here Sheikh Zayed would hold court with local tribesmen and receive the rulers and representatives of other emirates. Little wonder there should be a shrine. In a small, cloistered square the male line of the ruling Al Nahyan family features as gold-embossed leaves on the branches of a ceramic tree, while covering the walls are gold-framed portraits of Zayed, his immediate forebears, and all nineteen sons. Of his several daughters there is no mention.

My visit to the palace follows a week of relative progress. On Tuesday my passport was returned, duly stamped with a residency visa. This means I have an identification number which, in turn, allowed me on Wednesday to obtain a local driving licence. On Thursday I spent a couple of hours visiting car showrooms, while on Friday, being the quietest morning on the roads, I borrowed a car and survived my first experience of driving here. Today I return to Abu Dhabi to take up residence at the Oryx Hotel and start work. The apartment I have been promised is unlikely to be ready before January.

Some will wonder why it should take so long for Abu Dhabi Police to complete my induction; after all, I've been here seven weeks. Recent problems with accommodation may also beg questions about their ability to plan. But *is* it any wonder that administrative systems should be bureaucratic, inflexible and slow when, for all Abu Dhabi's material advances over the last half century, life in the corridors of power still reflects the values, customs and traditions of centuries of desert subsistence?

"*Shway, shway,*" experienced colleagues intone – which means much the same as 'One step at a time.'

Whether on the grass of al Ain or pavements of the capital, scratch the surface and you will find sand. Similarly, peer beneath the veneer of modernisation and you will see the ways of the Bedouin.

In her poem Maysun goes on to describe her husband, Caliph Muawiyah, as a 'fatted ass.' The story goes that when Muawiyah found out he banished Maysun to live with her cousins in the desert – which suited her perfectly. Sir Richard Burton used to recite the poem to his Bedouin companions during his secret pilgrimage to Mecca and Medina. 'They never hear it without screams of joy,' he wrote.

24. WORKERS OF CHOICE
Abu Dhabi, 24 November 2008

A fable is a bridge that leads to truth
- Arabic proverb

According to an article in yesterday's *National*, the UAE's honey industry has become almost entirely dependent on foreign workers. The indigenous Emirati bee is not suitable for commercial honey production so keepers have resorted to employing expatriate varieties.

But some expat workers are more productive than others. Australian bees are said to be too aggressive, while Italian bees, although acclaimed for the quality of their honey, are too timid. Bees from the Caucasus, Balkans and Ukraine are all highly rated, but Egyptian bees tend to be the first choice of keepers here.

As for the dwarf bee of the emirates, it's simply not keen on being put to work.

'It's very hard to domesticate them,' a local bee-keeper explained, 'They simply won't accept it.'

25. SLEEPLESS
Abu Dhabi, 2 December 2008

One hand cannot clap
- Arabic proverb

The revving of engines, squeal of tyres, and pip, blast and shriek of car horns, are set to continue long into the night. It's National Day in the UAE and people are partying.

In the street outside my hotel young Emiratis are cruising in cars decorated with flags and ribbons and portraits of sheikhs. Some have even had their vehicles decked with heart-shaped stickers, or entirely re-sprayed, in the red, white, green and black of the national colours. Bumper to bumper, drivers are revving their engines, blasting horns, burning rubber and back-firing exhausts, while passengers hang out of windows and sun-roofs, some sitting – even standing – on the roof itself, singing and waving and spraying confetti and crazy foam – in an authentic expression of patriotic pride and celebration.

When the British government announced its intention to withdraw from the Persian Gulf by the end of 1971, Abu Dhabi and the other Trucial States were faced with a stark choice: fragment and, in the absence of British protection, risk being picked apart by bigger and more powerful neighbours bent on expansion – or put differences aside and enjoy the strength, wealth and influence that only federation could bring. Sheikhs Zayed and Rashid, rulers of Abu Dhabi and Dubai respectively, pressed for union and invited the rest of the emirates to join them.

'Federation is the way to power,' said Sheikh Zayed, 'The way to strength, the way to well-being.'

Echoing Lawrence – 'Anybody who talks of Arab Federation talks fantastically' – many Middle East observers thought that union would never happen; after all, the Trucial arrangements had bound the feuding emirates not to each other but to Britain. Tribal instinct for independence was obstacle enough to a union, let alone the antipathies and mistrust born of generations of inter-tribal conflict. But while Qatar and Bahrain opted for separate status, Sharjah, Ajman, Umm al Quwain and Fujairah were persuaded to join with Abu Dhabi and Dubai, and on 2 December 1971 the United Arab Emirates was born. The seventh member, Ras al Khaimah, joined the following year.

Few observers thought the union would last – yet here it is celebrating its 37th anniversary. In the capital anticipation has been growing for days. Landmark buildings have been illuminated in the national colours and armies of expatriate labourers have been fixing flags on street lamps and lights to palm trunks on all major routes across the city. Despite the downturn in the global economy and unresolved conflicts elsewhere in the Middle East, the UAE is putting on a show of confidence. Blessed with vast energy and financial reserves the government claims that the federation is better placed than most economies to weather the storm, and though cracks are starting to appear (particularly in Dubai, where 500 job losses were announced two days ago by the property company that developed the recently-opened Atlantis, The Palm Hotel), construction continues, cities expand and the desert recedes.

In a region synonymous with conflict and instability, the UAE has become a beacon of political unity, religious tolerance and economic prosperity. Observers speak not only of its domestic growth but also social development and increasing role in global economics. So as Emiratis celebrate their nation's progress and achievement with a noisy display of patriotism, so may we who are condemned to a sleepless night console ourselves with the hope that a country which has twice confounded the doubters may in turn inspire others to strive against the odds.

26. ZAYED AND THE DREAM
Abu Dhabi, 3 December 2008

Even when fallen, a rose keeps wafting its fragrance
- Arabic proverb

This evening's all-singing, all-dancing tribute to the late and much loved Sheikh Zayed bin Sultan Al Nahyan is as entertaining and illuminating off-stage as on.

Commissioned by the government's Authority for Culture and Heritage to mark the 37th anniversary of the UAE, *Zayed and the Dream* was written, directed, choreographed and performed by members of Lebanon's Caracalla Dance Theatre – to a full house, mainly of Emiratis in national dress, at Abu Dhabi's National Theatre.

Song and dance are augmented by photographs, film and video clips, no less than seven Arabian horses and nine peregrine falcons. There are also guest dancers from China, Russia and Spain to reflect the idea that the whole world is now beating a path to the emirates, and a brief appearance from an Emirati heritage company which performs a traditional dance to the beat of hands from those in the auditorium.

Interaction is constant. The projection of an image of the Father of the Nation at the very start is greeted by spontaneous applause, and every time photographic, film or audio archives are played, or the narrator recites extracts from his speeches, or the actor playing his part appears on stage – locals clap and cheer and hold up their mobile phones to capture the memory on camera: for although directed that photography is not allowed and that mobiles should be switched off, everyone openly ignores the ban. Interestingly when images of Sheikh Zayed with other world leaders are flashed on the screen Her Majesty Queen Elizabeth receives one of the loudest ovations of all – albeit not quite as deafening as that which greets Yasser Arafat.

"Please remain in your seat during the short interval," says a voice from the loudspeakers – whereupon all jump up and wander round the theatre to talk to family and friends.

The performance relates not only the story of Sheikh Zayed's life, the transformation of Abu Dhabi and the founding of the federation, but also his vision for consensus and cooperation between government and governed. Unity, as well he knew from his dealings with the tribes of the interior, could never be maintained by force; popular commitment to the concept and institutions of union would only be sustained through mutual bonds of trust and provision, rights and responsibilities. So he grounded his dream for modernisation in a partnership with the people best epitomised by his faith in the relationship between individual enlightenment and national development.

'Be advised, my brethren, be advised,' he booms, as dancers dressed as Asian construction workers parade across the stage in red safety helmets and blue dungarees, 'Seek education that leads to work.'

To which Emiratis in the audience respond with a huge cheer, oblivious to the irony that while applauding their beloved Zayed's plea for self-help they are content to watch a troupe of non-nationals crown their country's anniversary celebrations with a show that acknowledges the vital role of expats in its development – and in which their own people feature hardly at all.

In August 2010 Zayed and the Dream was performed to less enthusiastic reviews in London. Here is an extract from The Stage:

'Tourists to the UAE would find this spectacle fascinating, but on stage at the London Coliseum it comes over rather like a school play, and a rather boring one at that ... Clearly, Sheikh Zayed will always be a star of the region and UAE citizens may love what is virtually a hagiography, but, for the rest of us, this dream is more educational than entertaining.'

27. FINAL FRONTIER
Abu Dhabi, 13 December 2008

The clever woman could spin with a donkey's foot
- Arabic proverb

Namira Salim, a Pakistani national who has lived in the UAE for twenty years, has secured a seat on one of the first commercial sub-orbital flights of Richard Branson's Virgin Galactic spaceship.

She has already planted the UAE and Pakistani flags at the North and South Poles, trekked through Nepal, qualified as a pilot, scuba-dived in the Bahamas and sky-dived from the world's highest drop zone close to the summit of Mount Everest. Now she has beaten some 44,000 other applicants to become one of just a hundred members of the Virgin Galactic Founders Club. She has already completed her initial training in zero-gravity conditions and is scheduled to be launched into space next year.

'I am not an outdoors girl,' says Miss Salim in a newspaper interview, 'But I have always wanted to explore the mysteries of the universe.'

After her space flight she has another adventure in mind.

'I would love to have a companion and children,' she confides, 'But I have always wanted to save myself for a soul mate.'

As for the type of partner she is looking for, he would not himself have to be the adventurous sort.

'He does not have to jump out of planes,' she says, 'Just as long as he does not mind if I do.'

In 2011 Ms Salim was awarded the Tamgha-i-Imtiaz (Medal of Excellence) by the President of Pakistan for her accomplishments in sport and for inspiring other Asian women. Her space debut is scheduled for 2013.

28. A GOODBYE KISS
Abu Dhabi, 16 December 2008

*Some talk flows like a stream,
some grinds like a mill, and some flies like a bird*
- Arabic proverb

There is much laughter this morning at a piece of video film on the internet which shows an Iraqi journalist throwing a pair of shoes at the President of the United States.

For Westerners such an act may appear ridiculous: in the Arab world it is an expression of revulsion that speaks louder than words.

I watch the recording as Mr Bush shakes hands with the Prime Minister of Iraq at a press conference in Baghdad on the occasion of his farewell visit.

"It is the farewell kiss, you dog," shouts Muntazer Al Zaidi as he throws the first shoe.

Mr Bush ducks – the shoe misses – Mr Bush rises.

"And this is for all the Iraqis you have killed and widowed and orphaned," says Al Zaidi.

A second shoe flies through the air – Mr Bush raises his arm to fend it off – the shoe falls wide.

Al Zaidi is quickly bundled to the ground and arrested.

In Arab culture the sole of a shoe is considered the ultimate insult and when American soldiers pulled down the statue of Saddam Hussein in Baghdad in 2003 many Iraqis threw their shoes at it. An Emirati colleague is deeply scornful of the President's reaction.

"He placed himself beneath the sole of the shoe. It is like putting himself in the dirt. He should not have ducked."

But throwing shoes at a visiting head of state flies in the face of traditional Arab hospitality and Al Zaidi's action was condemned as shameful by the Iraqi government. Many journalists, on the other hand, invoked the democracy and freedom promised by the Americans to defend their colleague and call for his immediate release.

Freeing Iraq from the tyranny of Saddam was one thing: but the subsequent suffering of the Iraqi people is quite another – and to be the target of flying shoes shows just how much George W. Bush is now reviled by the people he liberated.

When released from prison in September 2009 Muntazer Al Zaidi returned home to a hero's welcome. He was inundated with offers of jobs, proposals of marriage and expensive gifts – including, it's said, a golden horse from the Emir of Qatar, a limousine from a businessman in Bahrain, and a cheque for a million riyals from Saudi Arabia. Arab parents have named children after him and the company which makes the brand of size 10 shoes that he threw at Mr Bush has had to work overtime to meet demand.

29. WORLD IN A SPIN
Abu Dhabi, 19 December 2008

The times are pregnant with black demons
- Arabic proverb

People in the UAE love their cars: the bigger the better. And with petrol costing a mere fifth of the price in the UK, many expatriates living here seize the opportunity to indulge their dream of driving a luxury sports car or gas-guzzling four-wheel-drive. But times are changing.

The world economic downturn is hitting expatriate employment in the UAE and the credit crunch is starting to bite. This week some banks reduced credit card thresholds and introduced stricter criteria for borrowing. For many card holders it came without warning. Fearing that people facing redundancy might be tempted to run up huge debts and abscond, banks cut limits first and informed customers afterwards. Many people were unaware of the changes until they presented their cards while Christmas shopping. Meanwhile motor traders say that banks have raised down-payments and interest rates on car loans and are unwilling to lend any money at all to any expatriate employees of construction, property and financial companies.

The timing is unfortunate for Abu Dhabi's International Motor Show which is taking place this week under the patronage of the Commander General of Abu Dhabi Police. Overall it's a low key affair. Visitor numbers are said to be down on last year and several high profile manufacturers are conspicuous by their absence.

'It seems the global financial crisis is taking a toll,' admitted one official, 'We were certainly expecting greater number of visitors, but they have kept away.'

Among the attractions is a Volvo saloon mounted on a spit in which visitors can volunteer to be turned upside down. Operated by Abu Dhabi Police, it's not, I'm assured, a new aid to interrogation but an invitation to see what could happen if one drives too fast. The roads in the UAE are among the most dangerous in the world. Over two hundred pedestrians have been killed on the streets of the capital since March this year. In Dubai this month an average of one person a day has died as a result of a road accident and last week five Asian restaurant workers perished when their minibus crashed in al Ain. Besides publishing advice and warnings, police forces across the emirates are issuing ever increasing numbers of fixed penalty tickets to drivers and jay-walkers. More speed enforcement cameras are promised – but it's well known, and even officially publicised, that drivers are allowed to exceed limits by 20 kph before enforcement takes place. Meanwhile the carnage continues.

While hybrids on some stands fly the flag for greener motoring, most interest focuses on luxury brands and big four-wheel-drives. As for the star of the show, the weird-looking Spanish *Tramontana*, an ultra-high-performance, insect-like sports car attracts most admirers. According to its manufacturer it provides 'the closest experience to a Formula One racer that a road-going vehicle can deliver.' But a prize for the most glitzy would go to a custom-built French two-seater, its bodywork encrusted with Swarovski crystals – the same company whose crystals adorn the 1,002 chandeliers in the Emirates Palace.

At Dh625,000 (over £100,000) this bejewelled *Cevennes* has already been snapped up. For cash-strapped expats, however, the standard model is still available – at less than a quarter of the price.

30. GOD'S GIFT
Abu Dhabi, 23 December 2008

Camels are ships of the land
- Arabic proverb

Two of the great passions of the Arab are being brought together in a competition this week – so reviving a custom that predates Islam.

The Director of the Poetry Academy in Abu Dhabi's Authority for Culture and Heritage has advertised an oral poetry competition on the theme of the camel. It coincides with the forthcoming camel festival in Abu Dhabi's western region which, according to a statement from the organising committee, seeks to reflect 'the importance of the presence of camels in our lives, and the fact that they are among the prime elements of our heritage and the heritage of our fathers and forefathers.'

An aptitude for language and poetry has long been prized in Arabia's famously voluble society.

'The Arabs never perform the most trifling undertaking or engagement without an enormous expenditure of words,' wrote the nineteenth century English explorer James Wellsted – an observation no less pertinent today.

While all men once aspired to be brave hunters and fearless warriors, more aesthetic qualities were required to achieve stardom. In Bedouin society only three events would bring neighbours to offer their congratulations: the birth of a boy, the foaling of a noble mare – and the emergence of a poet to preserve the history, fame and reputation of the tribe.

In pre-Islamic Arabia seven poets achieved distinction as the authors of the so-called Golden Odes. Around the turn of the sixth century tribes from across the Arabian Peninsula sent their best poets to compete for glory at an annual market at Okaz in the Hejaz region of modern day Saudi Arabia. Tradition has it that the best poems would be inscribed in gold upon silk and hung on the pagan shrine (the *Kaaba*) at Mecca – hence their collective Arabic title, the *Mu'allaqat* (suspended odes), and colloquial name, the Golden Odes.

Passed down by word of mouth until committed to writing several centuries later, these suspended odes open a window on Bedouin life in pre-Islamic times. As well as recalling their conquests of women, the poets boast of their triumphs in war, their fondness for wine and gambling, the qualities of their horses and camels and their riding skills. Through images of pearls in the night sky, high-heaped dunes, dust clouds like smoke and winds cross-weaving furrows in the sand, we are drawn into the natural wilderness of the desert. And while public attitudes to wine, women and gambling may have changed, the landscape is eternal.

To the poet called Tarafa, whose life was cut short when he was buried alive, his hands and feet having been severed, for lampooning in verse the brother of a king, belongs a very special distinction. Relating the departure of his beloved and others of her tribe when moving camp in the desert, he described their caravan as 'ships tall-rigged' climbing 'the long wave-lines,' while of his own camel he said, 'ship-strong is she.' Since Tarafa is the only one of the Golden Ode poets to liken camels to ships, this is almost certainly the earliest such reference in Arabic literature.

Just as their coastal cousins harvested the seas, so the Bedouin ploughed the oceans of sand. The key to their survival was the single-humped dromedary, or Arabian camel. It provided meat and milk for food and drink; wool for tents, saddle cloths, ropes and girths; legs for transport and power for drawing water from wells; sun-dried dung for fuel; urine for washing hair – 'All the desert beauties use it,' wrote the explorer Bertram Thomas – and for rubbing on skin to protect from insect bites; even its vomit, induced by means of a rod, would be garnered for use as medicine for an upset stomach. No wonder they called the camel *Ata Allah* – God's gift. In Arabic the word for camel, *jamal*, derives from the same root as that for beauty and in traditional songs the Ship of the Desert features as a symbol of grace and nobility. Today camels entertain on the racecourse and compete in beauty contests, and no self-respecting tourist returns home without having their photograph taken perched Lawrence-like in the saddle.

As Christmas approaches, however, I shall conclude with an ancient image: one that pre-dates Tarafa, in which three wise men bearing gifts are guided by a star to Bethlehem, each mounted, popular portrayal would have it, on a camel.

In 2006 the Okaz souk was revived to promote the Kingdom's heritage and attract tourists. It has since become an annual event at which artists, actors, writers and poets participate in a cultural extravaganza and shopkeepers sell Bedouin souvenirs.

31. GIFTS AND GOODWILL
Abu Dhabi, 25 December 2008

To you your religion and to me my religion
- Arabic proverb

At the back of St. Andrew's church in Abu Dhabi, in the Anglican diocese of Cyprus and the Gulf, is a black and white photograph taken in 1966. It shows a young Sheikh Zayed, in the first weeks of his accession as ruler, with the Archbishop in Jerusalem (sic) at the laying of the foundation stone of the church on the sands of the Corniche.

In 1984 the original building was replaced by the present church sited near the racecourse in the middle of the island.

"We were asked to move," the priest tells me – presumably to make room for new development.

In each case the land was a gift: the first from Sheikh Shakhbut, the second from his brother, Sheikh Zayed, reflecting the common roots of Islam and Christianity and their tolerance of other religions. In *The Golden Bubble* the novelist and travel writer Roderic Owen tells of joining some expatriate colleagues and their families for Christmas Day in Abu Dhabi in 1955 and being visited by Sheikh Shakhbut who, to their surprise, apologised for there not being a church in Abu Dhabi.

'But wouldn't you disapprove of a church here?' they asked.

'Of course not,' said Sheikh Shakhbut, 'You need your religion as we need ours. Besides, good as you are, you'd no doubt be better if you went to church; and that would be to everyone's advantage.'

Christmas Day is not a holiday for Muslims. While the Holy Quran recognises Jesus as a prophet, it does not acknowledge his Resurrection or Divinity. The opportunity for me to attend church this morning is a concession from Abu Dhabi Police out of respect for the Christian religion.

In the crowded pews my neighbour is Cornelius, a retired priest who was born in India but now lives in Australia. Over fifty denominations worship in St. Andrew's, he informs me, sharing facilities at staggered times and on different days. According to Church leaders, there are too few churches to meet demand. Although only 3% of the residential population of the UAE are Christian their number has been growing year on year. Close to St. Andrew's is the Roman Catholic cathedral of St. Joseph where I saw scores of expats alighting from buses. A notice tells me that between seven o'clock this morning and eight this evening there will be Christmas Masses in English, French, Tamil, German, Arabic, Konkani, Italian, Polish, Singhala, Urdu, Filipino and Malayalam.

On a typical Friday (Holy Day in the UAE) Abu Dhabi's combined multi-denominational church complex is a place of worship for thousands of Christians in multilingual, back-to-back services which start before sunrise and continue long after sunset. But for hundreds of thousands of Hindus and Sikhs living here, the nearest temples are in Dubai.

Inside St. Andrew's an embroidery on the wall catches my eye: 'Water will gush in the wilderness and streams in the desert.' The words frame an image of a gazelle drinking from a pool, so linking the prophecy of Isaiah with the legend of the founding of the city when one foggy day hunter tribesmen from the interior followed footprints in the sand to the head of the island where cloud lifted to reveal a gazelle drinking at a spring.

Similar conditions prevail on the island this Christmas morning and it seems entirely fitting that to locate the spire-less church in thick fog I am guided by the dim outline of minarets on the neighbouring mosque.

32. BEAUTY AND THE BEAST
Madinat Zayed, 28 December 2008

Beauty doesn't exist: men only dream it
- Arabic proverb

'The smell of the camel is muskish and a little dog-like,' wrote Charles Doughty, 'The hinder parts being crusted with urine.'

Not so here today. You find me at Abu Dhabi's Mazayina Dhafra Camel

Festival where high stakes have attracted the owners and breeders of 24,000 of the most beautiful *Asayel* and *Majahim* dromedaries from Bahrain, Kuwait, Qatar, Saudi Arabia, Oman and the UAE. Forty million dirhams (£6.6m) is being offered in cash and prizes over ten days of auctions, racing and beauty competitions. Every winning owner will be given a Nissan six-wheel-drive vehicle, while others will receive Range Rovers, Land Cruisers and Toyota pick-ups.

Only purebreds can be entered. Should there be any doubt about a contestant's credentials its owner is required to take an oath:

'I swear by Almighty God that this camel is mine (or my legitimate heirs) and that it is purebred and God is my witness.'

The light-skinned *Asayel* – or red – camel originated in Oman and the UAE and is the lighter, friendlier and faster of the two breeds. A particular beauty called *Mabroukan* (her name means Blessed) was sold for Dh15 million (£2.5m) when auctioned last year and has already broken a racing record at this year's event. In the festival programme we are told that the Prophet Muhammad called the southern Arabian *Asayel* 'Blessed Red' and that Antara bin Shaddad presented some to his beloved cousin Ablah in Arabia's famous medieval tale of romance.

The dark-skinned *Majahim* variety, which came originally from Nejd in Saudi Arabia, is larger, stronger and heavier – and a formidable sight when moving at speed. As I drive along Shariah al Million (Million Street, named after the number of dirhams that change hands in camel sales) vehicles stop and heads turn as some thirty or more, half hidden in a cloud of dust, are herded across the sand by handlers in half a dozen four-wheel-drive vehicles – much as shepherds at home use quad-bikes to drive sheep.

'Camels are in our blood,' explained one of the organisers, 'They have been for a long time and they will continue to be. Now we are returning what they gave to us as a celebration. Some people love the camels like their own children.'

Their utility – whether for sustenance, shelter or transportation – is easy to imagine. But what makes for beauty in a dromedary? Each contestant is scored out of a hundred. Twenty-five points are awarded to head and neck; here the judges consider ear firmness, whiskers, nose shape, head size, neck length and posture. Fifteen points go to the front, where neck width and shoulder length count, and ten points to the rear, where leg size and straightness are critical factors. Twenty points are allocated to the upper body: while back height and length are important, the judges also consider the shape and position of the hump. Lastly, thirty points go to general shape and fitness; hair sheen and the spacing between toes can make all the difference.

When winners are announced the Arabs throw their *ghutras* (cotton head coverings) into the air, wave camel sticks and join in spontaneous dancing. Meanwhile Western visitors gaze bemused. Looking at its long neck, knobbly knees, disproportionately small head and truncated behind, they are perhaps reminded of the office joke that a camel is a horse designed by a committee. But nasal flaps and a double row of long, curly eye-lashes that protect against dust and sand are testament to evolution's role in the dromedary's design, and not even its smell could mask its beauty in Doughty's estimation.

'Yet is the camel more beautiful in our eyes than the gazelles,' he wrote, 'Because man sees in this creature his whole welfare in the *khala* (desert).'

Contrary to popular myth the camel stores fat in its hump, not water. But it is adapted to minimise water-loss through sweat and respiration. Thick body hair protects the skin from extreme heat and its nostrils moisten dry air on inhaling and cool exhaled air. It also has a very low metabolic rate, a perspiration thermostat which rises and falls with changes in external temperature, and is said to be able to detect water up to 3 kilometres away.

33. PUPPET SHOW
Abu Dhabi, 1 January 2009

Man thinks, God arranges
- Arabic proverb

Many Arabs believe they are powerless to control events: everything, they say, is in God's hands. Conversational references to the future are therefore often rounded off with the ritual refrain, '*Inshallah*' – which literally means, 'If God wills it.'

It is a resignation born of the sterile world of the camel-herding nomad. The Arabs of the desert, wrote Lawrence in *Seven Pillars of Wisdom*, 'knew themselves just sentient puppets on God's stage.' In a world of plenty, however, their fatalism is less an axiom of faith than a way to avoid responsibility and blame. So while *Inshallah* can suggest the possibility of something happening, it can just as likely mean something is definitely not going to happen.

For some weeks I have been led to expect a desktop computer to help me with my work.

"When will my computer arrive?" I ask from time to time.

"Next week, *Inshallah*," is invariably the answer – and it has only recently dawned on me that there may be no intention of supplying me with a computer but no-one will actually admit it.

Some three months after arriving in Abu Dhabi I am still living out of a suitcase in a hotel – my fifth. Although an apartment is pending, it's still in the hands of the builders. Last month I was assured that the apartment block would be ready for occupation by 15 December – '*Inshallah*.' But 15 December came and went and the apartments remained unfinished. Then last week I was told I should start buying furniture because the apartments would be ready by the weekend – '*Inshallah*.' Well, the weekend has come and gone and the apartments are still not finished.

Based on the inexpert evidence of my own eyes, the apartments will not be ready for at least another two or three weeks – *Inshallah* – and once the builders have made them ready the whole block has to be handed over to the landlord, which will probably entail bureaucracy and further delay ... and then, of course, there's God's hand in it.

Meanwhile Sheikh Mohammed of Dubai has been showing that it is possible to control events. Last night, in a move so sudden and unexpected as to prompt conspiracy theories of a terrorist threat, he cancelled all public New Year celebrations in the UAE's party city. It was explained as a gesture of solidarity with the Palestinians of Gaza who are currently being bombarded by missiles from Israel. Pictures of civilian suffering in local newspapers have been harrowing in their detail and people here are not only shocked but angry.

The question is: will the Arab world unite to resolve the problem – or simply wait for God to sort it out?

What became known in the Arab world as the Gaza Massacre continued until 18 January. Over 1,000 Palestinians were killed, of whom at least 430 were civilians. Israel suffered 13 fatalities, including 3 civilians. In February I received the keys to my apartment. Various components of a computer did eventually arrive on my desk, albeit in dribs and drabs – but without any connecting wires or power cable.

34. HAMMER BLOWS
Abu Dhabi, 9 January 2009

People are more like their times than their parents
- Arabic proverb

On two sides of my hotel foundations are being laid for new towers. On another an obsolete apartment block and multi-storey car park are being demolished. As old gives way to new the noise is incessant and I have learnt to sleep with a pillow over my head, as well as under, and ear-plugs in between.

So while the sound of hammer blows may have receded in Dubai, here it continues unabated. A bullish government has confirmed that work on the flagship projects of Abu Dhabi's Urban Structure Framework Plan 2030 – the Guggenheim, Louvre, National and Maritime museums on Saadiyat Island – has started and remains on target for completion by 2014. But almost every day fresh evidence emerges of the local impact of the global downturn, and in a new blueprint for economic growth published this week economists warn of the chance of recession hitting the UAE.

Their pronouncement comes in Abu Dhabi's Economic Vision 2030.

Tourism, financial services and the property sector *will* suffer, they say, and jobs *will* go. Recent market falls and volatility serve to confirm the fragility of economies dependent on oil. More diversification is recommended, underpinned by a bigger role for the private sector and greater development of what is described as the emirate's most important natural resource – its young people. Two-thirds of Emiratis are under the age of twenty-five and in an echo of the late Sheikh Zayed the report urges that more should be done through education, work experience and training to equip them for productive roles in the economy.

With greater economic participation will surely come demands for more political empowerment: after all, the constitution states that the country should be 'progressing by steps towards a comprehensive, representative, democratic regime.' At the moment government is concentrated in the hands of a few and democracy exists only in the form of a consultative Federal National Council of which half the members are elected by an electoral college of voters, the other half being appointed by the government. But this afternoon, in a rare and coordinated expression of anger across the UAE, I watched as several thousand people marched along the Corniche carrying flags and placards and shouting slogans in support of the Palestinians of Gaza whose bloody plight is daily splashed in graphic images on the front pages of our newspapers.

Arranged over the internet and by mobile text messaging, similar demonstrations were held simultaneously in Dubai, Sharjah and Ras al Khaimah. All took place with the approval of the Ministry of Interior and here in Abu Dhabi the police not only sealed the route to protect the protestors but handed out free bottles of drinking water to refresh them. By contrast, in neighbouring Saudi Arabia university staff and students were banned from holding peaceful sit-ins and a religious leader issued a fatwa describing public protest as 'moral corruption.'

In answer to a question about whether parliamentary democracy should be introduced in the UAE, Sheikh Zayed once responded:

'Why should we abandon a system that has satisfied our people in order to introduce a system that seems to engender dissent and confrontation?'

But now there is an undercurrent of feeling among educated young nationals that more people should have a voice in government and this afternoon's protests show how easy public opinion can be galvanised, particularly when governments seem incapable of resolving issues of concern.

The hammer blows raining on Gaza may yet herald an Abu Dhabi Democracy Plan.

In 2011, in the wake of violent protests elsewhere the Arab world, the UAE government announced an increase in the number of voters in the electoral college from 7,000 to almost 80,000.

35. VAULTING AMBITION
Abu Dhabi, 16 January 2009

Don't climb too high, lest you fall too deep
- Arabic proverb

On the front page of this morning's *National* there's a photograph of an electrical storm over the world's tallest building.

The picture was taken earlier this week when hail and thunderstorms wrought havoc in the northern emirates. A web of lightning illuminates the evening sky over the unfinished 780 metre-plus Burj Dubai, burnishing the glass and steel tower with a faint sheen of silver.

'Spectacular' is how the newspaper describes it. But the slender tower looks vulnerable to the atmospheric onslaught: lightning suggests doom and silver turns ghostly grey. 'Apocalyptic' comes to mind. Like a latter-day Babel in the Book of Genesis, the Tower of Dubai reaches for the heavens to glorify Man.

Come, let us build ourselves a city
with a tower that reaches to the heavens,
so that we may make a name for ourselves.

Dubai's vanity has taken a heavy knock of late. Tucked away in the business pages of the English language Arab newspapers this week was an announcement that construction of the world's tallest building has been halted for a year. This is a reference not to the Burj Dubai but the proposed Nakheel Tower, also in Dubai. Although the developers of tall towers tend to be cautious about disclosing the secrets of height, the Nakheel project is confidently expected to dwarf the Burj and rise more than a kilometre into the sky. Its foundations alone will take three years to complete and the delay announced this week is the starkest sign yet that all is not well in Dubai.

Some weeks ago a UAE national confirmed a rumour circulating among the expatriate community that Sheikh Mohammed of Dubai had recently visited Abu Dhabi to ask Sheikh Khalifa for help. It was said with some glee, reflecting competition – if not rivalry – between the two emirates. Both are trying to raise their profiles – but in different ways. While Dubai craves attention by building tall towers and breaking world records, Abu Dhabi pursues a more subtle approach based on art, sport, and culture. Unlike Dubai, however, Abu Dhabi is rich enough to withstand the current downturn.

In their pursuit of success the Abu Dhabi owners of Manchester City Football Club are now seeking to set a new record in the world of football. The Abu Dhabi Group for Development and Investment, a private equity company owned by Sheikh Mansour bin Zayed Al Nahyan, a brother of the President, is said to be prepared to pay £100 million or more to recruit Ricardo Izecson dos Santos Leite – more popularly known as Kaka – from AC Milan. Newspapers are speculating that the Brazilian star will be rewarded with wages of £20 million a year after tax – which amounts to a staggering £384,000 a week.

While opinion among professionals in the beautiful game is mixed, the chairman of a rival English premiership football club surely spoke for many when he said, 'It's totally barmy.'

Barmy it may be, but it's already helping to put Abu Dhabi on the map and would be one in the eye for Dubai.

Kaka turned down Manchester City's offer and remains with AC Milan.

36. GREEN DESERT
Abu Dhabi, 23 January 2009

All things but knowledge diminish if used
- Arabic proverb

The Bedouin lived a simple, noble and free existence in harmony with the changing seasons and natural elements of their harsh environment – or so romantics would have it. In reality life was impoverished rather than simple, as savage as it was noble, and more constrained than free. In Doughty's estimation the life of the Bedouin was the 'most miserable of mankind.'

Untrammelled by all but the most indispensable of possessions, however, the desert-dwellers of the UAE left no more mark on the environment than footprints in loose sand.

'They recognised the need to conserve it,' said Sheikh Zayed, 'To take from it only what they needed to live, and to preserve it for succeeding generations.'

What a contrast to the popular image of their modern day descendants: the oil rich sheikhs with their palaces, towers and gardens, sleek limousines and gas-guzzling four-wheel-drive vehicles – and the largest environmental footprint in the world. In his later years, when comparing the comfort and ease he observed in modern Abu Dhabi with his youthful memories of living with the Bedouin, Sir Wilfred Thesiger complained that the Arabs had been ruined by oil. But the poison is set to become the antidote. Driven by economic common sense to reduce dependency on oil, Abu Dhabi is set to reinvent itself and become an exemplar of environmental good practice – drawing on wealth derived from oil to fund knowledge and innovation in green technology.

Even now the world's first zero-carbon, zero-waste city is being created near Abu Dhabi airport. The six kilometre-square Masdar City – walled to protect it from hot summer winds, powered by electricity generated from sunshine and waste, and watered by solar-powered desalination – will be home to 50,000 residents and a place of work for another 50,000 commuters. No cars will be allowed – people will have to walk, cycle or ride along tracks in small driverless, subterranean podcars fuelled by solar energised electric batteries – and buildings will be equipped with dew-catchers, rain-water harvesters and sensors to detect leaks.

At the heart of Masdar will be the Masdar Institute of Science and Technology, a government-owned hub for energy research which is already investigating the impact of heat, humidity and dust on solar technology. Meanwhile a solar energy farm has been specially built to meet the power requirements of the city's construction. Energy from the sun is central to Abu Dhabi's vision for a greener future – hardly surprising given that it exists here in even greater abundance than oil – and at the World Future Energy Summit held here last week the government announced a target of producing at least 7% of the emirate's power from renewable sources by 2020.

Billions of dirhams have already been committed to wind and solar energy partnerships in the UK, Finland, the Netherlands, Germany, Spain and the United States. Meanwhile forty-one different solar systems are being tested here and on the eve of the summit came news that the first solar-powered desalination plant is up and running in the western region. At 550 litres per person per day, the UAE is one of the highest per capita consumers of water in the world and desalination plays a vital role in quenching the country's thirst. Most ambitious – and controversial – of all are plans to build a network to capture industrial carbon dioxide and bury it in depleted oil wells. Such a system would reduce carbon emissions in the atmosphere and free up the natural gas which is currently used to force oil to the surface.

One can almost hear the planet breathe a sigh of relief.

But how much more convincing the government's green conversion would be if motoring habits and the cost of petrol in Abu Dhabi reflected their environmental impact (it costs little more than £10 to fill the tank of my Honda Civic); if the newspapers, cans and plastic water bottles discarded daily in my waste bin did not end up in a conventional landfill site (of the emirates, only Sharjah has a formal scheme for recycling waste); if municipal authorities across the emirate were not hell-bent on greening the desert (irrigation accounts for 76% of water consumption in the UAE); if there was some sign that public authorities and residents alike even considered their impact on the environment – let alone cared.

A report in 2008 placed the six countries of the Gulf Cooperation Council (Bahrain, Kuwait, Oman, Qatar, Saudi Arabia and the UAE) in the top ten waste producers in the world. Led by Sharjah, Dubai and Abu Dhabi, facilities for recycling industrial, construction/destruction and domestic waste are gradually improving in the UAE. Changing habits may take a little longer.

37. THE AUDACITY OF HOPE
Abu Dhabi, 26 January 2009

Throw your heart out in front of you and run ahead to catch it
- Arabic proverb

'The happy fortune of rain' in Arabia is so uncommon as to prompt Emiratis to abandon the shelter of their homes and drive into the desert to marvel at a downpour.

Their joy is instinctive. 'The Lord be praised,' Doughty's Bedouin companions would cry when a shower heralded the prospect of fresh pasture for their camels.

Imagine then the excitement here over the weekend when it snowed in the mountains of Ras al Khaimah. Snow is so rare that the local vocabulary does not even have a word for it. *Barid*, meaning cold, is said to be the closest that classical Arabic has to offer. 'Unbelievable' was how a helicopter pilot described the scene.

It's only the second time in living memory that the Jebel Jais has seen snow. A mere dusting in 2004 was the first. This time, as the temperature plunged to -3C, the 1,737 metre mountain lay under a blanket of snow some 10-20 centimetres deep – and this in a country with an average annual temperature of more than 27C.

Ordinarily snowfall in the UAE would probably trigger suggestions in the national press of climate change and impending environmental catastrophe, particularly as Abu Dhabi's many low lying islands are at risk from any rise in sea level. But it comes at the end of an extraordinary week in which newspapers and television here have been focusing on an African-American with an Arab name as he assumes the office of President of the United States.

During his election campaign Barack Hussein Obama challenged Americans to believe in 'the audacity of hope.'

'Hope in the face of difficulty,' he urged, 'Hope in the face of uncertainty.'

Last week, in his inaugural address, he offered hope for peace between Israel and the Palestinians.

'To the Muslim world,' he said, 'We seek a new way forward based on mutual interest and mutual respect.'

How easy it would be to be sceptical: to point to the fact that the conflict has been going on so long as to be insoluble. But a rare display of unity among Arab nations following the recent massacre of Palestinians in Gaza, and the appointment of George Mitchell, a seasoned diplomat who helped to bring peace to Northern Ireland, as the President's Middle East envoy, have combined to lift the mood here.

And if, contrary to experience and expectation, it can snow in the sub-tropical UAE, why not peace in the Middle East?

George Mitchell resigned in May 2011. In the UAE there has been no more snow. President Obama's Middle East peace initiative continues.

38. LEAKING PIPES AND EXPLODING SOCKETS
Abu Dhabi, 6 February 2009

Better black bread in your own house than honey at your neighbour's
- Arabic proverb

About five minutes' walk west of my apartment block is a mosque. Of the hundreds in Abu Dhabi it is one of the smallest. Yet it must have one of the most powerful loudspeaker systems in the city and shortly after 5.30 in the morning I am woken by the dawn call to prayer.

I am living on the third floor of a square tower some eight storeys high in the suburbs of the city. To imagine it picture the block in a line of some twenty more towers of similar height, size and shape. At ground level, currently empty, there will be shops. Then the mezzanine designated for offices. Then four floors, each of four two-bedroom apartments, most now occupied by fellow expat advisors. All topped by two penthouse suites and, crowning all, a small cabin for the watchman.

Across the road is a parallel world of similar blocks of shops, offices and apartments. The two rows face each other about 150 metres apart, separated by a busy eight-lane highway lined along the middle and on each side by palm trees, grass and flowerbeds.

Water pipes leak and electrical sockets explode – but after almost four months of living out of a suitcase in a succession of hotels, having my own space is liberating, even though much of my freedom during these first four days has been spent scrubbing floors and cleaning cupboards. And while the interior of the apartment may be somewhat Spartan, all necessities for survival can be found in the world below: supermarkets and hardware stores, more barber shops and laundries than one would think viable in a single street, banks and bakeries, cafes and restaurants, grocers, newsagents, tailors and vehicle repairers.

During the day the neighbourhood is a hive of noise and activity. Rather than park their vehicles and walk to the shops, locals simply stop in the road and summon shopkeepers with a blast of the horn – repeatedly if necessary, until someone emerges to do their bidding – and every afternoon there's a huge traffic jam as pupils are picked up from the local school. After the sun sets the area becomes a haven of inactivity as the cool of evening draws men to the plentiful *sheesha* (flavoured tobacco) cafes. Then the air grows pungent with the sweet scent of apple and peach-flavoured smoke and tranquillity descends – but only intermittently because for as long as the shops and restaurants remain open drivers sit in their cars and blast on their horns.

If a place for recreation is required, about ten minutes walk to the east of my apartment block is a public park. To reach its pleasant green acres one must trudge ankle-deep across a broad strip of soft, red sand which serves to remind that not so many years ago all hereabouts was desert. Like all public parks in Abu Dhabi, this afternoon – being the Islamic Holy Day – it is full of families and groups of expatriate workers enjoying the holiday. Many have brought picnics, some are cooking on barbecues, and as children play football and adults chat I linger beside a group of young Africans who are singing and dancing beneath the shade of a tree to the accompaniment of tambourines and a makeshift drum.

Lying on the grass in the warm winter sunshine listening to the music of Africa, my eyes close and oblivion beckons … but another small mosque lies hidden close by, and I am suddenly brought back from the brink by the mid-afternoon call to prayer.

39. SCHADENFREUDE
Abu Dhabi, 7 February 2009

Every eunuch scoffs at his master's prick
- Arabic proverb

The credit crunch has hit the UAE. It's official – or rather, it can no longer be denied thanks to a British construction project manager and his Porsche.

When twenty-eight year old Andrew Blair was made redundant from his Dh395,000 (£63,000) a year job in Dubai last month he advertised for another – by scrawling a message in black ink on the rear of his white Porsche

'MADE REDUNDANT TODAY
CONSTRUCTION PROJECT MANAGER'

together with his name and mobile telephone number. A photograph of the car soon found its way into the Gulf press and, from there, to the international media. In local interviews the enterprising expatriate explained how he was having to adjust his lifestyle. No longer could he afford to spend Dh9,000 (£1,500) a month on entertainment and eating out. In eighteen months he reckoned he had only made three meals in his Dh7,000 (£1,100) a month rented apartment. Austerity measures include moving into cheaper accommodation and eating at home on a Dh30 (£5) daily budget. His visa runs out in two months, after which he will have to return home to recession-hit Bristol unless he finds another job.

Mohammed has also been made redundant. He too was employed in the construction industry. I met him this morning while walking with a colleague along the sea front. Seeing a couple of white faces he approached, politely wished us 'Salaam alaykum' – Peace be unto you – and held out an envelope. Inside was a testimonial from his former employers in Dubai commending him as a good worker and regretting the need to terminate his contract. His residency visa runs out in four weeks. Unless he can find another job here he will have to return home to his impoverished family in Pakistan.

Meanwhile some newspapers in the UK can hardly contain their delight – as if there were not more pressing problems at home to write about.

40. MARCH OF TIME
Abu Dhabi, 12 February 2009

Examine what is said, not him who speaks
- Arabic proverb

Britain's 'Pop Idol' and 'How do you solve a problem like Maria?' have their counterpart on UAE television.

Forty-eight poets chosen from some 16,000 applicants across the Arab world are competing over the course of sixteen weeks for prize-money totalling Dh22 million (£3.6m). Broadcast before an audience at the al Raha Beach Theatre in Abu Dhabi in a prime time Thursday evening slot, contestants are assessed and eliminated by a combination of votes from a panel of judges and the theatre and television audiences. Dh5 million (£833,000) will go to the winner of the grand final in March.

Sponsored by the Crown Prince of Abu Dhabi, the *Millions Poet* television show coincides with the emirate's recent camel festival poetry competition in which over four hundred poets from eleven countries celebrated the beloved animal in verse. The winning poet was invited to recite his poem on *Millions Poet*. Both competitions focus on preserving the Nabati (colloquial) style of poetry which is at the heart of Bedouin oral culture and quite different from classical Arabic from which it derives.

'The topics are more traditional,' explained one contestant, 'We talk about horses, hunting and cultural experiences using authentic imagery.'

Once the poetry of the Sands, it's now the poetry of the street and there's a contemporary bleakness which no number of beautiful metaphors can conceal. Last month's topics included the impact of the credit crunch, conflicts in Gaza, Lebanon and Iraq, and an Omani's reflections on the plight of his disabled niece which so touched members of the audience that they donated enough money to enable her family to send her abroad for treatment.

'It has become like football,' observed the grateful uncle, alluding to the growing popularity of colloquial verse.

For one show some fans flew all the way from Mauritania to cheer a favourite national poet.

While love of sheikhs and country are common themes, division and inequality have also featured. Attention currently focuses on a Saudi Arabian who recently spoke of the struggles of women poets in a field of expression dominated by men. And Aydah Al Aarawi Al Jahani certainly knows what she's talking about because she's under pressure from her family and her tribe to withdraw from the show – simply because she is female.

In the non-democratic kingdoms and emirates of the Gulf, Nabati poetry is providing a rare opportunity for popular expression, and audience participation in talent shows like *Millions Poet* is the closest many people come to having a political voice. Aydah Al Aarawi Al Jahani only avoided elimination by judges in the latest round when 59% of television voters rallied to her cause. Of just three female contestants who started out, she is the only one still in the competition.

I asked an Emirati if she thinks the Saudi Arabian poetess is helping to further the cause of women in the Gulf.

"You had George Eliot," she replied, "It takes time."

And the fact that a Muslim woman covered top to toe in a plain black *abaya* (long, loose robe) and *sheyla* (headscarf) is willing to have such a conversation with me – is proof itself of the march of time.

41. DOCTOR WHO AND THE SHAMAL
Abu Dhabi, 14 February 2009

Shut the door through which wind enters your house
- Arabic proverb

One morning this week I left a window open when I went to work and returned several hours later to find the entire apartment covered in dust.

The UAE is caught in a sandstorm whipped up by a north-westerly *Shamal* wind from beyond the far end of the Gulf. In Abu Dhabi visibility is down to a few hundred metres, the temperature has dropped ten degrees, and everything lies buried under a layer of fine silt from the Euphrates basin.

Meanwhile in the desert of Dubai a production team is waiting anxiously to film *Planet of the Dead*. The cast of *Doctor Who* has travelled all the way from Cardiff to record barren scenes for a BBC Easter Special – only to find their alien planet location in the grip of a lingering Shamal.

The sandstorm is not the first setback the team has suffered. Last month a key prop – a London double-decker bus in which the Doctor is transported to the dead planet – was wrecked when it was dropped in its container while being unloaded at the docks in Dubai. For a moment the entire project looked doomed – until someone had the bright idea of re-writing the script and incorporating the damage into the plot.

The Shamal, however, was not envisaged and time is fast running out.

Has he who defeated the Daleks finally met his match?

Planet of the Dead was broadcast on BBC television on 11 April 2009. Most of the footage from the first three days' filming proved unusable but the Shamal relented to give two clear days. After the bus crash-landed in the middle of a vast desert, a dazed Doctor observed: 'Call it a hunch, but I think we've gone a little bit further than Brixton.'

42. THE ROAD TO UNION
Semeih, 20 February 2009

A bundle of sticks is harder to break
- Arabic proverb

By local standards, Semeih is steeped in history – though you would not know it simply by looking.

For centuries a well here was a gathering place for tribes from Abu Dhabi to launch raids into neighbouring Dubai. The last time the two emirates engaged in war was from 1945 to 1948. A minor quarrel over borders quickly escalated into a matter of honour. Neither Sheikh Shakhbut of Abu Dhabi nor Sheikh Saeed of Dubai would back down. So it fell to two leaders in waiting – Sheikh Zayed and Sheikh Rashid – to restore peace.

Two decades later Sheikh Zayed and Sheikh Rashid, then rulers of Abu Dhabi and Dubai respectively, chose to meet at Semeih, located half-way between the two cities, to discuss proposals for union. Four weeks earlier the British prime minister had announced in the House of Commons his government's intention to reduce spending by withdrawing military forces from the Persian Gulf by the end of 1971. The news came as a shock to the vulnerable emirates. The rulers had been looking forward to enjoying their new-found oil wealth under Britain's continuing protection. Now they faced the prospect of having to fend for themselves.

Even before this announcement the British had been trying to encourage the idea of federation but opinions in the emirates varied as to the extent to which authority should be centralised. There were also tribal differences to be overcome and political minefields to be negotiated with Iran and Saudi Arabia, both of which felt threatened by the possibility of a strong union in the lower Gulf and saw the proposed British withdrawal as an opportunity to further their own influence in the region. Successive kings of Saudi Arabia poured millions of dollars into construction projects in the northern emirates while Iran made plans to seize three islands in the Gulf.

At Semeih Sheikh Zayed began by making a symbolic concession of disputed offshore territories to Dubai. This paved the way for agreement with Sheikh Rashid on the principle of merger and an invitation to the rulers of the other Trucial emirates (which included Qatar and Bahrain) to join them. It was the first step on a rough road to union. Agreement took many more meetings. At one point there was even a suggestion from some of the emirates that British forces should be paid to remain and provide protection. In the end Qatar and Bahrain opted for independence leaving the other seven Trucial States to pursue federation alone.

Forty-one years on there is little at Semeih to tempt the thousands of motorists who speed past every day to pause on their journey. No hotel, shops or cafe, not even the old rest house in which the two sheikhs held their initial meeting: just a small plantation of trees and a lake. My visit is prompted by a newspaper article in which it is suggested that something should be put here to commemorate that remarkable first summit of 18 February 1968: a visitor centre, perhaps, with facilities for educating schoolchildren about the nation's history.

While archaeological research across the emirates has unearthed evidence of Stone, Bronze and Iron Age settlements, historical records tend to be limited to the accounts of imperial administrators and travellers. For all the richness of their cultural legacy, no stones point to where the desert-dwelling nomads lived, no memorials mark their passing. Although memories of quarrels endure, fields of battle have long since been obliterated, and until relatively recently great leaders were commemorated not in literature, paint or sculpture but in the oral folklore of the tribes. Transformed utterly by oil, it's hardly surprising that the modern UAE, where the lives of young Emiratis bear so little resemblance to those of their grandparents, is struggling with a crisis of national identity.

If a window on the pre-industrialised country is required one need look no further than a new exhibition devoted to Sir Wilfred Thesiger's travels in Arabia at the recently restored Jahili Fort in al Ain. Twice he crossed the

Rub al Khali (Empty Quarter) in the late 1940s dressed as a Bedouin and travelling by camel and on foot. After the second occasion he stayed with Sheikh Shakhbut in Abu Dhabi and with Sheikh Zayed in al Ain, and the account of his travels, *Arabian Sands*, ends in Dubai. The exhibition is illustrated by photographs he took during his expeditions and as I reflect on the significance of the meeting at Semeih an image from a recent visit to al Jahili returns. It depicts an encampment of the Manasir tribe, allies of Abu Dhabi's Bani Yas tribal federation, inside Abu Dhabi's territory at Liwa in 1948. Those who stare out are the survivors of an attack just a few months earlier by tribes from Dubai. Fifty-two Manasir were killed. Now, thanks to the seeds of a vision sown at Semeih, former enemies cooperate in a federation of common interest which has allowed each emirate to pursue its own path – in peace and security.

A few kilometres beyond Semeih lies the border between Abu Dhabi and Dubai, and there, on land spanning the boundary and donated by each, the architects of the union planned to build a new federal capital. However, residual rivalry eventually put paid to the idea.

Union is one thing: unity quite another.

On 2 December 1971 a treaty was signed in Dubai between Britain and the brand new UAE recording their mutual determination to ensure that relations between them should be governed by a spirit of close friendship. They confirmed that they would consult over matters of mutual concern in time of need, encourage educational, scientific and cultural cooperation, and recognise close relations in the field of commerce. The 1971 Treaty of Friendship was reaffirmed by the UAE's Minister of Foreign Affairs and the British Foreign Secretary during Queen Elizabeth's state visit in November 2010. The Abu Dhabi Declaration celebrated the two countries' strong cooperation in areas such as defence, security, energy, trade, education and culture, and recorded their determination to build ever closer relations. To prove the point they promptly signed agreements on civil nuclear cooperation, consular issues and visas.

43. SHOW OF FORCE
Abu Dhabi, 27 February 2009

*Once you have decided to hit someone, then hit them hard
because the retribution will be the same whether you hit hard or not*
- Arabic proverb

A camel train trudges slowly across the desert. Sand blows in ... the camels and their riders disappear from sight.

This is the opening scene of a film entitled *Farewell Arabia* which was broadcast by Rediffusion London Television when the UAE was still in its infancy. As the wind drops and the dust settles, however, a new picture emerges: a huge American car appears over the crest of a dune – slithering and sliding through the sand. At the wheel is Sheikh Zayed, chanting in Arabic as he attempts to steer the emirates to a new future. And following close behind: half a dozen or so Land Rovers full of heavily armed soldiers. It's an image replete with symbolism: cast adrift by Britain, the vulnerable emirates have one eye on modernisation – the other on defence.

Less than two decades earlier Abu Dhabi and the Sultan of Oman had had to call on British help to evict an occupying Saudi Arabian force from contested territories in Buraimi. And no sooner had the British withdrawn their protection from the former Trucial States than Iran invaded two islands governed by Ras al Khaimah and another ruled by Sharjah, claiming historic title to all three. The occupation of the islands has remained a bone of contention between the UAE and Iran ever since. And earlier this month the Iranian government reiterated its ownership and also laid claim to the UAE's Gulf ally, Bahrain.

This week, as Iran began testing its first nuclear power plant and fuelled suspicions that it is secretly planning to build atomic weapons, defence is again uppermost in the minds of the leaders of the emirates. Over the last five days the Abu Dhabi National Exhibitions Company has hosted an International Defence Exhibition. Almost 900 companies from fifty countries treated over 150 official delegations from around the world and some 45,000 visitors to the very latest in global defence technology. A new quay was specially dredged near the exhibition centre to showcase units of the UAE's navy while overhead there was a display from the country's air force. Living between the airport and the exhibition venue I have been treated to a ringside view of week-long aerial activity.

Among the guests of honour was Sheikh Mohammed bin Rashid of Dubai, Vice-President and Prime Minister of the UAE. Famed for his horsemanship and his poetry, the UAE's Renaissance man was yesterday photographed holding a machine-gun. And while he may have had one eye on promoting local products and services, his other was surely keeping watch on developments on the other side of the Gulf.

Of such tensions are defence deals made and, despite the economic downturn and fall in the price of crude oil, the market for military hardware in the Arab countries of the Gulf is stronger than ever. Contracts worth over Dh18 billion (£3bn) have been agreed by the UAE alone – more than five times what it spent at the last event two years ago. Combat aircraft from Italy and transport planes from the United States, Swiss observation systems and Italian anti-submarine technology, guns from Germany, speedboats from the UAE's own naval ship building company – all these and much more are in the shopping basket.

'There's no arms race in the region,' said a UAE military spokesman.

'Deterrent defence,' is how the President describes it.

Let's hope our nuclear neighbour across the Gulf sees it that way.

44. THE LURE OF THE EAST
Sharjah, 6 March 2009

Believe what you see and lay aside what you hear
- Arabic proverb

James Joyce tells the autobiographical story of a young boy who visits the Araby Bazaar in Dublin in 1894.

The very name of the bazaar, which promised a 'magnificent representation of an oriental city' in marked contrast to the 'ruinous houses' of home, conjures 'an Eastern enchantment' over him. For days his head is filled with wandering thoughts of mysterious delight. But he arrives late, finds most of the stalls already closed and the remaining ones selling wares far from exotic.

The prospect of a visit to Sharjah prompts similar anticipation today. After all it's the UAE's capital of culture, a former Cultural Capital of the Arab World, and a temporary exhibition at the city's Art Museum promises to transport us to 'luminous desert sands, colourful street scenes, serene and opulent interiors – all inhabited by darkly enchanting peoples of the Arab and Ottoman worlds.'

The Lure of the East explores the West's fascination with the Middle East and North Africa through British Orientalist painting of the nineteenth and early twentieth centuries – a genre said to have been inspired by the popularity of exotic tales from the *Arabian Nights*, which created longing for a sun-burnished world of dromedaries and deserts, bazaars, harems and dusky-skinned maidens.

No artist in the exhibition captures the romance better than John Frederick Lewis (1804-76) whose work makes up almost a fifth of the one hundred and twenty paintings, prints and drawings on show. He leads us by camel train into the scorching desert in *Edfou, Upper Egypt*; portrays himself as a carpet-seller *In the Bezestein Bazaar, Cairo*; peeps into the shady *Courtyard of the Coptic Patriach's House in Cairo*; introduces us to *An Armenian Lady, Cairo*, and a *Circassian Girl* in Constantinople; steals into the delicate lattice-screened chamber of a sleeping woman in *The Siesta*; shares an intimate glimpse of *Hareem Life, Constantinople*; takes us into *A Kibab Shop, Scutari*; eavesdrops on *Indoor Gossip* and *Outdoor Gossip*; shows us the *Chapel of the Burning Bush, St. Catherine's Monastery, Mount Sinai*; and invites us into the *Interior of a Mosque at Cairo, Afternoon Prayer* – just as the late afternoon call to prayer rings out across the city.

But how do Lewis's paintings compare with the world outside? With the traditional architecture of its arts and heritage quarter, strict Islamic laws on alcohol and decency, historic creek and old wooden dhows crewed by the descendants of Sindbad, Sharjah is probably the closest the UAE comes to old Arabia – yet it pales against the colourful, stylized images of the British Orientalists. For my companion it is an uncomfortable experience as she finds herself the object of attention of hordes of young Asian labourers with little to do on their day off but congregate, lounge and stare.

"I'm old enough to be their mother," she says.

For James Joyce's young Dubliner Araby proved to be an illusion. Modern Sharjah, with its concrete towers, car congested streets, leering labourers and complete absence of dromedaries, may leave Western visitors with a similar sinking feeling.

Although Sharjah is popularly thought to be 'dry', by a quirk of law liquor is served at the expatriate Wanderers Rugby Club.

45. WHEEL OF CHANGE
Abu Dhabi, 12 March 2009

Two in harmony can take a town
- Arabic proverb

The police force in Abu Dhabi is being driven to improve performance, so you can imagine their delight at a ceremony last night when it was announced that they had won this year's Award for Excellence in Government. Berets, I'm reliably informed, were thrown into the air.

But more testing times lie ahead. The government of Abu Dhabi has published an ambitious agenda for social and economic modernisation and has called upon all public entities to contribute to change. Detailed expectations are spelt out in performance contracts in which government authorities and departments are required to improve their services in line with specific outcomes which reflect the ruler's vision of a confident, secure society underpinned by a competitive and sustainable economy.

Within this framework Abu Dhabi Police has been given a list of targets to improve confidence, safety and operational effectiveness (the emirate is so rich that economy barely enters the reckoning) and this week, in the sumptuous surroundings of the capital's Intercontinental Hotel, senior police leaders attended workshops over two evenings to review their focus and fine-tune their plans. But working to targets is a new experience for Abu Dhabi Police and our team of advisers from the UK is playing a crucial role in developing a planning and performance regime to enable the force to meet its contractual obligations.

Acknowledgement of our contribution came at the end of the second workshop when, in a speech about national security and the importance of family life, the General Commander thanked the team for helping to steer the wheel of change. And it was perhaps no accident that in a recent translation on the theme of Abu Dhabi Police being driven to improve performance, the English word 'driven' was rendered in Arabic as 'chauffeured' – which happens to capture the nature of our relationship rather neatly.

Since then, to combat waste and inefficiency, the government has started to hold departments to closer account for budgetary spend. It is also taking steps to reduce public sector dependency on expatriate labour and increase the employment rate of Emiratis.

46. THE FIRST DROPS OF RAIN
Abu Dhabi, 27 March 2009

We are all the children of nine months
- Arabic proverb

Hundreds of supporters travelled from neighbouring Saudi Arabia yesterday to cheer their favourite poets in the final of this year's *Millions Poet* competition in Abu Dhabi – though any women among them required the permission of their husband or brother to travel abroad and none would have been allowed to drive.

The latest series of this prime time talent show has attracted more attention than ever. An estimated 50 million people across the Middle East watched last night's contest on television. As to why, one need look no further than Aydah Al Aarawi Al Jahani, the schoolteacher from Medina whose veiled participation had earlier prompted threats from relatives and members of her tribe. Happy to relate, all were subsequently reconciled and yesterday she competed with their blessing.

'I hope to reach the *berag*,' she said, referring to the coveted winner's flag, 'That is the only reason I came on the show.'

And no matter which of the contestants won, there was never a doubt as to where the gold-embroidered *berag* would go – for all four finalists hailed from Saudi Arabia. In the event, however, the first prize of Dh5 million (£800,000), went not to Aydah Al Jahani, who finished fourth, but to Ziad Hajeb bin Naheet, a former policeman known as the 'Poet of the Nation.'

While victory for the first ever female *Millions Poet* finalist would have made for a fairytale ending, Mrs Al Jahani can take consolation from Ziad's admission that his winning recital was inspired in part by the diversity of his fellow competitors. Her perseverance may also encourage more female poets to apply to take part in the next series of the competition.

So time marches on and, hard on its heels, the cause of women in the Gulf. No where more so than in Saudi Arabia where for the first time, to the surprise and delight of many of his subjects, a modernising king recently appointed a woman to his Council of Ministers: the first drops of rain, a senior government official ventured, of an approaching thunderstorm of reform.

In September 2011 King Abdullah granted women in Saudi Arabia the right to vote and stand as candidates in municipal elections and to be appointed to the national consultative council – although not until 2015. Celebrations were cut short, however, when almost the very next day a woman was sentenced to ten lashes after being caught driving a car without a licence in Jeddah earlier in the year. Happily Shayma Jastaniah's sentence was quickly annulled by the King.

While there is no law against women driving in Saudi Arabia, they are not allowed to have driving licences – and it's illegal to drive without a valid licence. In June many Saudi women took to the wheel in a nationwide protest and drove through their local towns and cities. Their action followed the release from prison of Manal Al-Sharif, a member of the Saudi action group Women2Drive, who had been arrested for posting a video of herself driving on Facebook. According to the English-language Arab News the reaction of the police at the time was generally low-key. Some women drivers were reported for driving without a licence and a woman in Jeddah said she was detained by soldiers and escorted home. But many said they were ignored. 'No one tried to stop us. No one even looked,' said a government IT consultant who swapped places with her husband in the family Hummer for a 45-minute drive through Riyadh, 'We drove past police cars but had no trouble.' Her only problem was her husband. 'He kept telling me to slow down or speed up,' she said, 'He was very fussy.'

47. OPULENCE AND BLING
Dubai, 3 April 2009

Wealth and children are the ornament of this life
- the Quran

Well-heeled parents who want the best for their children are beating a path to Baby Bling in Dubai's Village Mall in Jumeirah.

Baby Bling is the brainchild of Camelia Mohebi, who launched her enterprise just over a year ago with an interest-free loan under a government scheme to help Emiratis set up small businesses. The idea was prompted by a trend to decorate maternity wards with balloons and ribbons. Now she sells baby costumes with the logo

VIB – VERY IMPORTANT BABY

embossed with Swarovski crystals and personalised ones which spell out the baby's name. For Dh18,000 (£3,000) one can buy an 18-carat gold and diamond dummy. If that seems too extravagant cheaper ones are available from Dh2,500 (£416) to Dh6,500 (£1,083).

'I have sold five of the Dh18,000 dummies in the last year,' said Miss Mohebi in a recent interview, 'And fifteen silver ones.'

She conducted her market research through Facebook and was inundated with enquiries. Most of her business comes from the oil-rich countries of the Arabian Peninsula. One customer paid her to fly to Saudi Arabia and bought products costing Dh90,000 (£15,000).

'People in the Middle East, especially Arabs, love opulence and bling,' she explained, 'It has been part of our culture for centuries and babies are the ultimate fashion accessories.'

Over a hundred years ago Charles Doughty described how Bedouin women would deck their young daughters with mother-of-pearl necklaces and 'load' their heads with bunches and strings of little silver coins.

This week Miss Mohebi's business acumen was recognised when she received an award from Sheikh Majid bin Mohammed Al Maktoum, chairman of the Al Tomooh Scheme for Financing Small National Projects, for the most potential business growth.

For although recession has started to bite in Dubai, the population of nationals in the UAE is still forecast to rise by almost 3.5% this year – so creating plenty of potential for Baby Bling.

48. ECHOES
Abu Dhabi, 9 April 2009

The wrath of brothers is fierce and devilish
- Arabic proverb

Conspiracy and murder descended on the capital last week in the shadow of the ruler's ancestral fort: brother killed brother, uncle murdered nephews, and a king was slain in civil war.

This violent sequence may ring a bell. And if I add that all unfolded on a stage before an audience in the theatre at Abu Dhabi's Cultural Foundation, Shakespeare's *Richard the Third* may come to mind. For Shakespeare it was – albeit transformed into a modern Arabic re-telling.

Commissioned by the Royal Shakespeare Company, *Richard 111: an Arab Tragedy* is set in the Middle East and was performed in modern dress by an almost exclusively Arab cast to the accompaniment of traditional music and dance from the Gulf. While script and cast were much altered from Shakespeare's original, some of the better known lines were retained in an English re-translation which was broadcast simultaneously in text on two large screens. Most famously, in his dying moments Richard offers his kingdom for a horse. But convention is challenged from the very start. The play opens not with Richard and his 'Now is the winter of our discontent' speech but with Queen Margaret, the exiled widow of a vanquished rival, who places a curse on him. Small suitcase in hand, she introduces herself as a refugee. She could be from Lebanon, Palestine, Afghanistan or Iraq. Displaced and dispossessed, her presence haunts the title role throughout and portends his ultimate doom.

The Kuwaiti writer and director, Sulayman Al Bassam, originally set his play in Baghdad. On reflection, however, he chose not to draw a direct comparison between Richard and Saddam Hussein, and by not limiting his territory to Iraq made all the Arab world his stage. Intrigue and ambition, tyranny, execution and murder are thereby portrayed as universal themes – unconstrained by geography, unfettered by time. And as the action shifts between medieval England and contemporary Arabia, from the Wars of the Roses to militant Islam, from political agents to American surveillance, I catch an echo of Abu Dhabi's past.

For almost two hundred years the fortress next door to the theatre was the home and principal administrative headquarters of the Al Nahyan family, from whom, by tradition, the Bani Yas tribes have chosen their leader. But tribal custom allowed those who elected the rulers the right to remove them as well, and the history of the ruling sheikhs of Abu Dhabi is an almost unbroken sequence of murder and insurrection. Of the thirteen sheikhs who ruled from the palace fort from about 1795 to 1966, most met a violent and bloody end: deposed (by a son); deposed (by a brother); murdered (by two brothers); joint rulers both murdered (by a distant relative); deposed and killed (by a cousin); died naturally; died naturally; murdered (by two brothers); murdered (by a brother); deposed and killed (by a brother); abdicated; deposed (by a brother).* Behind the scenes, meanwhile, protecting their commercial interests, the British grew ever more imperious and intrusive.

The turning point came in 1966 when Sheikh Shakhbut bin Sultan Al Nahyan, in the face of popular discontent and with no little encouragement from the British, was gently removed by his younger brother, Sheikh Zayed; many years before, after their father and two uncles had all been murdered, their mother, Sheikha Salama, had made her sons swear not to do as tradition and settle family disputes by bloodshed. Oil was behind the coup. Wary of change, Shakhbut would not spend his new wealth and the people of Abu Dhabi grew impatient for schools, hospitals and public utilities. So the moderniser confronted the traditionalist and the elder brother was sent into temporary exile.

The old fortress has long been abandoned for sumptuous new palaces, and if the present ruler is haunted by the past it is only the benign ghost of his late father, Sheikh Zayed, who, though dead these four years, still remains the guiding spirit of the nation. And there may lie the rub: Zayed's influence will surely wane and beneath the surface tensions persist.

An Arab Tragedy reminds us that the future resonates with echoes of the past – and even as I write a US warship is steaming towards the Horn of Africa to protect America's maritime interests in the pirate-infested seas off the coast of southern Arabia.

* Sheikh Shakhbut bin Diyab, the first ruler to make Abu Dhabi's fort his residence, was deposed by his eldest son, Mohammed, in 1816, who in turn was deposed by his brother, Tahnoon, two years later. Tahnoon bin Shakhbut lasted until 1833 when he was murdered by his brothers Khalifa and Sultan, whom he had banished from Abu Dhabi but unwisely allowed to return. In 1845 joint rulers Khalifa and Sultan were murdered after a feast by a distant relative, Isa bin Khaled Al Falahi, whose coup failed when he and all his sons were killed. They were followed by Khalifa's nephew, Saeed bin Tahnoon, who had been living in exile since his father's murder twelve years earlier. But Sheikh Saeed was deposed in 1855 after killing a tribal elder in retaliation for murdering his brother. Although Saeed managed to escape from the fort, he returned and captured the Maqta watchtower guarding the approach to Abu Dhabi island, only to be routed and killed by forces of his cousin, Zayed bin Khalifa, who had been elected to succeed him.

With Sheikh Zayed the First there followed a rare golden age of relative peace, unity and prosperity which quickly came to an end after his natural death in 1909. Zayed's eldest son, Khalifa, was chosen to succeed but refused. So the mantle passed to Zayed's second eldest son, Sheikh Tahnoon, who died from ill-health three years later. Again Khalifa bin Zayed was offered but declined the succession, whereupon leadership passed to another of Zayed's sons, Hamdan, who lasted until 1922 when he was murdered by his brother, Sultan, with the help of another brother, Saqr. Four years later Sheikh Sultan was shot dead by Saqr, who himself met a violent end two years later when he was pursued and killed after an assassination attempt instigated by his eldest brother, Khalifa, failed.

One of Khalifa's sons was then installed as caretaker ruler but it was only ever intended as a temporary measure. Khalifa wanted office neither for himself nor his sons and so backed his nephew, Shakhbut bin Sultan, who became ruler in 1928.

49. PRIDE AND PREJUDICE
Dubai, 14 April 2009

The dogs may bark but the caravan moves on
- Arabic proverb

'Hovering over Dubai,' wrote Simon Jenkins in *The Guardian* last month, 'Is a cloud called nemesis.'

The author has caused quite a stir in the city which he suggests is on the brink of being reclaimed by the desert. In the current downturn, he says, as businesses fail and expatriates lose their jobs and flee, Dubai's tall towers will prove to be 'casualties of architectural folly': unfinished, abandoned and decaying, walls will crumble and glass will shatter, empty shells will be overrun by squatters, basements will become breeding grounds for feral dogs and sand will drift relentlessly in. And he concludes with Shelley's traveller's tale 'from an antique land' of 'two vast and trunkless legs of stone,' near which, half-buried in the sand, lies the broken image of 'Ozymandias, king of kings,' bearing on its pedestal his proud boast:

'Look on my works, ye Mighty, and despair!'

English-language newspapers here have refrained from firing cheap shots at the UK in return – despite allegations of government sleaze, violent stories of feral children and news that the British economy remains deep in recession. But editors have leapt to Dubai's defence and the director-general of the Department of Finance this week sought to reassure us that the emirate is on the road to recovery. In the interim the British Foreign Office felt compelled to describe Jenkins' remark as 'over-exaggerated' and Lord Mandelson, Secretary of State for Business and Enterprise, distanced himself from the comments when he visited Abu Dhabi in a bid to extend British markets in the UAE.

Still the story rumbles: 'Dubai will survive,' insisted an expert in yesterday's *Khaleej Times*; 'Western expats full of praise for Dubai,' ran a headline in the *Gulf News*; while today, in a very public show of solidarity, Sheikh Khalifa of Abu Dhabi joined Sheikh Mohammed of Dubai on a presidential tour of the city which, besides hotels and beach resorts, offices, marinas and shopping malls, took in Union House, where the UAE was founded in 1971, and concluded with a trip to the top of the world's tallest building.

As I write I have in front of me a photograph that was taken in Abu Dhabi shortly after unification. It shows a Bedouin family sitting in a circle on the ground in a traditional hair tent drinking coffee while waiting for their government-funded house to be completed next door. This afternoon, as they stood side by side under the flag of union on the very spot where their fathers signed the treaty of federation little more than a generation ago, the President and Vice-President of the UAE spoke of the miraculous leap their country has made and of their vision for sustainable development. It's a startling achievement: from goat-hair tents and camel dung fires to glass towers and the prospect of civil nuclear power – in less than half a century.

'Yesterday these were disunited emirates suffering ignorance, poverty, illness and chronic disease,' wrote the Emirati poet, Hamad Khalifah Bu Shihab, 'And today the Lord has bestowed upon us His grace in uncountable abundance.'

Reputation and honour mean everything in Arab society and today, in Abu Dhabi's very symbolic display of public support for Dubai, we saw nothing less than a reaffirmation of union. When Britain withdrew its Trucial umbrella of protection thirty-eight years ago the seven emirates had the option to fragment but chose instead to join together. Today the bonds which unite them are hardwired to all the major economies of the world

– and if an ill wind blows a cloud over Europe, America or Asia, it also hovers over the UAE. Dubai's recession is but a measure of its progress.

Here's Hamad Khalifah Bu Shihab again:

'Yesterday, few people knew of our name and today our voice reaches all corners of the Earth.'

50. A ONE-ARMED BANDIT
Abu Dhabi, 17 April 2009

If God gives you anything, take it!
- Arabic proverb

Police in the UAE have adopted a novel approach to improve road safety: as well as issuing fines and penalty points for bad driving, they give cash and certificates for good behaviour.

Having learnt of the annual Road Star contest's impending arrival on the streets of Abu Dhabi this week, imagine my joy when, within moments of setting out from home on the day in question, I spotted a police car outside a local cafe. As I passed, it followed – so affording me the perfect opportunity to display some model driving skills. Nor should it be hard to make a good impression here: speed limits are universally ignored; tailgating is routine; lane discipline is non-existent; and most people find it impossible to drive without talking into a hand-held mobile phone. You will therefore understand my disappointment when the officer behind me grew tired of being held to the speed limit and overtook without so much as a glance.

I have since found out that twenty drivers were picked out for a cash reward of Dh750 (£125), a certificate of safe driving and a handshake from a senior officer in the Traffic Department. Some were rewarded for signalling while changing lanes – as rare an occurrence in the UAE as it is common in the UK – others simply for wearing a seat-belt or not speeding. Most, of course, feared the worst when stopped and none was more bemused than a driver who later confessed to a long history of traffic violations.

'I've got no idea why they chose me,' he said, 'I'm driving with a broken arm.'

51. TALE OF THE UNEXPECTED
Abu Dhabi, 19 April 2009

Every day of your life is a page of your history
- Arabic proverb

Some forty years ago, when Abu Dhabi was little more than a cluster of palm huts on a barren island, a young man from the north-east of England began work at a steel-making plant in Hartlepool. Here I shall call him by his Arab name: Mubarak bin Shot'n – the Blessed One from Shotton.

"The first job I was given was to stencil Abu Dhabi and someone's name, Sheikh someone, I forget who, on an order of 20-inch steel pipes," he explains, "It was the first time I ever heard of Abu Dhabi. I had to ask where it was. The Persian Gulf, I was told."

Today Mubarak is visiting Abu Dhabi for the first time and his reminiscences come as we wander through the congested streets of the high-rise city centre. Forty years ago we would have been walking on sand.

"This order went on for months," he recalls, "There must have been hundreds – no, thousands – of pipes sent over, each about sixty or seventy feet long."

These shipments coincided with the modernisation of the emirate after Sheikh Zayed took over the reins of government from his brother, Sheikh Shakhbut. Wary of change and loath to spend money, Shakhbut had recoiled when shown plans for the island's development.

'But this is Paris!' he said, 'We don't want a Paris in Abu Dhabi.'

Since his departure the city has never stopped growing, and forty years on the Louvre Abu Dhabi lies at the heart of the government's agenda for attracting more tourists. Poor Shakhbut will be turning in his grave.

Beyond Shakhbut's old fort, closed pending redevelopment, we turn off the main thoroughfare into a quiet side street. Ahead of us, mounted on low blocks along the edge of the pavement, is a rare stretch of exposed steel piping some fifty yards long. The joy of travel often lies in the unexpected and Mubarak is delighted to think we may have stumbled upon some of the very pipes he dispatched here all those years ago.

Standing some two feet or so above the kerb, the top of the pipe is perfectly pitched for sitting on, and as the sun sinks a dozen or more people are taking advantage of the late afternoon shade to perch and catch up with friends.

"It's certainly the right size," says Mubarak, running his hands over the pitted metal.

On each side curious spectators follow the movement of his fingers and listen as he strikes a note with his fist.

"Yes," he concludes with satisfaction, "It could well be one of ours."

As we leave I glance back and see that several of those who were sitting are now standing, their heads bent, eyes peering: seeing not the reflections of youth but only rust and peeling paint.

52. THE ARABIAN OSTRICH
Abu Dhabi, 30 April 2009

Justice is often a stick in the hands of the unjust
- Arabic proverb

Tucked away on the inside pages of today's *Gulf News* is a small article in which the Human Rights Office of Abu Dhabi's Judicial Department expresses concern about events depicted in a deeply disturbing video currently circulating on the worldwide web.

In the video an Afghan grain merchant is tortured for allegedly failing to repay a debt to a member of the country's ruling Al Nahyan family. The victim is electrocuted with a cattle prod, beaten with a piece of wood, run over by a car, and the ground on which he cowers is sprayed with a burst of bullets. The perpetrator is said to be Sheikh Isa, a son of Zayed and half-brother of the President, assisted by a man dressed in the uniform of a police officer or security guard.

Questions were raised by the Human Rights Office after the Minister of Interior, another senior member of the Al Nahyan family, buried his head in the sand. For him it was enough that the parties were said to have resolved their dispute without complaint on either side.

But it's not enough.

Global confidence is crucial to Abu Dhabi's long term economic development and while the government may be able to distance itself from Sheikh Isa, who holds no official portfolio, it risks the fate of the Arabian ostrich, once abundant in the emirates but now extinct, if it chooses to ignore international concern about justice in the UAE.

The Human Rights Division of the Judicial Department launched an investigation and in January 2010, following a three-month trial, Sheikh Isa bin Zayed Al Nahyan was acquitted of charges of sexual abuse, endangering life and causing bodily harm to Mohammed Shah Poor at his farm in al Ain in 2004. The security guard was also acquitted. Five other defendants were convicted and sentenced to terms of imprisonment.

The court found that Sheikh Isa could not be held liable for his actions because he was drugged and coerced with a view to blackmail by two former business partners, Bassan and Ghassan Nabulsi, who were each sentenced to five years' imprisonment in absentia. A cook was sentenced to one year in prison followed by deportation for helping to tie up the victim and two farm workers were given three years' imprisonment for taking part in the abuse.

After the verdict was announced Mr Shah Poor, who received compensation for his injuries in a private settlement soon after the incident, congratulated the sheikh and kissed him on both cheeks. The Nabulsi brothers, who were in America at the time of the trial, deny that they drugged Sheikh Isa.

53. PICTURES AT AN EXHIBITION
al Ain, 23 May 2009

What you can't see with your eyes, you'll see with your mind
- Arabic proverb

'It is our solemn responsibility to interpret the history of our ancestors. The events of their lives help us to understand the past and to plan the future.'

So begins the foreword to a booklet published to honour the legacy of Sheikh Zayed bin Khalifa Al Nahyan – Zayed the First, more commonly known as Zayed the Great, who ruled Abu Dhabi for fifty-four years – on the occasion of the centenary of his death.

Earlier this week a copy of this booklet was delivered to every apartment in my block, a gift from Abu Dhabi's Authority for Culture and Heritage which is campaigning to raise public awareness about how the UAE's past impacts on the present. So we learn that security at sea (as a result of fostering good relations with the British) and selective tax concessions to some important boat owners sealed Abu Dhabi's pearling dominance over the other emirates and not only provided Zayed with the wherewithal to improve agriculture and build a new fort in al Ain but gave him leverage with other tribal leaders and so helped to stall the expansionist incursions of Ibn Saud's marauding tribesmen from the Nejd.

As well as stability, security and prosperity, however, we also find unity, for it was under his leadership that the rulers of the Trucial States first came together to resolve differences peacefully rather than resort to war. In 1905, with curious similarities to what happened under his grandson at Union House some sixty-six years later, Sheikh Zayed presided over a meeting in Dubai of the sheikhs of Dubai, Ajman, Umm al Quwain and Sharjah to settle a tribal dispute and the following year they agreed a document which defined spheres of tribal influence.

There, in a nutshell, we have Zayed's achievement – carefully air-brushed of the violent discord within the Al Nahyan family that undermined his father's authority and blighted his own accession. We learn that his father died in 1845: not that he was murdered by a distant relative, who himself was then killed and all his sons besides. We are told that tribal elders invited young Zayed to become ruler of the Bani Yas tribes in 1854: not that they had first deposed his cousin, who refused to give up without a fight and was subsequently killed when he tried to regain the fort in Abu Dhabi. Nor is it explained that Ibn Saud's claim to Bani Yas territories in the Buraimi Oasis had been nurtured by his own father who paid tribute in return for Saudi protection from members of his own family. And perhaps just as well: because it's a long, complicated and sorry tale of Al Nahyan intrigue and Bani Yas in-fighting in which other Trucial rulers became deeply embroiled – and would run to an encyclopaedic-size volume.

On 19 May, exactly 100 years after Sheikh Zayed's death, an exhibition was launched to mark the centenary at Jahili Fort in al Ain – and it's there you find me today, eager to see what's on show. When Sir Percy Cox passed this way in 1902 he observed 'a nice new fort and a walled date and fruit orchard, at that time in its infancy, but very promising.' Following recent renovation the fort still looks 'nice' and 'new' and dozens of flags bearing the great Zayed's name flutter in the morning breeze to whet the appetite. But in the gallery there are just eight portraits, the paint barely dry and half of them derived from the same ancient grainy photograph taken by a German traveller called Hermann Burchardt of a white-bearded old man seated in a huddle of tribesmen outside the ruler's fort in Abu Dhabi in 1904.

"We've driven a hundred miles to see this," laughs my companion.

It's another triumph of pomp over circumstance, much like the pretty box, large enough to hold a double layer of chocolates, in which I recently received a sliver-thin theatre ticket. And what could we reasonably expect – Zayed's coffee pot, sword and seal? Some of his precious pearls, perhaps – or the saddle from the horse presented to him by an admiring Sherif of Mecca?

Yet there is a relic from his day – in the home of the exhibition rather than in the exhibition itself. Above the original entrance to Zayed's much extended and recently restored fort is an Arabic inscription which in translation reads:

> *A door of goodness is opened in glory's chapter*
> *Where joy and happiness with high glory reside,*

The blessings of honour said, 'Mark this house,
A house of high standing built by Zayed bin Khalifa.'

This, we may surmise, made a deep impression on his famous namesake who, after his father had been murdered by an uncle in Abu Dhabi in 1926, was brought up with his mother's family in al Ain and reared on stories of how his grandfather had once put an end to war by forging unity among the tribes – so inspiring his own dream of federation.

'History is a continuous chain of events,' the younger Zayed would preach many years later, 'The present is only an extension of the past.'

Perhaps his grandfather's legacy is what he had in mind.

54. THE DEVIL'S GAP
Ras al Khaimah, 29 May 2009

Take care not to let cares take you
- Arabic proverb

While sailing home from Madras in 1817, an officer of the Honourable East India Company called William Heude was suddenly awoken one night by a cry from his ship's captain calling on everyone to rise and defend themselves or else be murdered in their beds. A moment later, as he grabbed his sword and pistols, the door of his cabin burst open and he was confronted by a man with a sabre …

Ordinarily the greatest danger of a voyage came from rocks and storms, but not within the infamous Devil's Gap, a colloquial name among the East India sailors for the entrance to the Persian Gulf (whether on account of its adverse winds or 'the wickedness and profligacy of the people of its shores,' our narrator could not say): here it was pirates and all who entered the Gap were in constant fear of attack. A few days earlier they had watched warily while an Arab dhow weighed the odds of success before eventually sailing away. Doubtless, too, they had in mind the fate of the crew of the East India Company's *Minerva* in 1808. Contemporary accounts told how, after a sustained battle against a fleet of fifty or more dhows and some

5,000 pirates, the vessel was at last seized and purified with water, prayers and perfumes before survivors were ritually executed to cries to 'Allah! Akhbar!' – God is Great! – brutality said to have been learned from the Portuguese, who were the first Europeans to assert themselves in the region.

On this occasion, however, it proved to be a false alarm. In *A Voyage up the Persian Gulf* Heude tells us that his attacker, whom happily he quickly managed to disarm, proved to be none other than the captain himself – 'who, his wits having entirely forsaken him, had imagined himself beset, and had alarmed us accordingly.'

In 1819, after earlier attempts had failed to bring lasting peace, a fleet of nine British warships delivered a final, devastating bombardment on the pirate stronghold at Ras al Khaimah. The inhabitants were forced to retreat, pursued by an army of marines, to a small fort a few kilometres beyond the town at Dhayah. Some four hundred lives were lost before the Arabs surrendered and two hundred boats were either seized or destroyed. The British subsequently agreed a series of treaties with the coastal sheikhs which ushered in 150 years of maritime peace and security for the emirates.

A renovated fort now crowns the pinnacle of rock at Dhayah.

55. ECLIPSE
Sharjah, 6 June 2009

In the end everything is consumed by moths
- Arabic proverb

Hidden behind the tall, mostly nondescript concrete blocks which rise above the traffic-choked streets of central Sharjah is an airport control tower. And unbeknown to the many thousands of motorists who drive along King Abdul Aziz Road every day, a runway too – right beneath their wheels.

The story of al Mahatta airport begins in 1932 when the government of Persia withdrew permission from Imperial Airways (the forerunner of BOAC and British Airways) to fly civilian aircraft over the northern shore of the Gulf. So an alternative route was sought along the lower Gulf. On the whole the Trucial sheikhs were not keen to cooperate because some of the tribes objected to the idea of British aircraft landing to refuel on their territory. But with the collapse of the pearl market and the silting up of the creek on which the town's dwindling trade had long depended, the ruler of Sharjah jumped at the opportunity of a secure and regular income. So an agreement was soon reached in which Sheikh Sultan bin Saqr Al Qasimi, in return for rent, landing fees and a personal subsidy, would provide a landing site for aircraft and a rest-house for air crews, passengers and maintenance staff.

Imperial Airways had already commissioned Handley Page Limited, aircraft manufacturers of Hertfordshire, to build a fleet of eight luxury HP42 airliners to service its European and intercontinental routes. Those designed for Africa, the Middle East, India and beyond were equipped with a cargo hold for mail and baggage and seats for twenty-four passengers. All were given a name from ancient history or classical mythology beginning with the letter H. So it was, late in the afternoon of 5 October 1932, that *Hanno*, a four-engine biplane with a triple tail-fin and upper wingspan of almost 40 metres, became the first aeroplane to touch down on the rolled sands of al Mahatta, so giving Sharjah the distinction of being the first of the emirates to have an international land-based airport.

Two years later Imperial Airways extended their far eastern route to Australia. Soon one plane a week was stopping overnight, by which time the rest-house had been completed in the style of a fort to protect its occupants from bands of marauding Bedouin. Large, lumbering and nicknamed 'The Flying Banana' for the upward sweep of its rear fuselage, the HP42 had a range of 500 miles and took five and a half days to fly from Croydon to Sharjah at a return cost to each passenger of £168 (which, adjusted for inflation, equates to £8,742 today). What it lacked in speed, however, it made up for in safety and comfort; and in almost ten years of civilian service – and over 10 million miles of flying – not a single passenger suffered injury, which is thought to be unique for an aircraft of its time.

With the outbreak of the Second World War in 1939 the seven remaining HP42 airliners (*Hengist* had been destroyed in a hangar fire in Karachi two years earlier) were converted for military transport. Meanwhile al Mahatta became a base for Blenheim and Wellington bombers and remained an outpost of the RAF until British withdrawal from the Gulf in 1971. After the war the fledgling Gulf Aviation Company (now known as Gulf Air) operated an air taxi service out of al Mahatta for oil companies around the lower Gulf. But arrangements remained primitive. The old sand runway, on which oil would be poured to bake the surface, was frequently crossed by camel trains and goat herders and a loud bell would be rung to warn of the impending arrival and departure of aircraft. Not until the 1960s was it given a hard surface, by which time De Havilland Comets regularly landed for refuelling while on low altitude surveillance missions over the borders of Iraq and countries of the Eastern Bloc.

In the discovery of oil, however, lay the seeds of al Mahatta's decline. Demand for aviation in the rapidly developing Gulf quickly outgrew the little air base and in 1977 a new airport was opened well beyond the bounds of the expanding city. Meanwhile Sharjah itself was also eclipsed, economically and politically, by oil-rich Abu Dhabi and the merchant adventurers of Dubai. Its economy suffered to such an extent that the ruler turned to Saudi Arabia for help – which is why Sharjah alone of the emirates has a King Abdul Aziz Road, King Faisal Mosque, and strict Islamic laws banning alcohol and upholding public decency.

Visitors to al Mahatta today can see the cockpit of a Comet preserved in a hangar by the old rest-house. There are also four small passenger aircraft in the livery of the Gulf Aviation Company. But there's no example of an HP42. All that were pressed into military service in 1939 had been either lost or destroyed by 1941.

As for *Hanno*, in March 1940 he collided with *Heracles*, a fellow HP42, during a gale at Bristol airport and was ignominiously cast upon the scrap heap.

In March 1940 the HP42 known as Hannibal went missing during a flight from Pakistan to Sharjah. Its last known position was over the sea just 40 miles from its destination. No distress call was received, no wreckage was ever identified, nor were the bodies of its four crew and four passengers ever found. Rumours of hi-jacking or sabotage have been fuelled by official secrecy. Details are classified as secret until 2040 and amateur aviation archaeologists are said to have been discouraged from investigating too deeply.

56. RECRIMINATIONS
Abu Dhabi, 16 June 2009

*Do not keep very careful accounts with others
or God will keep very careful accounts with you*
- Arabic proverb

Recriminations are flying after the UAE's national football team was eliminated from the 2010 FIFA World Cup last week following a dismal run of results in the final round of qualifying matches.

The die was cast from the very start when the team lost at home to North Korea and Saudi Arabia, prompting some scathing remarks in the local press and the resignation of their manager, Bruno Metsu.

'If we had won those two opening games we would have had six points,' rued his successor, Dominique Bathenay.

How true – but the team did little better under his management, scoring just one point and finishing bottom of their group. In their final home game more than five thousand fans travelled to support the South Korean team while only fifty turned out to cheer the UAE.

'We seem to be playing our home game tonight,' a visiting journalist quipped.

And to add insult to injury, in their final match of the competition they were defeated by Iran, their troublesome neighbour across the Gulf.

Now Bathenay has also gone, and both managers – and, by implication, the whole national football establishment as well – have been the target of criticism from Salah Obaid, a former captain of the team, who is blaming the poor performance of his team mates on a constant diet of fast food from McDonald's.

He may have a point: burgers and fries seem to hold an irresistible attraction for many Emiratis. So much so that, according to the World Health Organisation, more than 25% of men and almost 40% of women are classed as obese.

'Al Rumaithi bites back' – is one of the headlines today as Mohammed Khaflan Al Rumaithi, President of the UAE Football Association, dismisses the claims of the former national captain and suggests that his outburst was prompted by resentment at being dropped for some recent games.

Speculation is now shifting from analysis of failure to plans for appointing a new manager. Favourite for the vacancy is Srecko Katanec, whose career as coach of the Slovenian national team ended in tears some years ago after his most talented player stormed off the pitch after an unwelcome substitution and branded him as useless.

Meanwhile McDonald's is maintaining a dignified silence – as befits the official sponsor of the 2010 World Cup Finals.

Having sunk to 124th position in FIFA's world rankings in 2009, the UAE national football team enjoyed a better year in 2010 with Srecko Katanec as coach, winning six of their twelve international matches, drawing two and losing four, so promoting them to 111th in the world.

57. LEAP OF FAITH
Abu Dhabi, 30 June 2009

Any door opens to keys of gold
- Arabic proverb

There is much rejoicing in government circles here today at news that the oil-rich UAE has won its bid to provide a home for the new International Renewable Energy Agency – IRENA for short – and so become the first country outside North America and Europe to host the headquarters of a major international institution.

Success follows a slick presentation to a meeting of members at Sharm el Sheikh – prepared, rumour has it, by the same company that helped President Obama to the White House – in which $136 million was pledged to support the agency for the first six years plus $50 million in annual loans to finance renewable energy projects in developing countries. At the last minute the UAE's only rivals, Austria and Germany, thought better of bidding and withdrew before the vote. Bonn and Vienna will each host a satellite office instead.

'This is an historic agreement,' said the chief executive of Abu Dhabi's sustainability project at Masdar, 'We are very proud.'

The UAE's success will surprise many. Not only has the country's spectacular rise been fuelled by oil, it has the fifth highest per capita consumption of energy in the world – and the largest environmental footprint of all. Hardly the greenest of credentials.

But plans to build Masdar City, a carbon-neutral, waste-neutral commercial and residential development on the margins of the capital evince green ambitions. IRENA's headquarters will lie at the heart of this new complex. Construction has already started on the Masdar Institute of Science and Technology using energy powered by the sun. IRENA will sit alongside in rent-free accommodation and combine to form a global hub for the research, development and dissemination of renewable energy technology and expertise. Given that world demand for energy is forecast to grow by half over the next twenty years, access, affordability and sustainability are critical challenges, particularly for emerging economies.

While the choice of the emirates may herald a more inclusive role for developing nations on the world stage, hosting IRENA is unlikely to change local habits – in the short term at least. Notwithstanding its commitment to draw at least 7% of its energy requirements from renewable sources by 2020, the government of the UAE still maintains that the industrialised countries of the first world should bear responsibility for global warming and the brunt of any counter-measures.

So there are still no official schemes in Abu Dhabi for recycling newspapers and cardboard, glass, cans or plastic. Demand for water (per capita consumption is currently amongst the highest in the world) is unsustainable without yet more environmentally damaging desalination plants. And only yesterday I was informed that my employer intends to withdraw my allowance for hiring an economical Honda Civic and provide me with a gas-guzzling four-wheel-drive vehicle – and free fuel card – instead.

In September 2010 Abu Dhabi hosted a World Renewable Energy

Conference. In his speech of welcome the Managing Director of Abu Dhabi's Environment Agency reiterated the UAE's commitment to reducing its own environmental footprint and becoming 'one of the leading countries' in sustainable development.

58. WHAT'S IN A NAME?
Abu Dhabi, 4 July 2009

More than one war has been caused by a single word
- Arabic proverb

In a secluded corner of the island capital, tucked away out of respect for local sensibilities, is a public beach much frequented by expats.

But the constant thud ... thud ... thud of heavy machinery this morning portends change: a wasteland nearby is being prepared for construction. Rumours are several: some have heard another palace is to be built, others say exclusive villas. The palms that used to screen the beach from the road have already been cleared and our swimming days are almost certainly numbered. Perhaps those of the fish and baby turtles, too. The hammour (or grouper) – a favourite food in the UAE – is already threatened by overfishing and the Arab Forum for Environment and Development recently warned that the delicate ecosystem of this shallow sea (no more than 110 metres at its deepest) is imperilled by rising temperature and salinity.

Nature must take some of the blame. Only one main source of fresh water drains into this near landlocked sea where hot summers and a prevailing south-westerly wind cause exceptionally high surface evaporation – so increasing salt content and density. The average temperature varies from about 18C in winter to over 35C in summer. For weeks now the water has felt like a bath – and the peak has still to come.

But Man threatens to tip the balance. Between them the countries bordering the sea operate 120 desalination plants around its rim. Each day they boil enough sea water to fill 4,800 Olympic-size swimming pools – and then flush tons of salt and treatment chemicals back into the sea. Colonies of coral near the shore are already dead or dying but attempts to remove minerals from the residual brine have so far proved commercially unsuccessful. The UAE is currently responsible worldwide for almost a quarter of desalinated water – most of which goes on greening the desert – and both Abu Dhabi and Dubai are planning to increase production as industry expands, population grows and groundwater becomes depleted in natural aquifers.

If you were to gaze upon the endless queues at the many public car-washes in Abu Dhabi you could be forgiven for thinking that water here is abundant. But in this perpetually dusty city it's against the law to have a dirty car, let alone drive one. It's also illegal to wash a car other than in a private area off-road. For most vehicle owners the only legal course is to pay a premium at the local car-wash, all of which happen to be owned by the government. The alternative is to pay someone to wash your car illegally in the street – or risk a fine yourself.

Meanwhile, as the sea is slowly poisoned those responsible argue about what it should be called. For centuries its name reflected the historical reality of a once powerful Persian Empire along its northern shore and a small scattering of Arab emirates to the south. But the emerging Arab nations of the oil era insist on their own epithet. So *The Persian Gulf* is not recognised in the UAE: here it is *The Arabian Gulf*. Global opinion is split. Iran, of course, insists on the traditional title. In the UK it's officially still known by the old name. Also in the United States – except by US forces based in the region, who are directed to use the new name. And on the internet a petition seeks to persuade Google Earth to delete the new and substitute the old.

This afternoon, in the ancestral home of the ruling Maktoum family in the Shindagha heritage district of Dubai, I saw a nineteenth century map of Arabia on which the letters P-E-R-S-I-A-N had been scratched out so that only GULF remains. A compromise, you may think. But no: to call it simply *The Gulf* would please neither Iran nor the Arabs – and likely upset both, which would be dangerous given the proliferation of military hardware in the region. Only last week a full page in *The National* was devoted to news of the development of a new missile defence system to protect the UAE's infrastructure from weapons of mass destruction – whence, we are left to surmise.

So if not *Persian Gulf*, *Arabian Gulf*, or simply *The Gulf*, perhaps we should look to the ancient Babylonians who, long before the Persian Empire rose on the northern shore, referred to this stretch of water in their epic account of the creation of the world.

For them it was the 'sea of bitterness.'

In 2010 Iraq's foreign minister added fuel to the fire when addressing an international security conference in Bahrain.

'We listened carefully to the debate about the naming of the Gulf, whether it is the Persian Gulf, the Arabian Gulf or the Gulf of Arabs,' he said, 'In fact, we found out that it used to be called the Gulf of Basra.'

Bahrain's foreign minister tried to play the issue down:

'It's just a body of water,' he said.

If only it were that simple.

59. OPEN SECRET
Abu Dhabi, 9 July 2009

The winds blow, yet the ships are becalmed
- Arabic proverb

Opening time passes, the doors remain closed: the queue grows longer and longer – and people wilt from the heat and humidity.

I am standing outside an office of the Abu Dhabi-based telecommunications company Etisalat which is in no hurry to welcome its customers.

In the great scheme of things a ten minute wait should hardly matter. But Etisalat is held up as a flagship enterprise, one of the very best the UAE has to offer. And even once inside, though I'm first in the queue, there's still another five minutes' delay.

They 'toil not' observed Charles Doughty of men of the desert. Bertram

Thomas was even more forthright: for him Arabia was 'the land of sloth.' In the UAE, according to a recent study by Dubai's Women's College of the work expectations of young nationals, jobs are often not taken seriously and punctuality is rare.

"We don't like to work," one openly admitted to me.

Most Emiratis want to start at the top, be paid more money for less work, and come and go as they please.

While waiting to pay my Etisalat broadband bill a slogan catches my eye.

'Reach out,' Etisalat implores its customers, 'The world is waiting.'

Advice it would do well to instil in its staff.

In a report about customer care in the UAE in September 2009 The National newspaper revealed that of 800 respondents in a survey 67% had experienced a serious problem with customer service in the last six months. One case cited was that of a woman who complained that she had had to wait outside a bank in Dubai for a full half hour after the official opening time of 9.00 am and, on being let in, had had a further wait while a member of staff was speaking on her mobile phone. The bank initially denied the allegations, insisting that it had been fully operational by 9.05 am and that staff were not allowed to use their mobiles while working. After CCTV tapes were viewed, however, the complainant received an official apology in which it was admitted that the bank had opened ten minutes late (later revised to eight minutes) and that the cashier had indeed been seen on film with a mobile in her hand.

60. ABANDON SHIP
Dubai, 11 July 2009

*Not every goal is attained by a trip:
winds sometimes blow against the ship*
- Arabic proverb

After running aground on a sandbank while embarking from Southampton, her arrival in Dubai could hardly have seemed more auspicious.

If not there in person the ruler Sheikh Mohammed bin Rashid sent his yacht, the biggest in the world, to lead a flotilla of small ships to greet her. Overhead there were fireworks and an aerial salute from a low-flying Emirates airliner. On board, above hundreds of flag-waving passengers, the UAE colours fluttered beside the Union Jack. And after bagpipes evoked her Scottish birth on the banks of the Clyde, Arabs performed a traditional dance to welcome her to her new home.

'QE2's roaming days are over' – was the headline in the following day's *National*.

After forty years at sea the QE2 was heading for retirement beside one of Dubai's iconic waterfront palms. But first a refit in the city's dry docks to transform 900 small cabins into 200 large hotel rooms and 130 apartments. Walls will be taken apart and fitted with air-conditioning. The engines will be stripped out to make space for a theatre. While gaming restrictions mean her casino will have to go, additional health and fitness facilities will provide a wholesome alternative. And although her 89 metre-high red and black funnel is destined for a maritime museum, it will be replaced by a replica – incorporating a sumptuous presidential-style suite.

Or such was the plan eight months ago.

A recent photograph in the UK's *Mail on Sunday* shows her languishing – 'forlorn and neglected' – in Dubai's commercial docks still waiting for the much publicised refurbishment to begin.

Should we be surprised? No. Before ever the cruise liner left the UK, with global finance squeezed, local economies shrinking and companies starting to shed jobs, the writing was on the wall for Dubai. But publicly the government would have none of it.

'We can confidently say that the Arab world has largely not been affected by the crisis,' said the Minister of Economy.

And Nakheel, the property subsidiary of the state-owned Dubai World conglomerate which bought her for a reported £65 million, remained upbeat about their vision for a world brand floating hotel that would attract tourists in their millions.

'Make no mistake,' a spokesman said, 'At the end of the day this is a business and our aim is to generate profits.'

But Nakheel was already sinking. Five hundred workers were laid off the very next month and another four hundred since. Plans to build a one kilometre tall tower have been put on indefinite hold and rumours of cash flow problems are rife. And still the market remains in the doldrums. So what next?

'Across the oceans again: QE2's owner plans trip to Cape Town' – is the headline in today's *National*.

The company has reviewed its plans and is now thinking about berthing the QE2 elsewhere. As host of next year's World Cup, South Africa is said to be top of the list. So I count myself all the more fortunate to have caught a glimpse of her while walking along the Shindagha waterfront in Dubai this afternoon – even if it was only the crown of her funnel over rooftops from afar.

After running aground on a sandbank while embarking from Southampton, some said it was a sign of her reluctance to leave. Should she leave Dubai for Cape Town – or indeed anywhere – it's unlikely there will be a repeat.

The QE2 did not go to South Africa and remains moored in Dubai. According to a story in The Mail Online workers employed to maintain the ship have spoken of hearing voices from its children's hospital and seeing a ghostly old woman wandering in the corridors. She appears no closer to being transformed into a luxury hotel.

61. GOAL DIFFERENCE
Abu Dhabi, 19 July 2009

We didn't sell the house: we sold the neighbour
- Arabic proverb

Families living in Mohammed bin Zayed City on the outskirts of Abu Dhabi are complaining about their neighbours.

One can hardly blame them. They live in desirable villas in a predominantly Emirati neighbourhood in an up and coming suburb named in honour of the Crown Prince – but in the heart of their community, just over the road from a glittering new mall, are row upon row of decrepit huts occupied by 100,000 expatriate labourers when they're not otherwise engaged in constructing and servicing the infrastructure of the city.

'Old and filthy' is how one woman has described the camps, laying blame for her children's asthma squarely on their stinking sewage systems. Besides the smell there's rubbish littering the streets, ranks of heavy construction vehicles, the incessant to-ing and fro-ing of hundreds of trucks, vans and buses belching fumes and whipping up dust, not to mention allegations of 'muggings, thefts, harassment and leering.' Her husband has even pronounced the mall a no-go area of an evening – which is no mean privation for a nation of shoppers. So you can imagine her delight at news that the camps are going to close and their inhabitants moved elsewhere.

'The sooner the better,' is the gist of what she told a newspaper.

The government, which is still smarting from a BBC *Panorama* programme which exposed squalid conditions in camps in Dubai earlier this year, is also keen to see them close. Sheikh Mohammed bin Zayed has called for all labour camps in Abu Dhabi to meet internationally accredited standards of health and safety – as befits an aspiring global capital. New rules mean that every camp in the UAE must have its own kitchen and medical facilities, adequate space for parking and recreation, at least one bathroom, two toilets, a laundry and shower for every eight residents, no more than ten people to a room and no less than three square metres of space per person.

But many of the labourers living in camps in Mohammed bin Zayed City have said they would prefer to stay where they are, despite assurances that alternative accommodation will almost certainly offer better facilities. Why? They say they are happy with things where they are, citing the convenience of shops and public transport. But the real reason is more likely to be money, for which many will sacrifice comfort. Accommodation in new camps will probably cost a lot more – and there's already precious little money left over to save and send home, which for most workers is the whole object of being here.

Meanwhile shopkeepers in Mazyad Mall are caught in the middle. Although happy to welcome men from the camps in their stores, they find that other customers, especially Emiratis, tend to leave quickly or go elsewhere. This has already prompted a ban on labourers frequenting the mall on the busiest evenings of the week, when entry is restricted to 'ladies, children and families only,' and at all times if not clean and tidy.

At least one shop, however, will be sorry to see the camps close. The best customers at the *Golden Goal* scratch card kiosk are not Emiratis – but labourers, who can win upwards of an entire year's wages at a single go. According to *The National*, for every five hundred tickets sold only one is bought by a local.

Such is the difference between living the dream – and dreaming of living.

Golden Goal subsequently closed and the notice restricting entry to the mall for labourers was replaced by a new non-discriminatory code of conduct.

62. FRUIT PICKING
Abu Dhabi, 20 July 2009

A secret is like a dove: when it leaves my hand it takes wing
- Arabic proverb

BlackBerry owners in the UAE have been mystified by a recent spate of problems with their e-mail handsets following a 'routine upgrade' supplied by the Abu Dhabi telecommunications company Etisalat.

A software patch purportedly intended to improve network quality has been draining batteries, over-heating handsets and leaving many users disconnected.

But a leading manufacturer of anti-virus and security systems for mobile technology has advised the BlackBerry's Canadian owners that Etisalat's patch contains an eavesdropping bug.

'No doubt about it,' a spokesman is reported as saying, 'It was intended to intercept people's e-mail and forward it on to someone else.'

Encryption used by BlackBerry makes it difficult for others to hack into messages and governments in the Gulf are becoming increasingly concerned about the security risks posed by unmonitored mobile traffic. Given the UAE's record of media censorship, this latest piece of spyware is thought to be a crude attempt at interception.

Meanwhile Etisalat has opted to remain silent – as are many of the UAE's 500,000 BlackBerry owners.

A few weeks later the UAE government announced that it would ban BlackBerry phones from using e-mail, instant messages and web-browsing services from 11 October 2009. A few days before the deadline, however, it relented, stating that BlackBerry had become compliant with UAE telecommunications regulations. Pro-democracy protests across the Middle East, many organised through social networking sites like Facebook and Twitter, have since raised fresh government concerns about the security risks posed by mobile technology.

63. TREE OF LIFE
Abu Dhabi, 25 July 2009

There is among trees one that is pre-eminently blessed: it is the date palm
- the Prophet Muhammad

Palm branches groan and trees drip: the season of mellow fruitfulness is upon us – and so, too, Abu Dhabi's annual date festival.

For a month or more I've been watching huge bunches of the UAE's favourite fruit turn from green to yellow, red, black or brown, according to the variety. The emirates are the world's leading cultivators of date palms and Abu Dhabi, with over 30 million trees, has the lion's share. Most are cultivated on commercial farms but over a quarter of a million decorate the broad verges and central reservations of the capital's roads where the fruit can be picked with impunity, provided one is not greedy.

During this week's festival in the Liwa Oasis newspapers have been singing the date's praises. We have learnt of its antiquity in Arabia; its importance as a staple of the UAE's pre-oil economy; its high fibre, mineral and energy content; not least, its medicinal properties, particularly for problems concerned with the bowels and other parts in close proximity.

Should anyone doubt its virtues, the authority of the Prophet can be invoked. He recommended that seven dates of the *Ajwa* variety should be consumed each morning to ward off disease and infection. Personally I prefer the *Medjool*, being twice the size and wonderfully soft, sweet and juicy.

Traditional Bedouin poetry often compared the utility of the date palm with that of the camel. The one furnished nutritious fruit to sustain man and beast, trunks and branches for building boats and houses, fibre for weaving baskets and rope, foliage for shade and oil for soap, while the other provided milk to drink, meat to eat, hides for leather, dung for campfires, mounts for warriors and transport for trade, not forgetting urine for preventing insect bites and cleansing the hair of lice. Useful qualities all.

'Which,' the poet would ask, 'Is the superior?'

But in the poetic debate camels and date palms were often mere metaphors for contrasting ways of life: the nomadic wandering of the pastoral Bedouin vis-à-vis the settled existence of the oasis farmer. While pronouncement could be made in favour of either, in reality neither was superior because each thrived only by exchanging goods with the other. Today public festivals dedicated to camels and dates are as much about Emiratis honouring their long-suffering ancestors, whether nomad or farmer, as they are celebrations of the animal and tree upon which their forefathers' lives once depended.

Over ten days at Liwa some Dh3 million (£500,000) are on offer in cash and four-wheel-drive vehicles. As well as contests for best date in class, based on variety and size, weight, beauty and taste, poets have been invited to give special readings, chefs to exercise culinary skills, and all and sundry to participate in heritage and handicraft displays – all on the theme of the cherished date.

In Islam there is a tradition known as *zikr* (the remembrance) in which Muslims finger beads on a circle of rope while reciting the ninety-nine most beautiful names, or attributes, of God. Usually such beads are made of precious stones but one creative entrant at this year's date festival has fashioned a string of beads from the seeds of the fruit. A commercial venture is thought to be in the offing – and given that some charred seeds more than 7,000 years old recently unearthed in an archaeological dig on Abu Dhabi's Delma Island are the earliest evidence of date consumption anywhere in the world, a more fitting tribute to the UAE's tree of life is hard to imagine.

But even date stone prayer beads are unlikely to tip the balance of utility in favour of the palm: for I've heard it said that God has a hundredth name known only to the camel – which, so they say, is the reason for its aloof and supercilious expression.

In April 2010 it was reported that scientists at the Zayed Complex for Herbal Research and Traditional Medicine in Abu Dhabi are the verge of finding a medicinal use for date stones. They have discovered that the stones have anti-viral properties which could help to cure infections. Meanwhile another team of scientists from the UAE University in al Ain has developed a new breed of palm which may be more commercially attractive than conventional trees – because it has no stones.

64. DWELLING IN THE PAST
Abu Dhabi, 6 August 2009

A rich man who is ungenerous is like a tree without fruit
- Arabic proverb

Forty-three years ago today the past relinquished hold of the future in Abu Dhabi and modern times began. It's even possible to pinpoint the moment. It was ten to three in the afternoon: because that's when an RAF Pembroke took off from al Bateen airport carrying the ruler into exile – and power transferred to Sheikh Zayed.

Some say it was abdication; others describe it as a bloodless coup. All we know for sure is that Sheikh Shakhbut had little choice but the manner of his going. Perhaps he reflected on the fate of his predecessors. His father became ruler after assassinating an elder brother, only to be eliminated himself by another brother, whose own rule was cut short when he was murdered at the instigation of their eldest brother, who thought better of taking over the reins and so handed the opportunity to his nephew.

So it was that in 1928 the mantle passed to Sheikh Shakhbut and remained with him for the best part of forty years, which was no mean feat given the difficult economic circumstances he immediately encountered, let alone the border disputes which followed closely the exploration for oil.

Hardly had he started when global recession undermined the pearling industry, then the mainstay of Abu Dhabi's economy and the principal source of the ruler's wealth. Soon afterwards Japan flooded the market with cultured pearls. In 1934, however, a British geologist spotted the potential for oil. An exploration concession followed, for which Shakhbut negotiated an annual income long before oil was ever found; in his expat memoir, *Arabian Destiny*, Edward Henderson described how he would deliver oil cash to Sheikh Shakhbut in a suitcase. Similar agreements were signed by sultans, sheikhs and kings across the region and the question of border precision assumed critical importance, so much so that long-standing disputes with Dubai and Saudi Arabia soon flared into open war.

Nor were Shakhbut's relations with the Bedouin any easier. For many the prospect of oil money was no substitute for independence. So they feuded and raided and generally made life difficult for the ruler, who would have struggled to maintain control but for his younger brother. At that time Sheikh Zayed was his brother's representative in al Ain with particular responsibility for relations with the tribes of the interior, and it was only through him that Shakhbut maintained any influence beyond the city. Encouraged by the American oil company ARAMCO (which had the Saudi oil concessions), the new Kingdom of Saudi Arabia reasserted an ancient claim to the Buraimi Oasis, then divided between Abu Dhabi and Oman. After occupying the

Omani village of Hamasah in 1952, Saudi Arabia offered money, presents and other inducements to local tribesmen to win their allegiance. In *Sultan in Oman* Jan Morris came upon a group of impoverished Bedouin, each keen to flaunt the expensive watch on his wrist. Although the Saudis were eventually expelled three years later, the story goes that they offered Sheikh Zayed $42 million – the largest bribe in history – to surrender sovereignty of a large chunk of Abu Dhabi's hinterland.

Meanwhile domestic development was next to non-existent. Although Sheikh Shakhbut received more money from the mere possibility of oil than ever he did from pearls, he was wary of the impact that a windfall might have on a people who had for centuries survived through mere subsistence. A story is told of a huge pile of banknotes found infested and half-eaten by insects in a room in his fort. Only when he learnt that he could earn interest did he deposit his money in a bank. And all the time people were crying out for houses, electricity and plumbing, schools, hospitals and roads.

The discovery of oil only served to fuel tensions. Export began in 1962 and quickly gathered pace – as did Shakhbut's income. By 1966 he was earning an estimated £25 million a year but was still loath to spend. So life in Abu Dhabi continued as it had for generations. It was only after much persuasion that he eventually agreed to a generator being installed in the fort. How people's hopes must have soared when the lights in the ruler's fort were first switched on – only to sink when months of expectation that they were next in line turned into several more years of waiting.

It was a different story in al Ain. There Sheikh Zayed restored and extended the traditional *aflaj* irrigation system, promoted trade and established schools and clinics. He also worked behind the scenes to foster a common sense of purpose and identity with the other Trucial emirates, thereby sowing the seeds for future federation. Above all Zayed was liked and respected – unlike his increasingly intractable brother, who became even more marginalised after a visit to Jordan in the spring of 1966 when, in response to warm hospitality, he donated some £700,000 to Jordanian good causes. His own police and defence forces had not been paid for several months. It was the final straw.

While Shakhbut's departure passed almost unnoticed, its impact was quickly felt.

'I want five years' development to be achieved in one year,' said the new ruler.

The pace of change has remained much the same ever since, so that all trace of Shakhbut's world vanished long ago except for the much restored fort and Maqta watchtower which stands guard over the narrow strait between the island capital and the mainland. Or so it seemed: because for many years his summerhouse lay unseen and forgotten behind a high wall.

Constructed of coral and sea rock, palm wood, gypsum and sand, Sheikh Shakhbut's summerhouse is the only example of a traditional stone domestic dwelling ever found on the island. Old men say it was built about 1946 as a rest house for visitors. Here Shakhbut would greet tribal chiefs and entertain VIPs or simply retreat to catch a cooling breeze. But the modern world stalked him: an airfield was built close by (the very one from which he was later launched into exile). And as the airport grew his summerhouse disappeared behind its perimeter, not to re-emerge until a new airport was opened on the mainland and the wall of the old one was taken down.

Since then, amid growing concerns about the erosion of traditional Arab culture and values, the summerhouse has been restored and converted to a heritage museum. But whereas in Shakhbut's day it stood on a remote shore overlooking mangrove forests and the sea, today it stands in the middle of a public park. The sea, now barely visible from its veranda, has been pushed back to make way for the eastern ring road.

This evening the doors are locked and I have to make do with a glimpse of some portraits of Shakhbut through barred windows and dusty panes of glass. As I turn to go, however, staff direct me to another museum only recently opened where visitors can experience scenes, sounds and smells from local history by taking a Jorvik-style journey through time – complete with veiled mannequins, stuffed camels and plastic fish.

While the past may have relinquished hold of the future in Abu Dhabi, it seems the future cannot let go of the past.

After a brief period of exile in Bahrain, the UK, Lebanon and Iran, Sheikh Shakhbut was allowed to return to Abu Dhabi and lived the remainder of his days as an honoured elder of the family at his favourite palace in al Ain. He died in 1989.

65. BLANK CANVAS
Abu Dhabi, 21 August 2009

For every glance behind us, we have to look twice to the future
- Arabic proverb

Sunshine filters into the gallery through a vast domed roof pierced with an Islamic pattern of stars. Rays of light move in time about the space within and sparkle on pools of water. At night the effect is reversed as beams of artificial light from within penetrate the darkness outside. The building itself is a work of art – not to mention the treasures inside.

Or so it will be: work on the Louvre Abu Dhabi has only just started.

I have joined a tour of the future of Abu Dhabi: for although it will be another four years or so before the Louvre itself is finished, the first acquisitions are currently on show at the Emirates Palace hotel to give a foretaste of the treat in store.

There's a Grecian jar, some two and a half thousand years old, depicting Heracles in the first of his labours killing the Nemean lion. A broach of garnet and gold bearing a cross and the head of an eagle transports us to the dying days of the Roman Empire. From second or third century Pakistan there's a statue of the Buddha, whose features reflect the conquering influence of Alexander the Great; opposite stands a life-size, fifteenth century wooden statue of Christ showing his wounds, his pierced feet worn smooth as glass by the touch of countless pilgrims' hands; and in between, some richly decorated pages from a Mamluk Quran of fourteenth century Egypt or Syria. From Renaissance Italy there is a Madonna and Child by Bellini. We learn that two paintings by Edouard Manet were originally part of the same canvas, separated during the artist's impecunious days to increase the prospect of a sale and now happily reunited in the Louvre Abu Dhabi collection. A seventeenth century French tapestry reflects Western fascination with the exotic mysteries of Imperial China, while some nineteenth century wooden furniture from Africa proves to be the inspiration for the decorative arts movement of 1920s Paris. Lastly a loaned painting by Cezanne of rocks and trees near his home in Aix-en-Provence takes us to the threshold of modern art and the final, abstract piece.

Piet Mondrian's *Composition with blue, red, yellow and black* was painted in Paris in 1922. A grid of horizontal and vertical black lines is part filled with blue, red and yellow. Much of the canvas remains blank, however, and we are invited to fill it with whatever comes to mind. Bought for some £20 million from the collection of the late Yves Saint Laurent, this abstract was the very first of the Louvre Abu Dhabi's acquisitions and its blank spaces evoke not only the emirate's silent past but its unfulfilled hopes for the future.

"Everything on this journey through the history of art leads to this one piece," enthuses our guide, "It's a mirror to the soul."

When Mondrian applied his final touch to the composition Abu Dhabi was no more than a fishing village. For generations the pattern of life had remained largely unchanged and unnoticed. As empires and dynasties elsewhere rose and fell, those who subsisted here left little clue to their existence, let alone any mark on history. Not until the accession of Sheikh Zayed bin Sultan in 1966 did Abu Dhabi emerge from slumber. Now Zayed's sons want to be noticed.

'Our goal, in keeping with the aspiration of the Abu Dhabi government, is to help transform the UAE's capital city into a global cultural centre that is universal in its appeal,' writes the chairman of Abu Dhabi's Tourism Development and Investment Company in his introduction to the exhibition.

So the Louvre will stand beside a Guggenheim, a performing arts centre and two national museums in a multi-billion pound cultural theme park on Saadiyat Island. Over £300 million has been agreed for the brand name alone. Management advice, the loan of art and special exhibitions will cost the same and more again.

Saadiyat translates as 'Island of Happiness' – but there are many in the world of art who are distinctly unhappy about the Louvre-Abu Dhabi deal. An on-line petition against the proposal attracted support from over four and a half thousand museum professionals and art enthusiasts.

'Selling our heritage,' is how some French people described it, dubbing it 'the Desert Louvre.'

'Only renting it,' countered the French government, promising that the Mona Lisa would never be allowed to leave.

'Putting economic interests first,' said objectors, alluding to parallel talks about trade.

'Promoting French culture,' replied the government, keen to foster closer ties with one of the richest cities in the world.

'But they'll censor our nudes,' came the cry … and so on.

What many objectors really fear is Arab oil money driving up the price of art, so putting it beyond the reach of public institutions in the West.

Proponents talk of building a bridge between Islam and the West. 'A beacon for cultural expression and exchange,' is how Sheikh Khalifa, the ruler of Abu Dhabi, describes it. But the question is – will people come to Saadiyat? Although local interest in art may be growing, there is no artistic tradition here and the project is counting on a threefold increase in tourists. So alongside the cultural hub a luxury resort is to be developed with twenty-nine hotels, a championship golf course and marinas with capacity for ten thousand yachts. It may still take a miracle in marketing, however, if demand is to be viable and sustained.

"Why come to Abu Dhabi to see the Louvre," an Emirati once asked me, "When you can go to Paris and see the real thing?"

Meanwhile, even as Arab oil money filters into programmes of refurbishment in cash-strapped museums in France, the controversy is set to rumble in Paris every time the Desert Louvre makes a successful bid for art. Many there have turned their noses up at Saadiyat:

'It will be like a Disneyland,' they say.

And the French more than most should know.

66. NIGHT OF THE CRESCENT MOON
Abu Dhabi, 19 September 2009

If the moon be with thee, thou needst not to care about the stars
- Arabic proverb

Across the emirates there is a vigil this evening. Plans are on hold and children are on tenterhooks. Will they or won't they? – that is the question.

All we know for certain is that Ramadan, the Holiest of months in the Islamic calendar, is drawing to a close. To understand its significance we must go back almost 1,400 years: for it was during the month of Ramadan in AD610 that the Angel Gabriel first revealed the Word of God to an Arab merchant called Muhammad. The revelation came at a time when Arab society lacked spiritual guidance and was becoming increasingly divided. The message that Muhammad came to preach was submission to God and social justice to one other. And ever since the Prophet's time, to remind his followers of the privations of the poor, Ramadan has been marked by fasting, prayer and charity.

But when does it end? No one is quite sure. It could be this evening. If not, tomorrow. It's up to the Moon Sighting Committee. All we can do is wait and see.

For the last twenty-nine days, from sunrise to sunset, Muslims in the UAE have been abstaining from food and drink. Fasting begins at the break of dawn signalled by the morning call to prayer (4.44 am today) and continues until the sunset call (6.24 pm this evening). As well as the customary five daily prayers, there are additional rituals late into the evening and people tend to catch up on sleep during the day. During waking hours television provides the main distraction and more time is spent watching the box during Ramadan than at any other time of the year. Others choose a more reflective path. Reading the Quran from cover to cover is a traditional option and devout colleagues have told me how they telephone relatives every day to update and compare progress.

In public non-Muslims are also expected to refrain from eating and drinking during the hours of fast. One told me how he was served food in a mall just minutes before the sunset prayer call only to have it snatched away by an angry security guard. He was fortunate: at least three people have been arrested for not observing local etiquette. At police headquarters, where all is more relaxed, half-hearted and languid than usual, nerves have been on edge for want of a regular fix of coffee.

The anticipation with which Ramadan is awaited is matched only by that which precedes its end. For the month of fasting is followed by Eid al Fitr – a festive celebration accompanied by three public holidays. For days, if not weeks, families have been preparing. From top to toe new clothes have been bought. From top to bottom homes have been refurbished. Then there are the presents for children and provisions for family gatherings. But when will celebrations begin? Islamic months are of either twenty-nine or thirty days' duration, which means Ramadan must end today or tomorrow. There's no fixed pattern to the length of each month: the end of one and start of the next is signalled by the new moon. While astronomical calculations predict such a moon this evening, tradition demands that the end of Ramadan can only be announced when the Moon Sighting Committee is satisfied that the crescent moon has been seen by the human eye.

In days gone by people would be listening for a shot fired from a canon at the ruler's fort. Today the Moon Sighting Committee's announcement is broadcast by radio and television. In my apartment I have neither – but it matters not: for a sudden cacophony of car horns in the street outside tells me that the month of fasting is over and that Eid celebrations have started.

67. THE RAINBOW SHEIKH
Shanayl, 26 September 2009

He who has gold can do what he likes
- Arabic proverb

A larger than life-size Land Rover in the oilfields of Abu Dhabi's western region signals arrival at the Rainbow Sheikh's private motor museum.

If history had taken a different course Sheikh Hamad bin Hamdan Al Nahyan might have been ruler of Abu Dhabi today. Instead he is famous for his passion for cars, trucks and custom-made caravans. As well as more than two hundred vehicles in this museum, and others in Abu Dhabi and al Ain, he owns hundreds in Saudi Arabia, Australia and Morocco – and is still gathering more.

His great-grandfather, the eldest son of Sheikh Zayed the First, declined the opportunity to become ruler in 1928 after the incumbencies of three of his younger brothers each ended in murder. But as patriarch of the ruling Al Nahyan family Sheikh Khalifa bin Zayed became the power behind the throne when he helped to install his nephew, Sheikh Shakhbut, as ruler instead. Almost forty years later the kingmaker's mantle passed to his son, the Rainbow Sheikh's grandfather, who was a leading advocate for deposing the unpopular Shakhbut and replacing him with the second Sheikh Zayed in 1966. There was even a suggestion that his son, the Rainbow Sheikh's father, would be appointed Crown Prince – which might have put the Rainbow Sheikh himself, onetime equerry to the late Sheikh Zayed, in line to succeed.

As Sheikh Zayed's own family grew, however, so the political influence of the senior Al Nahyan branch waned and they turned instead to the oil industry to prosper. The Rainbow Sheikh's father was the Wali (administrator) of Das Island, which became the centre of Abu Dhabi's offshore oil production. And it was among the Land Rovers and pick-up trucks of the pioneers of oil exploration that the young Rainbow Sheikh's enthusiasm for motor vehicles began.

Turning off the highway beside the giant Land Rover visitors are confronted by the largest two-wheeled caravan in the world. There's a certificate from the *Guinness Book of Records* on show to prove it. With a lounge, kitchen, eight bedrooms – each with its own bathroom – and three garages below, it is probably also the slowest two-wheeled caravan in the world: a mobile Bedouin encampment no less, that travels no faster than a camel. Close by is another caravan which, albeit large, is remarkable less for its size than shape: it's a globe mapped with oceans, seas and continents, one millionth the size of planet Earth. While the Rainbow Sheikh may have lost a kingdom, here he can retire to a world of his own.

The rest of the collection is housed inside a huge air-conditioned pyramid: Hummers, sports cars and Minis, Chevrolets, Buicks and Cadillacs, a Rolls Royce or two, a Model T Ford and a host of other makes and models

– many bearing their owner's hallmark rainbow body stripes. Seven Mercedes Benz saloons point to how the sheikh came by his name: six are painted in a different colour of the rainbow, while the seventh combines all seven colours – every one with matching interior trim. It's said they were bought as a wedding present for his bride. But all pale in the shadow of the centrepiece of his collection: a special edition of the four-wheel-drive Dodge Power Wagon, the vehicle of choice of oil prospectors in the 1950s, which towers under the apex of the pyramid.

It was commissioned to celebrate the oil boom – and a more fitting monument would be hard to find: for at 50 tons and several times the size of an original, no one but an oil sheikh could possibly afford the fuel to run it.

68. THE FALCON AND THE FALCONER
Abu Dhabi, 2 October 2009

It is easier to lead a herd of a thousand camels than a company of two men
- Arabic proverb

Almost five years after his death the Founding Father of the Nation is still making newspaper headlines in the UAE.

Sheikh Zayed bin Sultan Al Nahyan's name recently appeared in *Newsweek* magazine in a list of 'postwar transformers' – leaders who have 'wrought drastic social, economic or political change' – alongside President Nasser of Egypt, Deng Xiaoping of China, Jomo Kenyatta of Kenya, Lech Walesa of Poland, Nelson Mandela of South Africa, Helmut Kohl of West Germany, and Margaret Thatcher of Great Britain.

The local press have seized on this opportunity to laud the oft-repeated achievements of the much loved leader who wrought Abu Dhabi from an obscure and backward desert kingdom into the capital of a regional powerhouse with global aspirations. Yet the photograph which accompanied the announcement in yesterday's *National* newspaper pictured the late sheikh not among oil wells, a glitzy cityscape or other world leaders – but with a falcon.

Meanwhile representatives of 114 countries have been meeting in Abu Dhabi under the auspices of the United Nations Educational Scientific and Cultural Organisation (UNESCO) to consider preservation of the intangible cultural heritage of humanity. While money can be earmarked to maintain buildings and monuments, the preservation of rituals and customs, poetry, dance and so on depends on the will of people to perpetuate them. This week UNESCO has been discussing cultural intangibles at risk and a case is being led by the UAE to add falconry to the list.

'Falconry is perhaps the most prominent tradition of the UAE cultural scene,' claims Abu Dhabi's Authority for Culture and Heritage, 'Dating back to pre-Islamic times.'

Now a sport, life once depended on it.

'A good falconer may almost daily mend the weak fare of his nomad household,' wrote Doughty – a favourite prey in Arabia being the plump houbara bustard, a resident breed whose numbers were supplemented every winter by others migrating from Asia. A single falcon could kill half a dozen or more in a day. Coveted for its (supposed) aphrodisiac properties, the houbara was hunted to near extinction in the UAE and now only survives here thanks to a conservation project inaugurated by Sheikh Zayed.

Should any of the UNESCO delegates have been in doubt about the falcon's importance in Emirati culture they had only to visit the Abu Dhabi National Exhibitions Company which this week happened to be hosting the annual International Hunting and Equestrian Exhibition: for there, among horses and hunting dogs, was a display of falcons to help raise public awareness.

Besides various bits of hunting paraphernalia, horses, dogs and falcons, and a musical ride by Her Majesty Queen Elizabeth's Household Cavalry, visitors to the exhibition were treated to a demonstration of traditional Emirati dancing. The *Ayyala* is a celebration of victory. Men stand arms-linked in two rows facing each other, waving camel sticks, swords or guns while swaying back and forth to the beat of drums, each row chanting in turn to the other and boasting of their courage and skill. Traditionally it was accompanied by the *Na'ashat* dance in which Bedouin women would roll their heads from side to side to show off the beauty of their long hair and so remind the men what they had fought for. Such rituals take us back to a time not so very distant when conflict between tribes was common. Performed today as a dance of welcome, the *Ayyala* serves to emphasise Sheikh Zayed's transformational achievement – wrought with the skills of a falconer.

Paintings and photographs at the exhibition show Zayed young and old practising the sport of his ancestors. As his brother's representative in al Ain we see him mounted on a camel with a falcon on his wrist. As ruler of Abu Dhabi we see him leaning out of the window of a car – with a falcon on his wrist. As President of the UAE we see him in formal attire – with a falcon on his wrist. Even in his twilight, when touring the inaugural Hunting and Equestrian Exhibition in a golf buggy, we see him pausing to admire a falcon and speak to its handler.

Among the fiercely independent tribes of the Trucial States rule was never a right but a concession. Zayed's Bedouin roots taught him that the relationship between a ruler and his subjects should be that of falconer and falcon. He therefore sought to nurture trust among the tribes as he would train a falcon: treat them well, sustain them, win their confidence and respond to their needs. It wasn't enough simply to share the fruits of oil: he wanted to win hearts and minds to a vision of unity capable of withstanding the centrifugal tendencies of an historically divided people. We therefore find him constantly alluding to traditional customs and imagery to remind people of their common past and conjure a new sense of national identity.

'He who does not know his past cannot make the best of his present and future,' he used to say.

So it was that the falcon, a symbol drawn from hunting in the desert, was chosen as the national emblem of the fledgling federation in 1971. But Sheikh Zayed also expected the air-conditioned beneficiaries of oil-funded modernisation to embrace new values, particularly education and work. Despite enforced discrimination to boost Emirati employment in the private sector, however, unemployment among nationals remains high, especially in Abu Dhabi. Private companies complain that many local applicants lack the necessary qualifications and experience for many professional roles, while low pay and long hours put them off applying for unskilled jobs – let alone a generous benefits system which coddles from cradle to grave.

Meanwhile the public sector, in which pay tends to be higher and working hours shorter, is awash with them.

It may also be telling that when the state schools in Abu Dhabi resumed after Ramadan and the recent Eid holiday, as few as one in ten pupils turned up. Parents said it was because of the risk of swine flu. Teachers said it was because parents simply couldn't be bothered to send their children to school for the last two days of the week. Is it any wonder that educational attainment is said to be woefully low?

And what of traditional values as the sons of Zayed strive for a seat among the world's economic superpowers? Globalisation is already eroding their potency. At Burger King baseball caps are fast replacing the *ghutra* among young men, while in marble malls young women allow ever more of their designer jeans and T-shirts to show beneath loose and brightly embroidered black *abayas*. Islam and family bonds are cornerstones of UAE society – but many of the majority expatriate population show scant regard for Muslim standards of conduct and dress, Emirati parents entrust the care of their children to nannies and housemaids with little or no knowledge of Arab culture or the Arabic language, and almost one in two local marriages ends in divorce. While competitions for camels and date palms, falcons, poetry and Saluki hunting dogs may open windows on the past, their force for unifying – let alone motivating – an increasingly divergent and dependent society looks set to diminish over time.

Nor are federal relationships without their strains. Abu Dhabi and Dubai often seem more bent on competition than collaboration. In the meantime the gulf between the big two and the other five is growing wider.

In *The Second Coming* the poet Yeats used the image of the falcon wheeling ever higher and wider in the sky above its handler as a metaphor for tension and conflict.

> *Turning and turning in the widening gyre*
> *The falcon cannot see the falconer;*
> *Things fall apart; the centre cannot hold ...*

Asking UNESCO to add falconry to the list of the world's endangered cultural assets may well help to safeguard the traditional sport of sheikhs. Preserving unity in the post-Zayed UAE will probably be more challenging.

In November 2010 UNESCO officially designated falconry on the Representative List of Intangible Cultural Heritage of Humanity.

69. LIFE ON MARS
Abu Dhabi, 6 October 2009

The eyes are of little use if the mind be blind
- Arabic proverb

As defending champions of the government's prestigious Award for Excellence, Abu Dhabi Police is on a journey without end.

A road map sets out the government's vision for a secure, confident and safe society in which justice and freedom prevail and the police respond to people's needs and expectations. Meanwhile a gazetteer of priorities, targets and performance indicators provides milestones along the way. But our tortuous path leads uphill and over the horizon and it would be easy to get lost or left behind.

Happily an instrument of navigation has been developed which, like a satellite in the sky, allows an overview of what's going on below. New software with colour-coded labels shows at a glance whether key policing indicators are on track to achieve their targets. All it requires is data to be fed from all quarters of the organisation, albeit by hand and with little enthusiasm or transparency, and the computer does the rest. Green means performance is above target. Yellow signals all is still well. Only red begs a serious question.

In time these colours may come to be seen as aids to interpretation and understanding of performance – not results in themselves. But not yet …

"That can't be right," cries one unhappy junior officer seeing red at a recent review of his department's performance, "Your targets must be wrong."

We check.

"No, the targets are correct."

"Then the figures we gave you must be wrong," says he.

So it proves: somewhat miraculously errors are found in his calculations which, when put right, turn each red bright yellow.

But with honour at stake and fingers ever poised to attribute blame, nothing less than green will do.

"They will not like yellow," he says desperately – they being his seniors who have their reputations to consider. Heads could roll – figuratively, of course.

Just as conversation turns to further substitutions, however, a colleague has a brainwave.

"That's not yellow," he says, "It's gold."

There's a pause while this revelation sinks in.

"Gold is good?"

"Gold is fine."

So we settle for a compromise – of green burnished with gold.

As I reflect on progress in promoting a performance regime in Abu Dhabi Police, a remark from my induction twelve months ago comes to mind.

"Welcome to Life on Mars," a colleague said, alluding to the popular UK television police drama in which the main character finds himself trapped thirty years in the past.

Emiratis tend to be less cryptic.

'It needs time,' they say.

70. GRAND PRIX FEVER
Abu Dhabi, 16 October 2009

Money can build roads in the sea
- Arabic proverb

Abu Dhabi's ambition is to become 'the capital of the world.' So says the exuberant chairman of Abu Dhabi's Yas Marina Circuit, home of next month's Formula One Grand Prix, in a front page article today.

Over the last three years Khaldoon Al Mubarak has overseen the transformation of a desert island into a world-class sporting and leisure venue with a five and a half kilometre motor racing circuit, marina and seven hotels – one of which straddles the track. And there's more to come. Already the mainframe of the world's first Ferrari World theme park is standing, as is a sign for Yas Mall although construction has yet to begin. A Warner Bros movie theme park, water park, two golf courses and much more are set to follow.

Anticipation is building with the countdown to 1 November. A fan zone with race simulators has been set up on the refurbished Corniche, hotels are fully booked and worldwide some 600 million people are expected to watch on television. This will be the long awaited moment when the eyes of the world focus on Abu Dhabi. Given the prospect of other attractions too – the Louvre, Guggenheim and so on – the city could certainly be said to be on the way to becoming a world capital.

But capital of the world? Unlikely as it may seem, another article on the same page of the newspaper reminds us that anything is possible here. Under the headline 'Abu Dhabi plans desert lakes to save wildlife,' we learn that thirty lakes are being constructed in protected areas of the desert at the instigation of Sheikh Mohammed bin Zayed, the Crown Prince of Abu Dhabi.

It's not a novel idea. Archaeological evidence tells us that lakes and human settlements existed in the emirate's interior under more benign climatic conditions. While surface signs have all but disappeared, rain from several thousand years ago remains trapped underground and Sheikh Mohammed's project to create new lakes and verdant oases encompasses several themes of government. Research and development into new ways to tap and produce water accords with plans to shift economic dependency from hydrocarbons to knowledge, while using solar power to generate pumps and filtration systems will help to optimise the emirate's natural resources and promote renewable energy. The object is to create a habitat for endangered indigenous species like the Arabian oryx, once abundant but declared extinct in the wild in 1972 – so helping to preserve the nation's culture and heritage. And if all goes well, environmental tourism will prove a popular spin-off, so building international relationships and boosting foreign income.

'You can't repeat the past,' said Nick in *The Great Gatsby*.

'Can't repeat the past?' cried Gatsby incredulously, 'Why of course you can!'

Any such suggestion might receive a similar retort from the Crown Prince: for deep in Abu Dhabi's desert we are told the first of the lakes is already finished and a herd of reserve-reared Arabian oryx has been released close by. In little over a year all thirty are scheduled to be completed.

But even Sheikh Mohammed might balk at Abu Dhabi's claim to the future.

A case of Grand Prix fever perhaps?

71. THE PEARL FISHERS
Ras al Khaimah, 23 October 2009

The sea is treacherous: they who escape it are newly born
- Arabic proverb

Imagine diving 30 metres or more from an open boat to collect oysters from the sea bed: your ears plugged with wax, leather caps over your finger tips, a bone peg on your nose, dressed – if you're lucky – in a cotton suit to protect from jelly fish stings, equipped with a basket for your catch and a heavy stone on a line to speed your descent to the bottom: and remaining there, scrabbling in the dark, for up to a minute and a half, until you can no longer hold your breath: then, after tugging on a rope, being hauled, lungs bursting, to the surface; and after five minutes' rest, diving again – up to sixty times a day, every day for four months, at the hottest time of the year.

Such was the lot of the Gulf pearl diver.

Go back some 4,000 years to the earliest written form and we find a similar image in the great Mesopotamian Epic of Gilgamesh. With heavy stones tied to his feet, Gilgamesh plunges into the sea to pluck the flower of immortality from the floor. But according to Hindu myth it was the god Krishna who fished the first pearl from the sea when he sought a present for his daughter, Pandaia, on her wedding day.

A pearl found by archaeologists in Kuwait is thought to be 7,000 years old. For the ancient Arabs pearls were gifts from heaven, formed from raindrops caught by oysters at night, and, just as the Bible likens the Kingdom of Heaven to 'one pearl of great price,' in the Quran 'ornaments' from the depths of the sea feature in descriptions of paradise and are presented as proof of God's bounty.

The Greeks thought that pearls were made by lightning striking the sea. The Roman historian Suetonius tells the story of General Vitellius pawning a valuable pearl from his mother's ear to help fund his posting to Lower Germania. In his first century *Naturalis Historia* Pliny the Elder wrote that 'the very highest position among all valuables belongs to the pearl' and 'those are most highly valued which are found in the vicinity of Arabia, in the Persian Gulf.' He recalled seeing Lollia Paulina, wife of the Emperor Caligula, 'covered with emeralds and pearls, which shone in alternate layers upon her head, in her hair, in her wreaths, in her ears, upon her neck, in her bracelets, and on her fingers, and the value of which amounted to 40 million of sesterces' – in modern terms, over $200 million. He also relates that Cleopatra once boasted of her great wealth to Mark Antony by dissolving one of a pair of pearl earrings worth 10 million sesterces (some $50m today) in vinegar – and then drinking it.

In the twelfth century the port of Julfar, near the modern day city of Ras al Khaimah, was described as a long established pearling centre by the Arab cartographer, Al Idrisi, and by the end of the nineteenth century, with an average annual export value exceeding £1.4 million, pearling was by far and away the most lucrative industry in the lower Gulf. It provided income not only for pearl merchants, boat owners, captains and crews but for the ruling sheikhs through taxation, much of which would be distributed among local tribes to maintain their support.

In 1917 a single gram of Gulf pearls was worth the same as 320 grams of gold or 7.7 kilograms of silver. With a fleet of over 400 boats Abu Dhabi became the wealthiest and most powerful of all the coastal sheikhdoms. The ruler earned some £60,000 a year from pearling taxes and tribes would divide their labour between pearling in the summer and date cultivation, camel husbandry and goat herding the rest of the year. The other emirates had some 800 boats between them.

But the world financial crash in 1929, coupled with the commercial development of cultured pearls in Japan in the 1930s, was catastrophic for the Gulf economies. Prices fell by as much as 90%. As Indian pearl merchants departed, the pearl fishers of Abu Dhabi reverted to their desert roots. For many in Dubai there was no such cushion: so people starved and the ruler struggled to maintain authority. A ban on imported pearls by the new government of independent India in 1947 proved the final nail in the coffin. Although restrictions were lifted the following year, the Gulf pearl industry had already collapsed. By then the sheikhs were dreaming of oil.

Today the story of the UAE's pearling heritage is told in museums across the emirates. One can learn about the craft of boat-building, the various types of vessel used, life at sea (breakfasts of dates and coffee, in the evening rice and fish, and nights sleeping on a cramped open deck), the tools of the trade, the sizing and grading of pearls, the markets (principally India, Persia and Turkey) and the rewards (relatively meagre for the divers and haulers, many of whom were slaves).

> *Welcome back, God is generous.*
> *Diving days are finished, God is generous.*

So went a traditional Gulf pearling song.

But while diving days are done, pearling is not. In 2004 Ras al Khaimah began producing pearls again: only this time the cultured variety – in partnership with Japan.

The Emirates and Japan Pearl Cultivation and Trading Company grows cultured pearls in submerged cages at an oyster farm off the coast of Rams.

72. COUNTDOWN
Abu Dhabi, 1 November 2009

Everyone puts his own loaf as close as he can to the fire
 - Arabic proverb

At last the long awaited day has arrived when the eyes of the world will focus on Abu Dhabi. More important still for locals: the moment when Abu Dhabi finally emerges from the long shadow of its upstart neighbour and assumes its rightful position of precedence.

"Do people in the UK know about the UAE?"

The question comes from an Emirati resident of Abu Dhabi.

"Many in the UK have heard of Dubai," I reply, "But Abu Dhabi is less well known. So when I say I live in Abu Dhabi, some people ask, 'Is that in Dubai?'"

My answer clearly irks. While both are members of the UAE, Abu Dhabi, larger albeit less populous than Dubai, is the capital and richer by far. But there are growing signs that Abu Dhabi wants to grab the limelight. Several weeks ago, just as Dubai was preparing to launch the UAE government's first satellite into orbit, news emerged of a deal between an Abu Dhabi government-owned investment company and Sir Richard Branson's Virgin Group for exclusive rights to host space flights in the Middle East.

Since then DubaiSat-1 has beamed backed photographs of one of Dubai's distinctively shaped man-made palm islands to its mother base in Dubai. Meanwhile Abu Dhabi has been releasing more details of its plans to promote space tourism in the UAE. One of its investment companies has bought a 32% stake in Virgin Galactic which plans to launch the world's first commercial flights into space. Passengers will be carried six at a time more than 100 kilometres above the surface of the Earth where they will be able to float in zero-gravity. Some 85,000 expressions of interest have already been registered and three hundred seats have actually been sold. There's also talk of building a space station in Abu Dhabi which would include facilities for launching satellites, so combining the emirate's ambition to overtake Dubai as the region's capital of tourism with aspirations to promote home-grown scientific and technological research.

If you sense some gamesmanship going on, you may well be right. For all their cordiality there's a long history of rivalry between the two emirates. Go back two hundred years and the Al Nahyan and Al Maktoum ruling families were members of the same Bani Yas tribal federation led by the Al Nahyan sheikhs of Abu Dhabi. But in 1833 the Maktoum branch split following in-fighting among the Al Nahyans and established themselves independently in Dubai, which, to add insult to injury, was until then ruled by the sheikh of Abu Dhabi. For the next century and more the Maktoums and Al Nahyans frequently fought over contested territories and relations sunk to their lowest in 1948 when tribesmen from Dubai killed fifty-two Manasir tribal allies of Abu Dhabi in a border dispute – which makes all the more remarkable political union between them only twenty-three years later. There has been peace ever since, if not always harmony. Here's my Emirati colleague again:

"When I am asked where I come from, I do not say Abu Dhabi: I say the UAE. But when people from Dubai are asked where they come from, they say Dubai."

Recent weeks, however, have been all about 'the Monaco of the Middle East' and I could not help but feel a touch of sympathy for our neighbour a few days ago when, in a newspaper article buried deep beneath layers of newsprint about the forthcoming Grand Prix, a former captain of the Australian national cricket team commended Dubai's new international stadium as 'the best cricket facility I've seen' – as if anyone at the moment cares.

For the last two and a half years or so tens of thousands of expatriates have worked round the clock to enable Abu Dhabi to host a sporting event almost as popular as football's World Cup and the Olympic Games. An idea of the scale of activity can be gleaned from food consumption in the nearby labour camp: 17 tons of rice, 8 tons of chicken and 156,000 chapattis –

each and every day. In all more than 184 million man-hours have been expended on the Yas Marina project – and since those who have made the race possible laboured night and day to do so, it seems only fitting that today's Grand Prix should be the first to start in daylight and finish in the dark.

Should anyone be inclined to dismiss it as just another motor race, however, I would draw on Bill Shankly's famous football dictum and say, 'It's much, much more important than that.'

This is what another Emirati has to say about it:

"It's like National Day but international, too, because many kings and famous people are coming from other countries."

For behind Abu Dhabi's desire to attract attention is its ambition for a role in global affairs commensurate with its wealth and strategic location. Only yesterday, while the media focused on final preparations on Yas Island, the city was the venue for an unpublicised meeting between US Secretary of State Hilary Clinton and the Palestinian President, Mahmoud Abbas, to try and revive faltering peace talks with Israel. And hand-in-hand with development of the new racing circuit we have seen new hotels, roads and bridges open: the first steps of a master plan that is shaping Abu Dhabi for the future.

For months posters here have posed the question, 'Where will you be on November 1st?' and a clock on the Corniche has been counting down the days. Well, as the sun goes down over the Yas Marina Circuit this afternoon and locals lord it over Dubai, I will be at the carnival on the Corniche with countless other expats with little or no interest in Formula One motor racing: watching the Grand Prix on a giant screen and knowing that Abu Dhabi will never be quite the same.

Commercial space flights on the Virgin Galactic Enterprise are scheduled to take off in 2013. Passengers must be over eighteen, healthy – and have $200,000 for the fare.

73. FIELD OF DREAMS
Abu Dhabi, 10 November 2009

Knowledge is light and all who contribute bring light to our world
- Arabic proverb

No longer is culture on Saadiyat Island simply a concept. True the main developments remain mere lines in the sand but already an exhibition centre has opened for visitors. And driving along the new Saadiyat highway last week from neighbouring Yas Island, where the motor racing circuit and hotel complex have sprouted in less than three years, I sensed for the first time the imminence of the cultural district and the enormous impact it will likely have on attracting tourists to Abu Dhabi.

Meanwhile only the most curious or lost of visitors are likely to turn off the ten-lane highway and follow signs for Manarat al Saadiyat – because there's no indication of what lies in store, except for those with some knowledge of Arabic. *Manarat*, which means place of light, derives from *manar*, which was the name given by the conquering Arabs of seventh century Egypt to the Greek Pharos, the great lighthouse off the coast of Alexandria which ranked among the Seven Wonders of the Ancient World; although almost a thousand years old, the 400-foot tower was then still in working order, using a system of mirrors to reflect the sun by day and fire by night. In the context of Saadiyat, therefore, *manarat* may be translated as place of enlightenment, linking, as it does, to Abu Dhabi's ambition to foster a knowledge-based economy. *Manar* is also the root of the English word minaret, but that's another story.

Enlightenment on Saadiyat lies at the end of a sand-blown road. The building itself would be unremarkable but for a vast latticework screen of stars through which sunlight casts shadows on the front wall – so mimicking the effect we can expect of sunshine filtering through the Islamic dome of the Louvre Abu Dhabi. Soon interactive displays featuring models and plans will explain the cultural, leisure and environmental vision for the island and next year items from the Louvre and Guggenheim collections will be put on public display. In the meantime visitors can enjoy temporary exhibitions, the first of which was launched to coincide with the recent Grand Prix.

Inspired by the popular Art Car movement of Europe and America in the 1950s and '60s, which proponents say can be traced back over 3,000 years to the highly gilded chariots of King Tutankhamen, Abu Dhabi Tourism Authority has taken thirteen classic vehicles and given each an artistic makeover. Exhibits include a 1939 Cadillac LaSalle, once the most fashionable car in America, a rare 1968 Mercedes, 1976 Rolls Royce Silver Shadow, 1996 Mini Cooper and a brand new Aston Martin DBS. But gone are the standard bodywork finishes: each has been customised with a unique, often garish and sometimes disturbing pattern of colours and images, symbols, shapes and words, by artists from France, China, Singapore and the UAE. I need only add that at least one artist has admitted to being offered a large sum of money NOT to daub paint on a car.

But Manarat al Saadiyat's inaugural exhibition is not simply a celebration of cars as art. Art Cars reflects Abu Dhabi's underlying journey from dependency on oil to a broader based, sustainable economy in which tourists flock to the emirate for culture, sport and leisure. And Saadiyat Island, with its museums and galleries, hotels and golf courses, beaches, marinas and lagoons, lies at the very heart of that vision.

Surveying the barren sands of Saadiyat today, notwithstanding the rapid development of Yas Island, one could be forgiven for being sceptical. But only three years ago the chief executive of Etihad Airways said that the goal of the fledgling national airline was to become the best in the world – and last night, at the World Travel Awards in London, Etihad was duly voted the world's leading airline. Nor was it the only local winner: Dubai's iconic Burj al Arab was voted the world's leading hotel, the Emirates Palace won the title of world's leading conference hotel, Dubai was recognised as the world's leading cruise port, and Dubai International Airport was voted best airport.

A line from the film *Field of Dreams* comes to mind: 'If you build it, he will come.'

Substitute *they* for he and you have Abu Dhabi's strategy for tourism in a nutshell.

74. THE DOWNSIDE
Abu Dhabi, 21 November 2009

The man who touches honey must lick his fingers
- Arabic proverb

'We are on the road to recovery,' says Sheikh Hamdan bin Mohammed of Dubai, 'Our economy is humming again.'

His upbeat message at a World Economic Forum summit in the UAE yesterday follows a speech by his father earlier this month in which Sheikh Mohammed reasserted the economic fundamentals of Dubai, reaffirmed the strong bonds which unite the emirates, and sought to reassure doubters of the close-knit ties between the ruling families of Abu Dhabi and Dubai.

'The success of Dubai is an extension of Abu Dhabi's success,' said Sheikh Mohammed, 'And vice versa.'

Referring to 'the blessed march' of federation started by his father and the late Sheikh Zayed, Sheikh Mohammed went on to explain how Dubai's position between East and West, its modern infrastructure and friendly business and investment environment have all helped the UAE's second city to weather the global financial storm. More than that, he spoke of his optimism for future growth. No more the ominous silence which greeted the melodramatic suggestion from Simon Jenkins in *The Guardian* in March that Dubai is on the brink of being reclaimed by the desert.

If pressed for evidence Sheikh Mohammed could have cited the success of the UAE sweets and confectionery business. Just days before his speech Dubai's World Trade Centre had hosted Sweets Middle East, an international exhibition for sweet and confectionery manufacturers. According to a special report in the *Gulf News*, the Middle East market is one of the top ten in the world and in the UAE domestic consumption and exports are both growing. Dubai alone is home to some twenty manufacturers of sweets, chocolates, biscuits and oriental delights – not to mention toffees and lollipops, date sweets, cookies and the 'first and finest' camel milk chocolate.

But turn the pages of the same edition of the *Gulf News* and a headline about a10-year project to tackle diabetes in the Gulf catches the eye. There follows a sorry tale. Nearly 10% of national budgets in Bahrain, Saudi Arabia, Kuwait, Oman and the UAE goes on tackling the disease. The UAE itself has the second highest rate of diabetes in the world. More than a million people – some 20% of the population – are diabetic and over 30% of deaths are diabetes-related.

Post-industrial lifestyles are being blamed for the pandemic of largely preventable type-2 diabetes.

'The desert Arab found no joy like the joy of voluntarily holding back,' wrote Lawrence in *Seven Pillars of Wisdom*, 'He found luxury in abnegation, renunciation, self-restraint.'

Today people have taken to their cars, jobs are sedentary, tastes are sweet and fast food all too convenient. Two years ago, in a study of 7,000 UAE residents from a hundred different countries, 62% of people were found to be overweight. Among nationals the rate was higher still: 75%. And the problem is getting worse. More than 25% of men and almost 40% of women are obese. Children are at greatest risk. A recent survey of students' eating habits in the UAE found that 25% do not eat vegetables, 47% don't eat fruit, and 56% eat fast food more than three times a week.

How different it was in Doughty's day. Then the 'lean nation' of *Arabia Deserta* was perpetually hungry and he described how men, when reposing at home, would 'lie heels out backward, about the hearth, as the spokes of a wheel, and flat upon their bellies' – in the belief that pressing upon their stomachs appeased 'the gnawing of hunger.'

'Get active!' urges Abu Dhabi's Imperial College London Diabetes Centre, 'Live healthily.'

But how do you persuade an indolent population described by the World Health Organisation as among the fattest in the world to get off their couches and out of their cars? The answer: by holding a walkathon.

Walk UAE is part of a campaign to encourage people to take regular exercise to lower the risk of developing diabetes. Last year some 7,500 people gathered in Abu Dhabi for a walk along the Corniche. Yesterday I joined an estimated 10,000 walkers for this year's event. Evidence that the message is winning hearts and minds? It would be nice to think so: but the fact that the route took us once round Abu Dhabi's new motor racing circuit probably had more to do with it.

If participation and enjoyment are measures of success – then the walk was indeed successful. But if it was about changing people's habits an opportunity was missed: for delighted as we were to be given free commemorative T-shirts and baseball caps bearing the *'Diabetes: Knowledge: Action'* awareness campaign logo, there was no information about screening services, no advice about exercise, and no suggestions for healthy eating.

'Hovering over Dubai,' wrote Simon Jenkins, 'Is a cloud called nemesis.'

Perhaps there is – and not just over Dubai but the whole of the country. But it may have less to do with the downturn in the global economy and more to do with the downside of the UAE's economic boom.

75. THE FRUIT BEARING TREE
Dubai, 11 December 2009

The fruit of timidity is neither gain nor loss
- Arabic proverb

A man sits with book in hand. Beside him stands a five year old boy. Both pairs of eyes are fixed on the open page, so much so that neither father nor son appears to be aware of the photographer. It's a typical domestic scene, repeated the world over – or so a quick glance would suggest. But peer more closely and it's just possible to make out the name of the Iraq Petroleum Company on the cover. This is no ordinary bedtime story: it's an oil company handbook.

The image takes us back to 1954, a full fifteen years before Dubai first exported oil. But in the faraway looks of Sheikh Rashid and young Mohammed – the former then Crown Prince (later ruler) of Dubai, the latter ruler today – dreams are already taking shape.

The photograph hangs in the family's ancestral home beside the saltwater creek in the heart of this cosmopolitan sprawl. The very name of the city is said to derive from the Arabic word *dabba*, meaning 'to creep,' which may allude to the flow of water inland from the Gulf. A notice in al Fahidi Fort museum tells us that it once crept all the way to the oasis of al Ain –125 kilometres away – though now entirely confined to Dubai itself. Long ago its natural shelter provided a safe haven on the ancient trading route between Mesopotamia and the Indus Valley. More recently it sustained the fishing, pearling and sea trade on which the city flourished under the liberal tax regime of the Al Maktoum sheikhs. Before oil wealth filtered through, Sheikh Rashid borrowed £500,000 to dredge the silted channel and so enable large ships to berth; until then they had to anchor at sea and off-load their cargoes into barges. And although two seaboard ports have since been created to accommodate even larger modern vessels, it's the creek, with its souks, quays, spluttering *abras* (water-taxis) and old wooden Gulf-plying dhows, which epitomises more than any beach resort, shopping mall or tall building Dubai's continuing love affair with the world.

It's a love warmly reciprocated in the region. Only 17% of Dubai's population are UAE nationals, who are outnumbered three to one by a thriving community of merchant Iranians. Although partying, champagne-swilling, Porsche-driving yuppies may constitute the popular Western image of expatriate life, a far richer vein of humanity resides here. Over two hundred nations are represented. When Somalian smugglers ferry refugees across the Red Sea to Yemen's impoverished shore it's said they point to the nearest mountain and say: 'Dubai's over there.' Much as Dick Whittington was lured to London by tales of streets paved with gold, mere mention of the UAE's fabled city is sufficient to conjure dreams of a new and better life. And while the many poor and dispossessed who come here may not aspire to be lord mayor, every month millions of dirhams are exchanged for foreign currencies and remitted to distant families at home. 85% of expats are Asian, and for India, Pakistan, Sri Lanka and Bangladesh cash transfers make up a significant proportion of GDP. And it's not as though these armies of largely low skilled workers are wanted in their own countries – leastways by their governments who have problems enough already with poverty, unemployment, extremism and unrest.

But it's a love not reciprocated in the UK press which sees only sleaze, self-indulgence and exploitation. 'A monument to vanity and greed,' is how I saw the city described under the recent headline 'Bye-Bye Dubai.' Rather more circumspect, another newspaper posed the question: 'Is this bye-bye Dubai?' And most outlandish of all, one that suggested we are witnessing 'the modern equivalent of the last days of Rome.' Have readers at home had enough of stories about domestic recession, spiralling unemployment, the £400 billion bank bail-out and looming £200 billion budget deficit?

Gloom and glee were prompted by the Dubai Government's announcement, on the eve of a prolonged public holiday, that it intends to seek a 'standstill' on Dubai World's debts, which amount to $59 billion – almost three-quarters of the emirate's total deficit. World money markets plummeted, lubricated by the revelation that the government had no legal obligation to underwrite the company's debts even though it is government-owned. Worst hit was the banking sector. Shares in HSBC Holdings, one of the larger UK creditors, fell by 4.3% – although its $16 billion exposure in the UAE represents a mere drop in the ocean of its global business. Belatedly the government explained that it only wanted to reschedule $26 billion of debt arising from Dubai World's troubled Nakheel property holdings, whereupon markets promptly bounced back. In the meantime supporters were quick to point out that Dubai World's international ports division – the third largest maritime operator in the world – is weathering the global downturn and still making a profit.

'It is the fruit bearing tree that becomes the target for stone-throwers,' said a defiant Sheikh Mohammed on the eve of National Day last week.

Perhaps he reflected on the public consternation that greeted his late father's plan to build a 39-storey tower in the 1970s. Not only would it be the tallest building in the Middle East, but the site chosen for it was beyond the confines of the old town in open desert beside the Abu Dhabi highway. 'He must be mad,' they said. Yet the Dubai World Trade Centre was to become the city's commercial hub and a catalyst for global enterprise and growth. Similar doubts were expressed about the construction of Jebel Ali port, the world's biggest man-made harbour, built all of 30 kilometres out of town. Even his son asked him to stop. Yet Jebel Ali is now one of the busiest container ports in the world – it's said to handle one every 25 seconds – and trade is by far and away more important to Dubai's economy than real estate or oil.

Looking back one can see that Sheikh Rashid always had his eye one step ahead. Much as he may have dreamed of oil, he knew that one day it would run out and therefore sought to invest its precious fruit in schemes which would sustain the emirate in the future. He used to say:

'My grandfather rode a camel, my father rode a camel, I drive a Mercedes, my son drives a Land Rover, his son will drive a Land Rover, but his son will ride a camel.'

In the light of recent events his observation sounds prophetic. Oil reserves are dwindling and in less than twenty years will be exhausted. But suggestions of Dubai's imminent demise are probably premature. Zero corporation and income tax and exemptions from import and export duties make it a good place to conduct international business. The city's guiding principle is reflected in another of Sheikh Rashid's favourite sayings:

'What is good for the merchants is good for Dubai.'

What's more it is politically stable in a region notoriously unstable and sits at the international crossroads between East and West. Perhaps most important of all, it enjoys very close ties with Abu Dhabi, which possesses abundant oil and, rumour has it, maintains a covetous eye on the family silver, especially Emirates Airlines.

So what next? That's what I was asked as I drove through Dubai this morning. For five kilometres or more along the middle of Sheikh Zayed Road the question 'Nakheel: What Next?' is repeated every couple of hundred metres or so on billboards alternating with advertisements promoting Nakheel's iconic palm island and waterfront developments. The media at home have already answered: the man-made palms, they say, are sinking into the Arabian Gulf from which they were claimed. I imagine they are having a field-day with headlines such as 'Dubai's Sinking Feeling' or 'Just Deserts.' As for the rumour, Nakheel has denied it – but who's listening?

In the first flush of oil Sheikh Rashid dreamed that Dubai would one day become a household name all over the world. Some forty years later it is – though not as he would have wished, nor as it deserves.

By mid-2011, helped by a migration of people from Bahrain to Dubai in the wake of political unrest, there was a sense that the worst was over. Traffic through Dubai ports increased by 14% in 2010 and, boosted by a buoyant oil market, Dubai's growth grew by 2.4%. Projected growth for 2011 is 3-3.5% – performance which would have the UK's Chancellor of the Exchequer green with envy.

76. IT'S BEGINNING TO LOOK A LOT LIKE CHRISTMAS
al Ain, 19 December 2009

Man is the enemy of what he doesn't know
- Arabic proverb

'It's beginning to look a lot like Christmas
Ev'rywhere you go ...'

The seasonal carolling of Bing Crosby reverberates from loudspeakers in the Rotana Hotel in al Ain.

The lyrics resonate. Outside the front door, in warm winter sunshine, a herd of wicker reindeer shelters from glass-fibre snow in a forest of little firs. In the foyer a huge tree decked with silver and gold completes the festive scene.

'There's a tree in the Grand Hotel,' croons Bing, 'One in the park as well.'

It's much the same in the many tinselled malls where expats can buy turkeys, plum puddings and cream; brandy butter may be a little harder to come by. Although Islam is the official religion of the UAE, it is indeed beginning to look a lot like Christmas here – ev'rywhere I go.

Strange? Not necessarily. Over coffee I read in the newspaper that Jesus appears in the Quran more than the Prophet Muhammad. Sometimes he's called the Word of God. Other times the Spirit of God. More often than not he's the Son of Mary. But he's never the Son of God. While the Quran confirms the Virgin birth, for Muslims the birth of Jesus is proof not of his divinity but of God's omnipotence:

'God creates what He wills. He says to it only, "Be!" – and it is.'

Given the common roots of Islam and Christianity and their shared acknowledgement of Jesus as the Messiah, we should perhaps not be surprised that Muslims respect the festival celebrating Christ's birth. On the other hand – why should they be tolerant when others are intolerant of them?

While the Swiss referendum vote to prohibit the construction of minarets and the French proposal to ban the burqa may be the most recent examples of Western antipathy towards Muslims, the UAE is still smarting over the refusal of the United States to countenance Dubai taking over the cargo operations of several US ports almost four years ago. Dubai acquired the franchises when it bought Britain's Peninsular and Oriental Steam Navigation Company (more commonly known as P&O) in 2006. But the might of post 9/11 American xenophobia was galvanised against the idea of a freewheeling Arab state taking control of its critical infrastructure, forcing Dubai to back down and sell P&O's US assets.

In reality, of course, reindeer, snow and fir trees have as much relevance to the traditional story of the Nativity as al Qaeda has to do with authentic Islam. But Muslims here are keen to foster a new spirit of respect, tolerance and understanding – and in the shared miracle of Christmas may lie our best hope for the future.

If reindeer, snow and tinselled trees add to the cause, so much the better.

77. RUBBLE AND DUST
Fujairah, 25-29 December 2009

Nothing but a handful of dust will fill the eyes of man
- Arabic proverb

In the museum at Fujairah there's a photograph of a barren landscape of rubble and dust. But for the caption – 'A picture showing the surface of the planet Mars taked (sic) by the Viking Spaceship after landing' – one could be forgiven for thinking it's a typical view of the landscape of Fujairah.

The UAE's easternmost (and second least populated) emirate is almost entirely mountainous and drops abruptly into the Gulf of Oman. Imagine bare, jagged peaks and scree-covered slopes with hues of red, brown, green and grey – and you pretty much have it. The exception is a narrow coastal plain which every day expands as the crumbling Hajar mountains recede.

Archaeological exhibits in the local museum point to organised communities along this coastal margin as long as 5,000 years ago. Pottery, jewellery, knives and arrow-heads have been unearthed in communal tombs that suggest trade links with Bronze Age Mesopotamia. Fast forward to the Islamic era and a year after the Prophet's death in AD632 his followers sealed the conquest of Arabia in a famous battle at nearby Dibba. So we may surmise that there has long been human activity in these parts.

'Fujairah is growing' boasts a sign beside a parking lot for giant stone-crushing vehicles, cutters, cranes and dumper trucks. The slogan is accompanied by a picture of a new waterfront development to show what's in store – which is along similar lines to Dubai's man-made palms, only smaller and shaped like a stick with a curved handle. So it is that rocks formed beneath the ocean millions of years ago and forced up above the Arabian Peninsula are now being returned to the sea to underpin land reclamation. Meanwhile land cleared of rock is being back-filled with new industrial development. Besides a growing number of aggregate and cement works and burgeoning industry of oil, gas and chemical bunkering, there's an international airport and thriving free trade zone to which foreign companies have been attracted by liberal tax regulation and easy access to the Indian Ocean.

Offshore are some of the busiest and most pirate-infested shipping lanes in the world. Container vessels line up for the port of Khor Fakkan, while outside the charmless city of Fujairah there's a constant queue of tankers, each waiting its turn to on or off-load. During the day they are barely visible in the sea haze; at night they light up the horizon like a city on a neighbouring shore. Although only six tankers can be accommodated at any one time, capacity is set to double. In the meantime vast new storage facilities are being built in the shadow of the mountains between Fujairah and Khor Fakkan. Quarries, cement plants and stone-crushers have never been busier.

No wonder the dust is flying: developers are working against the clock. Iran's nuclear programme has struck fear into its neighbours. Kuwait, Bahrain, Qatar and the UAE depend on the vulnerable Arabian Gulf for their oil exports. A fifth of the world's oil is shipped through the narrow Strait of Hormuz which Iran has repeatedly threatened to block if attacked.

'The Persian Gulf will be safe for all – or nobody,' a former Iranian president once said.

The Gulf is also the main route for much of the oil exported from Iraq. Only Saudi Arabia has an alternative sea-way. To be on the safe side Abu Dhabi's National Oil Company is laying a 360-kilometre pipeline to link one of its oilfields with its eastern gateway. There's talk that other Gulf oil producers may join in constructing a grid. Nor is it only oil at risk. Abu Dhabi is also building the country's biggest power and water treatment plants here as well as facilities for storing imported grain. Prospects for little Fujairah have never looked so good.

As the mountains crumble new beach resorts are opening north of the city of Fujairah and Khor Fakkan. Little more than a decade ago there was only one hotel in the emirate. Now there are about half a dozen – and more on the way – where Western tourists in Speedos and bikinis mingle with locals covered head to toe in national dress. With pristine private beaches, swimming pools, tennis courts, spas, multiple water sport opportunities and plentiful cafes, bars and restaurants, there's no need for tourists to leave the confines of their hotel. And many don't. When I visited a small mall in Fujairah for coffee I was virtually mobbed for my custom by three competing Filipinas and ended up buying coffee from one, cake from another, and water from the other. For the more adventurous there are tours of the mountains or coach trips to Sharjah and Dubai. Of local interest there is little and hotel staff, denied access to guest leisure amenities, readily confess to boredom on days off.

Among the old buildings of the emirate, however, there is a rare gem. Constructed of stone and mud-bricks and dressed inside and out with coarse plaster, al Bidiya Mosque is a small, low building, little more than 20 feet square and not quite as high, topped by four shallow, irregularly shaped domes supported inside by a single fat column. Radiocarbon analysis suggests it may date to the fifteenth century. Not only is it the oldest functioning place of Muslim worship in the UAE, it is one of the few remaining mosques built in the original style – that is to say, without a minaret. Tradition has it that in Prophet Muhammad's day the call to prayer was given from the roof of his house, which also served as a place of worship. But the use of towers was soon expressly forbidden lest the vantage of height should allow the muezzin to intrude, intentionally or otherwise, on the privacy of people below. Within a century of the Prophet's death, however, minarets had become a common feature of mosque architecture across much of the Middle East. The earliest are thought to have been appropriated from the original Roman towers of the former Byzantine church of St. John in Damascus in the eighth century. The name derives from the Arabic name (*manar*) for the Greek lighthouse (the *Pharos*) at Alexandria and may allude to a small prayer chamber that the conquering Arabs of the seventh century are said to have installed within it.

Happily some traditional features of local architecture are reflected in the design of the hotel in which I am staying: a complex of low, mud-coloured buildings with domes, decorative wind-towers and shady colonnades. Not so at the sky-scraping Meridien Hotel next door. But even that carbuncle pales against ambitions for the rock-strewn landscape which lies beyond it: for this barren site is earmarked for paradise – or rather, the $800 million al Fujairah Paradise Resort. A promotional video shows one thousand 5-star villas, a luxury hotel, mosque and mall, set in an oasis of lakes, palm trees, rivers and waterfalls, against a backdrop of mountains overlooking the sea.

Such is the future face of the rising star of the emirates – and not a pile of rubble nor speck of dust to be seen.

78. GOING ROUND THE BEND
Oman, 30-31 December 2009

Be good or the Shihuh will come and get you
- a traditional warning from parents in the northern emirates to encourage good behaviour in their children

A cry goes up: "There!" It's the dolphin-spotters' truncated equivalent of Herman Melville's whale hunters' alert, 'There she blows! – there she blows!'

From stillness all becomes animation. Fingers point, heads turn and the boat lists as people hurry from one side to the other – only to see a tail-fin disappear beneath the surface. Two minutes ago the cry came from the other side and we are lost as to where to stand or look next. I am on a dhow off the Musandam Peninsula – the north-eastern tip of Arabia, little more than 50 kilometres (31 miles) from the shores of Iran – slowly going round the bend.

The mountains of Musandam go right down to the sea. Or rather – they rise from the sea: because their rocks were formed beneath the ocean and are being forced up at a rate of some five centimetres a year by tectonic movements of the Earth's crust. Although they belong to the same Hajar range as the predominantly red peaks of Fujairah, here the mountains are higher (reaching almost twice as high as the loftiest of England's Lakeland summits) and mostly grey, yellow and brown. Known locally as the Ru' us al Jibal – the Heads of the Mountains – they lie not in the UAE but Oman, though they happen to be cut off and physically disconnected from the rest of the sultanate to the south.

Since time immemorial these mountains have been home to the mysterious Shihuh people, a primitive tribe once notorious for carrying out raids on neighbouring Ras al Khaimah. 'Wild and untamable,' is how Bertram Thomas described them following a visit to Musandam in the mid-1920s, noting their habit of carrying a *yurz* – a small-headed axe on a long slender handle.

Thomas believed the tribal map of this tip of Arabia resembled the setting for the biblical story of suffering in which three friends, each of a different tribe, counselled the hapless Job. He suggested that Musandam's aboriginal population could be descended from the ancient race to which one of the friends, Bildad the Shuhite, belonged. Whatever the truth, dialect and temperament have long set the Shihuh apart from other tribes in the region.

Sovereignty over Musandam was for a long time contested by the Qawasim tribes of Ras al Khaimah and the Sultan of Oman. Neither managed to subdue the Shihuh, however, and the mountainous peninsula remained largely independent until the discovery of oil elsewhere in the region dictated the need for territorial demarcation. When the Shihuh were asked whether they wanted to be aligned with the emirates or Oman they chose the more distant sultanate. So in my hotel I find no portraits of sheikhs but a rather faded picture of Sultan Qaboos.

From the western border to the main town – Khasab – is a 40 kilometre drive best undertaken when time is not an issue and the scenery can be enjoyed. The winding road is sandwiched between the sea and the mountains and, judging by two gaping holes in the concrete retaining wall, warning signs depicting falling rocks are not to be taken lightly. Although prehistoric animal carvings in Wadi Quida and ancient tombstones in the mountains point to a long tradition of settlement in these parts, today's inhabitants barely scrape a living. Certainly there's none of the glitz of Abu Dhabi or Dubai. Fishing, farming (chiefly goat-herding), trade and tourism are the official mainstays of the economy. Unofficially there's also smuggling and in the harbour I watched several crates being unloaded from a small boat under cover of darkness and placed in the back of a Nissan pick-up. The fibreglass speedboat equipped with two powerful outboard engines is said to be the hallmark transportation of smugglers from Iran who, rumour has it, ferry goats across the Strait of Hormuz in exchange for computers, televisions and American cigarettes. Given the extraordinary proliferation of goats here – literally round every corner – I can well believe it.

Beyond Khasab the road ends. To the south dirt tracks, often tortuous, steep and narrow, link farms and villages in the mountains and the inhabitants hail any passing vehicle for a lift.

"Salaam alaykum," I say in greeting when flagged down by a local man.

"Good morning," says he.

After this promising start we quickly reach our lingual limits, though he continues to chatter none the less. He has with him a large sack, tied at the neck, which he places in the back, and I can't help but wonder what it contains. Probably a goat. Without warning, as I'm driving up a steep incline with a vertiginous drop on one side, he suddenly pulls out a small-headed axe on a long handle, the *yurz* stick hallmark of a Shihuh tribesman, and proudly points to an inscription in Arabic.

"Saeed bin Saif," he says, thrusting the blade under my nose.

Assuming this to be his name I resolve to try to write it in blood should he strike and leave me for dead.

In the north and east, where a scattering of small communities depends entirely on fishing, boats are the main means of transportation, and the waters of the Khor Ash Sham, a 17 kilometre-long fjord which runs east of Khasab, are dominated by tourist dhows looking for dolphins. Our route takes us round a bend to a protrusion of rock that hardly merits the description 'island.' Here we anchor and, after clambering over the ruins of some vanished habitation, I swim around it in less than five minutes. Isle or islet would be nearer the mark.

Yet this tiny island was home to the British telegraph relay team who operated the submarine communication cable that was laid through the Gulf in 1864 to link Basra and Bombay. The *Illustrated London News* of the day informed its readers that those stationed here had 'boats for exercise and amusement, and a regular supply of English newspapers and periodicals' – concluding with the assurance that 'time passes away very quickly.' Not so: for the heat, boredom and monotony of life on Telegraph Island, hidden, as it is, round a bend in a remote fjord off an isolated peninsula, drove those compelled to live here to utter distraction – and so coined the popular phrase for going mad. The island was abandoned in 1867 – not a moment too soon for the sanity of its inhabitants.

During the voyage I fall into conversation with Arun, an Indian IT worker, who has come here with his family 'to get away from Abu Dhabi.' He's employed in the real estate sector and has had, as you may imagine, a difficult year. Odd, we reflect, that the very seclusion which drove members of the telegraph relay team round the bend is, in today's globally-connected world, one of Musandam's principal attractions.

But our introspection is suddenly interrupted by another cry: "There!"

A finger points to the narrow channel between our boat and another tourist-laden vessel. There indeed – there! Just beneath the surface, swimming side by side and seemingly grinning, are two bottlenose dolphins putting on a show. Pausing just long enough for excited spectators to lean over the rails and gasp, the pair simultaneously spring out of the water before diving deep and out of sight.

For a moment there is silence … then everyone starts clapping.

79. AN UNEXPECTED TWIST
Dubai, 9 January 2010

From you the money, from me the dance
- Arabic proverb

Earlier this week it was announced that what we have become accustomed to calling the Burj Dubai (i.e. tower of Dubai) will henceforth be known as the Burj Khalifa bin Zayed Al Nahyan – in honour of the ruler of Abu Dhabi and President of the UAE.

Sheikh Mohammed bin Rashid's gesture, made on the occasion of the inauguration of the record-breaking skyscraper five days ago, appears to have caught everyone by surprise – 'You're joking!' replied a friend when I texted him with the news – perhaps even Sheikh Khalifa himself because he was not among those who attended the pyrotechnic celebration which doubled as a party to mark the 4th anniversary of Sheikh Mohammed's accession. This morning road signs still point to the Burj Dubai and souvenir vendors have yet to discard T-shirts and miniature models bearing the old name.

Why the sudden change? While much has been written about the achievements of Sheikh Mohammed, the design of the 828 metre-high Burj and the challenges of 'super tall' construction, there has been only passing reference to the new name in the English-language newspapers – and no speculation whatsoever.

Officially the name was changed to reflect the greatness of the UAE personified by its head of state. But if we go back to last month's $10 billion rescue of Dubai World's subsidiary Nakheel, which saved Dubai – and vicariously, the rest of the UAE, too – from certain humiliation and shame, other possibilities emerge. On several front pages next day there was a telling photograph of Sheikh Khalifa and Sheikh Mohammed walking side by side on a swathe of red carpet flanked by a guard of honour. It was taken at Abu Dhabi airport just before the Vice-President saw the President off on an international engagement. While those behind can be seen huddled in conversation, the two principals march in silence and apart: Sheikh Khalifa fixing the camera with a steely stare, Sheikh Mohammed with his eyes cast down. Neither sunshine nor ceremony can conceal the chill.

So although dedicating the world's tallest building to Sheikh Khalifa may indeed be an expression of esteem, it could also be tacit acknowledgment of Dubai's debt to Abu Dhabi or even atonement for risking the reputation of the UAE. Cynics suggest it's the price exacted for support and rumour-mongers go so far as to say that the Burj – and much else here – is now owned by Abu Dhabi. Whatever the truth, it has prompted a great deal of humour in Abu Dhabi at Dubai's expense.

If good has come of Dubai's misfortune it lies in a strengthening of bonds with Abu Dhabi. Historically the two pillars of the federation have not always seen eye to eye. Even union in 1971, after more than a century of border disputes and intermittent fighting, failed to instil any sense of coordination and common purpose. While happy to join a flexible alliance of emirates, Sheikh Rashid of Dubai refused to entrust the security and economic development of his emirate to a central government. So the constitution to which he agreed remained provisional and, besides local health and education departments, special clauses allowed each member state to maintain an army and control its own natural resources. And every attempt by Sheikh Zayed of Abu Dhabi to increase federal control was resisted by Sheikh Rashid.

When each emirate was asked to subscribe a quarter of its oil revenue to a national budget, he opted out. Again, when contributions were sought from local militias for the fledgling Union Defence Force (UDF) he declined; he even threatened to leave the federation altogether when Sheikh Zayed merged his own militia with the UDF and appointed one of his sons as commander-in-chief. Above all, when Saddam Hussein sought to force up the price of oil to re-build his economy after the war with Iran, Abu Dhabi was willing enough to observe OPEC's production limits, while Dubai, which was not a member of OPEC, ignored them – behaviour described by Iraq as 'economic aggression' and later used to justify its invasion of Kuwait.

Although Sheikh Rashid was not the only ruler to take a stand against closer union, he was the most powerful, and it was only after his death that the process of integration could continue. By that time the writing was on the wall for Dubai: oil reserves were beginning to run low and Rashid's successors knew that revenue would be better spent on growing the economy than sustaining a standing army. So it was, in 1996, that the temporary constitution was at last made permanent, paving the way for control of Dubai's army to be surrendered to the Abu Dhabi-led UDF.

Which is why for many Emiratis 1996, rather than 1971, marks the real start of the union, and they more than most will marvel that the former home of the last bastion of provincial independence should have become the setting for a new symbol of federal subordination: for on the site vacated by the Dubai Defence Force Sheikh Mohammed ordered a new district to be laid out, once crowned by the Burj Dubai – now by Sheikh Khalifa's tower.

80. THE VIEW FROM SHEBA'S PALACE
Ras al Khaimah, 15 January 2010

Trust not the sea, trust not the times
- Arabic proverb

I am on the trail of one of the earliest known Islamic settlements in the UAE. Not Abu Dhabi, Dubai or Sharjah, nor any of the other four emirate capitals. Julfar exceeds all in antiquity.

But where is Julfar – or rather, where was it? From earliest Islamic times it featured in Arabic travelogues as a rich and bustling port in the Arabian Gulf and early European cartographers placed it on the southern shore of the Strait of Hormuz. By the late eighteenth century, however, all reference had ceased. More recently its very location was in doubt. Historical sources and archaeological evidence put it close to the city of Ras al Khaimah – and that's the starting point of today's quest.

A sign for Ahmad ibn Majid Road suggests I am not far away: for it commemorates Julfar's most famous son, remembered in the West as the navigator who guided the Portuguese explorer Vasco da Gama to the Malabar coast of India in 1498. My first stop is the stretch of coast immediately to the north of the modern city where a sand bar, 200 metres or so offshore and several kilometres in length, would have provided shelter for shallow-draught ships. There, under mounds of sand, archaeologists have found abundant evidence of a large, post-fourteenth century settlement – but nothing to indicate earlier occupation. In recent times the area has been used for fly-tipping and fragments of pottery and porcelain, some quite possibly hundreds of years old, lie scattered in the dunes among scraps of plastic, rubber and rusting tin.

Clues then take me two or three kilometres inland to Shimal, a small village at the foot of the crumbling Hajar mountains once guarded by an extensive hill fort known as Sheba's Palace. Here, where Bronze and Iron Age tombs had already been exposed, archaeologists discovered a wealth of material to indicate a thriving trading centre with pre-Islamic origins. In the lowest levels was pottery from fourth century Persia. Above they found later Persian pottery, pottery from India too, a tenth century gold coin from Oman, ceramics from twelfth and thirteenth century China, and a twelfth century carbonised coffee bean – the oldest ever found. Could this be the site of our lost port? Only if the landscape has changed. A twelfth century account places Julfar on the banks of a river at the foot of some mountains – and although there are mountains here there is no river. But the author of the report never visited Julfar and his second-hand description may have confused a khor (or creek) for a river – because geophysical studies here have revealed traces of an old sea inlet long silted as a result of mountain erosion and tidal currents. Excavation has also confirmed the remains of a medieval wall and ditch that used to run from the foot of the hill on which Sheba's Palace sits all the way to the shore.

From the vantage of the palace ruins, as the mid-day prayer call echoes across the plain, I watch a drama unfold. It begins before the dawn of Islam with a community of traders from the last great empire of Persia living on the banks of a muddy creek which provides a safe anchorage on the sea route to and from the East. Then in the seventh century Arab fleets and Muslim armies arrive to consolidate Islam across Arabia. With Islamic conquest comes peace, the port prospers from trade and the plain sustains a growing population. But in the fourteenth century tidal patterns change, a sand bar appears offshore, the creek begins to silt and larger vessels are no longer able to venture inland – so the hub of the city shifts to the coast where it reaches the peak of its prosperity under the protection of the kings of Hormuz, an island on the Persian side of the Gulf.

To sustain its protectors much of Julfar's hinterland is given over to cultivating date palms and a defensive wall is constructed, fronted by a ditch, all the way from the mountains to the coast to protect the plantations from marauding inland tribes. But danger comes not from the interior but the sea. Following Vasco da Gama's pioneering voyage round the Cape of Good Hope and across the ocean to India, the Portuguese vie for control of sea trade with the East. In 1507 they occupy Hormuz and for over a century Julfar remains a Portuguese dependency – until, getting caught in the backlash of a Persian offensive to regain ascendancy in the Gulf, it rebels in 1621. Retaliation is brutal. The suburbs of the city are burnt, its inhabitants murdered. But the balance of power is shifting. In 1633 the Portuguese are driven from Julfar by a confederation of tribes from Oman, who in turn are forced out by an army of Persians, themselves expelled by local Arabs in 1746 – by which time silt renders the harbour unnavigable for all but shallow-draught ships. By the late eighteenth century there's a new port nearby in a rising town called Ras al Khaimah, power base of the newly-arrived Qawasim tribes from the northern shore and islands of the Gulf – and over time Julfar sinks into the sand.

But where, you may ask, does the Queen of Sheba fit? She probably doesn't. In Arabic the ruin to which her name is given is called Qasr al Zabba – the palace of Zabba, a name used to describe a female warrior. Experts have suggested it should never have been ascribed to the Queen of Sheba, who lived, some say in Arabia (others Africa), about 3,000 years ago, but to Zenobia, warrior queen of the third century Roman colony of Palmyra in modern day Syria. The chances are, however, that neither lodged here because there is no evidence that any of the tumbled walls, cisterns or watchtowers pre-date Islam. But the local tourist board seems happy enough to perpetuate the myth and the suggestion of such legendary provenance lends lustre to dry stones.

With Shihab Al Din Ahmad ibn Majid, the self-styled Lion of the Sea, we are on surer ground – or so I thought. After all, he was the leading Arab navigator of his day, master of ocean winds and currents and author of many works on the theory and practice of navigation. Nor is his connection with Julfar disputed. The story goes that Vasco da Gama met him on the coast of East Africa and persuaded him to guide his fleet across the Indian Ocean to Calicut. By doing so, however, Ibn Majid opened up Arab sea trade with India to competition from Europe, and once the damage to their centuries' old monopoly became apparent Arab historians said it must be a case of mistaken identity. They claim he was elsewhere at the time, or, if it was him, that he only agreed to help after the Portuguese had plied him with drink – a desperate excuse for a Muslim if ever there was. Sheikh Sultan bin Mohammed of Sharjah feels so strongly about the stain on Ibn Majid's reputation that he has written a book in which he lays blame on an Indian navigator from Gujarat. Contemporary Portuguese records merely refer to an unnamed astronomical navigator.

In the dawn of history myth and reality merge. Perhaps the future is more certain. For while Arabs, Persians and Portuguese may have shaped Julfar's development, the sea was always the chief architect and arbiter of its existence – and this week a government-sponsored report warns that a rising sea threatens much of the coast of the UAE.

Some 85% of the UAE's population and over 90% of its infrastructure are said to be at risk, and in the race to shore up the most critical places all traces of Julfar will likely be washed away.

Although the Arabs lost their trading monopoly to the Portuguese, they stole from them a new design for their ships. Until Vasco da Gama appeared on the scene Arab vessels were double-ended (i.e. bow and stern were both pointed). Afterwards Arab ship-builders copied the square-stern of the European style which can still be seen in dhows today.

81. DISORIENTATION
Abu Dhabi, 23 January 2010

The well is deep but the rope is short
- Arabic proverb

It looks like a scalextric set in slow motion. In Yto Barrada's *Gran Royal Turismo* three black Mercedes Benz limousines emerge from a tunnel and make their stately way towards a village. A VIP is coming to visit and as the convoy approaches some last minute embellishments are added to impress. An avenue of trees suddenly pops out of the ground to line the road. Kerbs are freshly painted, a red carpet is rolled out and street lights are switched on. A little further on flags begin to flutter. Then I notice that the front of a scruffy building is set to spring open. Surely an ambush ...

Coming to the end of my tour of *Disorientation 11: the Rise and Fall of Arab Cities* in Abu Dhabi's first purpose-built public art gallery at Manarat al Saadiyat I expect nothing but the worst. This exhibition is the antithesis of Orientalist art. Here there are no sun-baked desert caravans or verdant oases to lure the romantic Western traveller. Forget rich and colourful costumes, bustling bazaars and harems hidden in cool, cushioned chambers. *Disorientation* is an Arab perspective on the failure of pan-Arab nationalism. There is no enchantment: only war, civil war, displacement and disillusion. Hope has given way to despair.

Steel yourself for a taste: children re-enact on video the assassination and funeral of President Sadat in 1981; a human-size model of a skyscraper recalls a tower in Beirut which was commandeered by various militias during the Lebanese civil war, the higher storeys once occupied by snipers, its basement used as a prison; a map of disconnected Palestinian territories in Jerusalem is engraved on hundreds of cubes of olive soap from the West Bank; young unemployed Algerians are photographed staring wistfully over an impassable blue Mediterranean from a breakwater barrier of huge concrete blocks; six members of former Christian militias in Lebanon talk on film of their involvement in the massacre of Palestinian refugees in 1982 ... after which the 'scalextric set' seems quite benign.

There is more in similar vein. Underlying the exhibition is a lament for the failure of the vision of Egypt's President Jamal Abdel Nasser for Arab unity in the 1950s and '60s. His United Arab Republic – a union principally between Egypt and Syria – lasted only three years. And although he was the inspiration for successful republican movements in Libya, Algeria, Yemen and Iraq, similar attempts in Lebanon, Jordan and Saudi Arabia were not successful. Since then, in the aftermath of Anwar Sadat's Camp David Peace Agreement with Israel in 1978, Egypt's influence in the Middle East has waned, superseded by fragmentation and growing dependency on America to put things right.

In the establishment-inclined English-language *Khaleej Times* last week, as newspapers round on President Barack Obama at the end of his first year in office for his failure to make significant progress towards peace in the Middle Peace, the opinion editor wrote of an 'existential crisis' and 'intellectual wilderness' in the Arab and Islamic world and deplored the lack of leadership.

His tirade coincides with the bleakest news yet from Yemen. On top of a rebellion in the north of the country, a separatist movement in the once independent south, diminishing oil and water resources and growing evidence of al Qaeda and Islamic radicalisation, today's *National* warns of a population explosion. For a year or more the United States has quietly been building the military and intelligence capabilities of President Saleh's precarious military dictatorship. Now it has offered $63 million for development and next week Western leaders meet in London to discuss a coordinated response. Closer to home the UAE has pledged $650 million to improve civil infrastructure, while Saudi Arabia has promised $1.25 billion in aid on top of millions for military assistance and a new border fence.

Osama bin Laden's ancestral homeland is the poorest of Arab nations. Over a third of the population of the Arabian Peninsula live in Yemen, of whom almost half subsist on less than $2 a day. Each year some 700,000 more mouths are added, at which rate the population could double during the next twenty years. At the same time the water table is falling and San'a faces the prospect of becoming the world's first waterless capital. Water extraction is four times greater than replenishment. About 90% is used for agriculture, of which half is expended on growing qat – a narcotic leaf chewed as a national habit. To ban qat would be to incite riots. But if it's not banned there will be riots when wells run dry. Meanwhile oil exports, which currently constitute 75% of national income, are also falling and are likely to cease altogether within a decade.

With Yemen seemingly teetering on the brink, other countries in the peninsula are worried that chaos may spill into their territories. Not without cause – because it already has. Over a hundred Saudi Arabian soldiers have been killed by Houthi rebels in skirmishes and incursions in the north where the two countries share an 1,800 kilometre mountainous border. While the Saudi government accuses Iran of supporting the rebels it is becoming increasingly concerned about al Qaeda's presence in the region. Last year the Saudi defence minister was lucky to escape with his life when a suicide bomber struck in Jeddah during the Holy month of Ramadan. Since then stories have emerged of al Qaeda's growing influence in Yemen and the Nigerian arrested for attempting to blow up an aeroplane over Detroit on Christmas Day is thought to have been trained there – which is why the world is starting to take notice.

At Manarat al Saadiyat's scalextric village it turns out there is no terrorist ambush. Inspired perhaps by the story of the Russian Prince Potemkin's efforts to spruce up villages in the Crimea for a visit by Catherine the Great in 1787, the grubby front wall flips over to reveal not masked gunmen but a bright, clean façade. And as the visiting VIP is hoodwinked or turns a blind eye, *Disorientation* shows what can happen when leadership fails: for if America and the West, however well intentioned, are seen to be interfering in Yemen's internal affairs, President Saleh will likely be deposed and in the vacuum that could follow al Qaeda would find the country even more fertile ground for recruiting new operatives.

'We need a Mandela like figure,' writes our opinion editor, 'Someone who could heal and unite us.'

But he offers little hope of such a Colossus from Arab ranks.

'Ours is a world of short-sighted pygmies,' he rues.

Once the VIP has passed through the impoverished village the grubby wall flips back, the palm trees disappear, the red carpet retracts, flags cease fluttering and the place reverts to its customary desolation. But wait two or three minutes for the convoy to re-emerge from the tunnel and it happens all over again: round and round, *ad infinitum*.

In June 2011, amid increasingly violent unrest in Yemen, President Saleh was seriously injured in an assassination attempt and taken to Saudi Arabia for treatment. He has since returned – whether to hand over power or make his last stand, it remains to be seen.

82. THE ENVY OF ICARUS
al Ain, 29 January 2010

Climb like a cucumber and fall like an aubergine
- Arabic proverb

Let me introduce you to – here conjure, if you will, a roll of drums and clash of cymbal – the magnificent Mr Ali Ozturk of Turkey!

Some hurrahs would not go amiss at this point.

Ali and his legendary flying machine, *Purple Violet*, are the top attraction at the al Ain air show: four days of aerobatics, showmanship and competition. Promotional notes tell us that *Purple Violet* is built like a Formula One racing car – though clearly with wings top and bottom rather than a wheel at each corner – and that it's possibly the fastest biplane in the world.

After craning my neck to watch several fly-passes by a huge airbus from the UAE's Etihad Airways, which, we are reminded, has been voted the world's leading airline, the commentator announces Mr Ozturk's impending arrival.

"Look down to your left," he advises, "Ali's flying low."

Seconds later, to huge applause from spectators, a purple (and violet) single-prop biplane races past the stand, almost scraping the ground before climbing into the sky and looping the loop. For a quarter of an hour or more Ali rolls, tumbles, dives and loops. How Icarus would have envied him the durability of modern wings. Several times the plane stalls and drops in a spin seemingly out of control and certain to crash – only to spark into life and, when almost beyond recall, soar upwards again leaving a trail of smoke. At one time it's transformed into a helicopter and we marvel as it crawls upended across the sky by its nose. Although there are many more aerobatic displays, none today quite compares with Ali and his *Purple Violet*.

But showmanship is not limited to the sky. Among the food stands (which offer a welcome fish and chip lunch), entertainment booths and static displays is David Webb from England. Basking in mid-winter sunshine of almost 30 degrees, Mr Webb can hardly believe his good fortune: an all expenses-paid trip to the emirates with the cockpit of a 1950s Hawker Hunter jet. His story begins in 1972 when the former Royal Navy plane crashed on take-off from HMS Daedalus, a land base at Lee-on-Solent, after the pilot was forced to eject following an instrument failure. It careered through a fence, across a road, over a 30-foot cliff and row of beach huts – and plunged into the sea. Salvaged two days later it was sent first to Farnborough for weapons trials and afterwards suffered further indignity with the UK Atomic Energy Authority in Oxfordshire where it was regularly bombarded with improvised lightning strikes. Rescue came in 2007 when Mr Webb, a technician with the Ministry of Defence, acquired the battered fuselage and painstakingly restored the cockpit section.

"Every single part was removed, cleaned and re-assembled," he explains proudly, "And the paint is an exact match for its original livery. It even has the name of the pilot on it."

He points to some stencilled letters: Lt. Mike Sharp.

"Toffee Sharp they called him. It would be the icing on the cake if I could make contact with him."

Mr Webb now accompanies the gleaming cockpit to air shows where long queues gather to squeeze and have their photograph taken inside a piece of British aviation history. Meanwhile several people who witnessed the crash have made contact with him. One man has told how, at the age of seven, he and his four year old sister were throwing stones into the sea when their mother suddenly screamed and, looking up, they saw the pilotless plane pass about six feet above their heads.

So far Flight Lieutenant Sharp has not been in touch. Not his best memory, I suspect. As for HMS Daedalus, it has long gone – and maybe just as well: because in Greek mythology Daedalus was the mastermind behind the waxed wings which gave way when Icarus, his son, flew too near to the sun, plunging him into the sea.

A fine name for a ship perhaps – but not for a naval flying station.

83. ON THE ROAD
Sila, 5 February 2010

Better a free dog than a caged lion
- Arabic proverb

From the city of Abu Dhabi a road runs due west for some 350 kilometres to the border with Saudi Arabia. The map shows a coast-hugging highway with the prospect of long views to the north over the Arabian Gulf and scenic sands to the south.

The reality is very different. The road crosses *sabkah* – salty mud flats – with few features apart from oil pipelines, electricity pylons and power cables. There is not a sand dune in sight and barely a glimpse of the sea. Even the hardy ghaf, an indigenous evergreen which thrives where most trees would wither, is a rare feature beyond the green fringes of the highway. For centuries it sustained nomadic wanderers with fuel, fodder, shelter and medicine. Now modern development and diminishing ground water endanger its very survival.

For much of the first 250 kilometres (156 miles) or so the monotony of the desert is concealed behind dusty curtains of watered palms that line the middle and sides of the road. Seaward, on a shelf overlooking the Gulf where a cluster of dilapidated Nissen army huts recalls the last days of British protection, a carpet of tiny shells is evidence of the sea's encroachment much further inland. Earlier still a large river flowed here and fossils of fish and fresh-water shells have been unearthed during recent surveys for a railway that will join the emirates and eventually link with Oman, Saudi Arabia and other Gulf countries. Archaeologists have also found two fossilised crocodile skulls and bits of elephant, hippo, monkey and giraffe, evincing an ancient landscape of swamp, grassland and trees. This morning all we see is one camel – in the back of a Toyota truck.

At the end of the green corridor a sign beckons to 'The Desert Islands' and out to sea lies a chain of islands where mounds and cairns, flint tools and arrowheads, point to human settlement going back more than 7,000 years. On one there are remnants from a pre-Islamic Christian church, while on another are traces of an early mosque.

But for many the history of Abu Dhabi begins with oil and in 1963 this part of the coast saw the emirate's first shipment of crude oil from an onshore field. The export terminal at Jebel Dhanna still dominates the shore, overlying mining shafts and tunnels of an earlier trade in sulphur. Widely used in the manufacture of gunpowder, medical and veterinary treatments, sulphur production is thought to have peaked between the eighteenth and early twentieth centuries when gunpowder played a key role in defence of competing trading interests in the Gulf. But I've read that even quite recently Bedouin would search here for sulphur crystals to make potions for ulcerous camels. Just as sulphur gave way to oil, however, so oil will one day come to an end – and next door to Jebel Dhanna is the face of Abu Dhabi's emerging economy: a 5-star hotel, beach resort and leisure complex.

Leaving the trees behind we continue over wide open *sabkah* relieved only by outcrops of sandstone sculpted into strange shapes by the wind.

> BEWARE OF
> ROAD SURPRISES

warns a sign, as befits the most lethal road in the emirate. And sure enough: out of the blue we see a lorry pulling a trailer displaying an address in Barnsley – so imbuing the Yorkshire town with a touch of the romance more usually evoked by the Silk Road cities of Asia.

Our destination is Sila, the most remote town in the UAE. Beyond lies the border with Saudi Arabia where during the pilgrimage season, when precedence is given to travellers bound for Mecca, queues of trucks can build in sweltering heat and crossing often takes up to a week. 'Checkpoint Gnarly' is what *The National* nicknamed it during delays last summer. Trucks backed up for over 30 kilometres (19 miles) and hundreds of motorists required treatment for heat stroke. One driver was found hallucinating and covered in dust after trying to swim his way across the sand.

Some thirty years ago people in these parts wandered freely between Abu Dhabi, Qatar and Saudi Arabia – many of Sila's residents still prefer to cross over the border (no visa is required by UAE citizens) to do their shopping rather than travel along the UAE coast – and there was little here but for a solitary ghaf, under which travellers would rest, and a well by which they would camp. The late Sheikh Zayed is said to have had a particular fondness for the tree. The story goes that he once found a branch had fallen off, whereupon he ordered that poles should be placed to hold the others up and that a forest should be planted around it. He also arranged for houses to be built to improve the lot of the people. So it is that Sila boasts the oldest and tallest ghaf tree in the UAE, albeit propped up and sustained by artificial irrigation, and the former tent-dwellers live in government villas with every mod con.

But the tree, once a welcome landmark in an empty landscape, is now inaccessible and barely visible inside a fenced plantation, while the people are said to yearn for the freedom of Bedouin life. In the summer most residents remain in their air-conditioned houses, but in winter many escape to traditional woollen tents over the border or to their own campsites on the periphery of the town.

'My God!' cried Dean in Jack Kerouac's great road odyssey, suddenly awestruck by the vast emptiness of the Mexican desert and the freedom that comes of nomadic wandering, 'It's the world!'

The sight of a large sculptured globe on a traffic island in the middle of Sila prompts a similar exclamation from my companion today. For us, however, there's no going on, and we turn and retrace our steps.

From the border with Saudi Arabia a road runs due east for some 350 kilometres to the city of Abu Dhabi. The map shows a coast-hugging highway with the prospect of long views to the north over the Arabian Gulf and scenic sands to the south.

The reality is very different ...

Following seismic studies the government announced that four nuclear power plants are to be built on the shores of the Gulf some 300 kilometres west of the capital not far from Sila. When I visited in August 2010 work had already started on clearing houses along the beach and preparing the site. Construction is set to begin in 2012 and the first plant is scheduled to come on stream in 2017. Demand for electricity in the emirate is expected to more than double over the next decade.

84. WAITING FOR GODOT
Abu Dhabi, 11 February 2010

The absent one carries his excuse with him
- Arabic proverb

On his pioneering journey across the Empty Quarter in 1930/31 Bertram Thomas was frustrated to find that the Arabs whom he had contracted to accompany and guide him would not be bound by a daily programme of start and finish times or fixed breaks for food and rest.

The discipline of scheduling has still not been fully assimilated into local business practice and appointments tend to be erratic.

"You will not need that," said an officer when I produced a diary soon after my arrival.

Her laughter rings in my memory.

This morning I am gathered with several other police advisers awaiting the arrival of a senior officer. Having received an urgent summons to brief him about the performance of his department, we have all hastily undone our scheduled plans in order to meet with him. But meetings invariably start late, if at all, and today's is no exception.

The Arabs who accompanied Thomas insisted that the welfare of the camels was their priority: so they would camp where there was water, regardless of how far they had travelled that day, pause when they came across a few bushes, and if necessary ride into the night to find the next pasture.

Like Godot in Beckett's play the officer never comes and we eventually give up and drift away.

Somewhere, I like to think, some camels are happily grazing.

85. SINDBAD AND THE MOUNTAIN OF COPPER
Oman, 20-25 February 2010

An enemy does not become a friend until the ass becomes a doctor
- Arabic proverb

Across the UAE drivers flash their car headlights to say, 'Get out of my way!' In the mountains of northern Oman headlights are flashed to say, 'Hello.'

Historically the area around Ibri had a fearsome reputation. 'The tribes occupying it are one and all thieving, treacherous and turbulent,' wrote Colonel Samuel Barrett Miles, British Political Agent and Consul in Muscat in the late nineteenth century, 'The quantity of available rascaldom is pretty considerable, and the quality of ruffianism is quite in keeping.' Yet today people smile and wave – so much so that I can't help but wonder whether I've been mistaken for a VIP whom they've been told to look out for but who is trailing some distance behind.

Beyond Ibri I come to ancient Nizwa, a hotspot for tourists from the cruise ships which berth at Muscat. Outside the castle my attention is drawn to a man dressed in the traditional full-length *kandoura* (long-sleeved, ankle-length shirt) and chequered cloth turban – because he's not an Arab but a Dutchman. To top it all he's wearing an indigo *besht* (long cloak with gold trim), the hallmark of an ambassador if not a sultan or sheikh, and has a *khanjar* (curved dagger) tucked in his belt. I shudder to think what might happen if a foreign tourist tried the same in Abu Dhabi where it's frowned upon simply to do something considered disrespectful with a newspaper bearing the picture of a sheikh, let alone impersonate one, yet Omanis point and laugh and children want their photographs taken with him. Nor is reaction in Nizwa exceptional. When I see Stefan again it's in a crowded souk in Muscat where he enjoys the same adulation.

But strangers have not always been assured of a friendly greeting. Defensive fortifications – walls, castles and watchtowers – in almost every town and village reflect not just centuries but millennia of suspicion, hostility and mistrust.

'The tribes are perpetually at war with each other,' observed the fourteenth century Muslim traveller Ibn Battuta.

No wonder the *khanjar* is part of national dress.

In the great citadel of Nizwa great delight is taken pointing out the pitfalls – quite literally – faced by unwelcome visitors in the past. Attackers had to breach seven reinforced doors on a winding staircase and avoid a succession of concealed pits underfoot while defenders poured scalding date syrup through 'murder holes' above.

The fort at nearby Bahla, centrepiece of a UNESCO world heritage site, looks even more formidable so I stop to take a closer look – only to find it closed.

"When does it open?" I ask.

The man hesitates and looks at his watch.

"In about five years," he says, explaining that it's undergoing extensive restoration – and has been ever since 1987: a world away from the breakneck speed of the youthful UAE.

In a small village in the wadis west of the Hajar mountains, over traditional coffee, home-grown dates and sweet cake, I ask a bedridden elder of the Al Nasri clan how long his family have lived there. Before answering he asks me how long some prehistoric hill tombs have stood in a neighbouring village.

"Up to five thousand years," I reply.

"Same," he says in answer to my question, "Same."

Even then the caravan route which passed on this side of the mountains was already ancient, perfum'd with frankincense from the monsoon south, and on ridges and hilltops for miles around archaeologists have found evidence of far flung connections in countless stone burial mounds. The best preserved cairns are shaped like beehives. Similar tombs exist in Bahrain, Abu Dhabi and the northern emirates, and fragments of pottery link each place with Bronze Age Mesopotamia. Excavations continue in the winter months and near the village of Bat I meet an archaeologist sifting the site of a circular structure.

"This is of the Umm al-Nar period," he explains – that is to say, from about 2600 to 2000BC.

Here we have an Abu Dhabi connection. Umm al-Nar is an island off the coast of Abu Dhabi (now occupied by an oil refinery) where, just over half a century ago, archaeologists discovered evidence of a Bronze Age civilisation which now bears the island's name. Although communal tombs from the Umm al-Nar period have already been found near Bat, my archaeologist thinks this particular circle of stones is what remains of a fortified tower.

"We've found some pottery," he says, "But no bones."

Meanwhile Mesopotamian clay texts of the same era record imports of copper from a land called Magan (or Majan) – which, according to experts, is almost certainly an early name for the copper-bearing region of modern day Oman.

There's still a village called Majan near the copper mountains west of Sohar, a port on the northern coast once capital of Oman and an early centre of trade with India, Africa and the Gulf. Revived by oil, aluminium and steel, no trace of the city's antiquity remains – except for a fort, which like that at Bahla happens to be closed for restoration. But folklore has it that Sohar was the birthplace of Sindbad the Sailor (though Scheherazade spoke of her hero being a merchant from Baghdad), in as far as his mythical adventures are said to have been inspired by the pioneering voyages of Omani merchants across the Indian Ocean and China Seas in prehistory. One such was Abu Ubayda bin Al Qasim who sailed from Oman to China about AD750 and whose 6,000 mile journey was reconstructed in 1980 by Tim Severin in a faithful replica of a traditional double-ended Omani sailing ship. The 80-foot vessel, named *Sohar* in honour of Sindbad's spiritual birthplace, is now beached on a traffic island outside the al-Bustan Palace Hotel in Muscat. Four hundred miles of hand-stitched coconut twine hold its wooden planks together – and not a single nail.

In modern times hydrocarbons have dominated the economy. An Oil and Gas Exhibition at the headquarters of Petroleum Development Oman in Muscat relates how exploratory drilling in 1956 missed its mark by less than 500 metres. Although reserves are relatively modest compared to the

UAE, there is a parallel with Abu Dhabi: for when the oil money did begin to flow the ruler refused to spend it and, just as Sheikh Shakhbut was forced from office in Abu Dhabi in 1966, so Sultan Said was overthrown in 1970. A tableau shows that enough barrels of oil are now produced every year to reach end to end more than half way from Muscat to the moon.

Under Said's son, Sultan Qaboos, the fruits of oil have been invested in modernisation and several people I meet who have observed Oman grow over the last thirty years speak of its dramatic but sensitive development. In marked contrast to the UAE, the indigenous population constitute the majority in their country: only about 25% of people in Oman are expats – almost the complete reverse of the 80/20 split in the emirates. Omanis therefore undertake all manner of labour and do for themselves rather than rely on foreign help. And except for one very tall minaret which towers above the low dome of the Grand Mosque in Muscat, here only mountain tops scrape the sky. Yet still the mosque lives up to its name: imposing, albeit austere, on the outside, reflecting the colours of mountain, plain and desert, and elaborate and highly decorated inside, with colourful Islamic motifs, Quranic calligraphy and geometric patterns laced with gold. If a boast was to be made it would be of the second largest hand-woven carpet in the world – the largest being in the Sheikh Zayed Grand Mosque in Abu Dhabi.

But in the wadis under the mountains, thick with the dust of Bronze Age dead, the worlds of Sindbad and Ibn Battuta linger. In the village of the Al Nasris, on the slopes of a low hill topped by a cairn, old mud-brick houses, some in ruins, others abandoned or given over to farm animals, moulder beside modern concrete boxes. And all around are gardens of date palms and vegetables to which water is still delivered as it has been for over two thousand years – by *aflaj*, an ancient irrigation system which distributes water from the mountains in underground channels. Here, too, the ubiquitous watchtower.

"Two people stayed there every night," explains the elder's son, Said Al Nasri, "Drink coffee, no sleep."

"How old is it?" I ask.

"Before my grandfather's time," he replies, consigning it to antiquity.

Although the tower has not been used for more years than Said can remember, he tells me rivalries still persist, and from the top of the hill he points to a distant football pitch where some young Al Nasris are squaring up to a team from a rival clan.

"Ah," I say with a knowing nod, "Football instead of fighting."

"No, no," says he, "Football then fighting."

While there is no law in the UAE preventing non-Emiratis from wearing national dress, those who do are expected to behave like an 'ideal' Emirati and refrain from any behaviour inconsistent with local values. Wearing the abaya and sheyla is particularly popular among non-Emirati women. 'It hides all the flaws,' explained one. Adopting the formal attire of a sheikh would probably be unwise.

86. THE MERCY
Abu Dhabi, 5 March 2010

Sunshine all the time makes a desert
- Arabic proverb

A 'nightmare' is how one colleague described last week's storms after being woken by thunder, lightning and lashing rain and spending the small hours mopping up water and bolstering domestic flood defences.

It's the same every year. Gutters and drains simply cannot cope, villas and apartments leak, roads turn to rivers and people quickly become stranded or trapped.

Of the seven emirates Sharjah was worst hit. Residents who at the height of last summer wilted as electricity ran out and cooling systems failed now found themselves drowning in a Venetian landscape of urban canals graced not by stately gondolas but clogged with submerged vehicles and floating debris. As access to Sharjah became impossible by road so commuter traffic built up in neighbouring Dubai causing long queues and turning major highways into car parks. In Abu Dhabi at least one person was killed and many more injured in a spate of collisions. In Ajman, where there were power blackouts, children were given an unexpected day off school. A man in Umm al Quwain said that he was watching news on television of the earthquake in Chile when rain started pouring in, while residents in Ras al Khaimah found themselves without television as a storm blew satellite dishes off rooftops. Only Fujairah, on the eastern coast, seems to have escaped serious disruption. Everywhere else it was the same story: flooded streets and leaking homes, traffic chaos, broken sleep and unplanned time off work.

'The water was too much,' was an Indian man's neat summation.

But to every cloud there's a silver lining …

Here rain is seen as a blessing from God. 'The mercy,' is how one editorial described it. It clears the air of dust, washes trees clean, refreshes parched plants and replenishes underground aquifers.

'The date farms need water,' said one excited observer, 'People living here are so happy.'

Some even risk life and limb to see dust-dry wadis transformed into turbulent rivers.

'In the UAE people miss the rain,' said one storm-chaser, 'They look forward to it like Europeans look forward to the sun.'

Nor does one have to venture outside to enjoy the thrill of the storm. One of the most popular television programmes here at the moment is a reality show called *Rijal al Awasef* – Men of the Storm. Although scheduled to coincide with the season for rain and therefore due to end shortly, there's now talk of a summer series – on dust storms.

Meanwhile, on the sand-rooted palm trees below my window, bunches of tiny green fruit have suddenly appeared. As yet they are no bigger than shrivelled peas. In the coming weeks, however, they will grow and ripen into honey-sweet dates on which to feast long after the floods of winter have seeped from memory.

87. GODS, GRAVES AND SCHOLARS
Umm al Quwain, 14 March 2010

Every sun has to set
- Arabic proverb

Intrigued by tales of pre-Islamic sun worship and sacrificial rites associated with human burial, I have been brought to Umm al Quwain by a camel.

The animal in question died some 2,000 years ago and was found with a dagger between its ribs in grave at Ed Dur, which some believe may be the site of Omana, a first century port that has long disappeared from maps.

I have come to find out more about this neglected corner of the emirates, the name of which officially means Mother of Two Powers. While the remains of a defensive wall, several watchtowers and an old fort on a peninsula in the Gulf testify to Umm al Quwain's onetime dominion over land and sea, today it holds little power over either. With just 1% of the UAE's landmass, it is the second smallest and least populous of the seven emirates. And not blessed with oil, it's also one of the poorest. Fishing and dates are the mainstays of its economy.

Whereas modern development has transformed the other emirates, Umm al Quwain lags behind. But fading images of new resorts on hoardings along the coast suggest that change will come in time. In the meantime Dreamland, a water park popular with day-trippers, and a small museum in the old fort, once home and seat of government of the ruling Al Mu'alla family, are the best the emirate has to offer visitors – unless one includes the Palma Beach Hotel which combines old and new in an Egyptian-themed resort with colourful murals, bird-headed gods, obelisks, pyramids and inscrutable sphinxes.

I start at the fort, which is guarded by ancient canons and a rusting British Scorpion tank, where I am welcomed (according to his name badge) by Hadid, a policeman entrusted with protecting the national heritage. My enquiries about Ed Dur meet with a blank. Instead he turns, rummages among some framed pictures stacked against the wall and pulls out an old photograph of a parade of police officers on the occasion of a VIP inspection.

"Ah, Sheikh Zayed," I say.

To which he nods and taps his finger repeatedly on the image of one of the young officers.

"Ah, Hadid," I say, much to his delight.

The photograph must be all of thirty years old yet his pride is undimmed and he puffs out his chest as he once did for the Father of the Nation.

In the dusty rooms of the fort an exhibition of bronze bowls and weaponry, coins, glass and jewellery illustrates the story of Ed Dur, a prehistoric coastal site on the edge of the town. Excavation has uncovered a square fort with round towers at each corner, a temple dedicated in Aramaic to the sun god Shamash, numerous tombs for humans, some pathetically small for children, and also several large burial pits for ritually-slaughtered camels. Its location beside a lagoon raises the possibility of a port and rich finds from places as far away as India and the Mediterranean point to international contacts and commerce. Coins from the first century AD bear the stamp of Greek originals – with Zeus and Heracles serving as models for Shamash – while fragments of painted pottery from Mesopotamia testify to settlement and trade here in prehistory.

For all its antiquity, however, Ed Dur shared a golden age with Imperial Rome when Roman demand for Eastern treasures led to a boom in maritime trade in the Gulf – which is why the long-abandoned first century coastal site in Umm al Quwain has been linked with the lost mercantile town of Omana in Greek and Roman literature.

In the earliest account of Western sea trade with the East, the *Periplus Maris Erythraei* (literally Voyage round the Red Sea which, to the Greeks, also included the Indian Ocean and Arabian Gulf), written about AD50, we find Omana described as a market town of Persia located about six days' sail from the Strait of Hormuz which, among other things, traded wine, dates and pearls with India in exchange for copper, sandalwood and teak. But the author, thought to be a Greek merchant of Roman Egypt, neglected to say whether it was six days' sail westwards (so making Ed Dur, 120 kilometres/75 miles from the Strait, a possible candidate) or east, while reference to Persian sovereignty, which may have been political rather than geographical, only serves to compound ambiguity.

Proponents of Ed Dur's claim therefore tend to invoke the principal Roman authority of the day, Pliny the Elder, in whose encyclopaedic *Naturalis Historia*, completed about AD77, Omana is unequivocally placed on the coast of Arabia – though precisely where, we can only speculate.

It's time to see for myself so I join the Sharjah-Ras al Khaimah highway and head north along the coast. Already I am in the realms of history: for the construction of the road was funded by Saudi Arabia in the run-up to British withdrawal with a view to cultivating influence in the vulnerable northern emirates. The Saudi contractor was Mohamed bin Laden, father of the infamous Osama, and on the outskirts of town I spot the Bin Laden company name on a roadside compound. After driving a few kilometres fragments of pottery scattered over a wide area of scrub and sand suggest I have found the site of Ed Dur and excavated temples and tombs soon confirm it. But there's no information to promote the past – unlike the future. Where the pre-Islamic sun-worshippers of Ed Dur once fished and welcomed ships from far-flung places, an advertising hoarding heralds an exclusive marina with 6,000 villas and 2,000 townhouses, parks, playgrounds, hotels and shops, and promises investors 'a coastal paradise where life comes full circle.'

So it would seem: for a marketing picture on the internet shows a family of modern day waterfront dwellers gazing worshipfully at the sun – just as those living here two thousand years ago might have done, only without any suggestion of a camel sacrifice.

In the second of his Ibn Battuta trilogy of books, The Hall of a Thousand Columns, Tim Mackintosh-Smith suggests that Umm al Quwain may derive not from the Arabic word quwwah (power), as officially suggested, but from qayw (meaning frequent and intense vomiting). As to why the place should be called the Mother of Vomiting, he explains that the original settlement used to share an island in the lagoon with a large nesting-site for regurgitating cormorants – and so intense was their smell that visitors also used to vomit.

Muslims have long celebrated the end of their pilgrimage season with Eid al Adha – the Festival of Sacrifice – when camels, sheep and goats are slaughtered to mark the deliverance of Ishmael, son of Abraham and father of the Arab nation, whom God preserved when he was sent into the wilderness. Animal sacrifice also has a role in secular festivities. When crowds gathered in Benghazi's Freedom Square to celebrate news of the death of their former ruler, Muammar Gaddafi, eight camels were publicly beheaded and their carcases butchered and shared among the masses.

88. PRE-NUPTIAL DISAGREEMENT
Dubai, 29 March 2010

A house divided cannot stand
- Arabic proverb

Turning to the 'Today in History' column in the *Gulf News* I find that today is the anniversary of the creation of the Dominion of Canada in 1867, the withdrawal of the last American troops from South Vietnam in 1973, and the election of Yasser Arafat as President of the Palestinian Liberation Organisation in 1989 – but there is no mention of the massacre which happened on the newspaper's very own doorstep this day in 1939.

The story begins in the Great Depression of the 1930s. The good times which Dubai had enjoyed before the Wall Street crash and the development of Japanese cultured pearls were a dimming memory. Indian merchants had long returned home, businesses had contracted or gone bust, schools were closed and food so scarce that the hungry resorted to eating lizards, bugs and leaves.

From discontent grew contempt for the ruler's authority. In the first waves of the pearling crisis Sheikh Saeed bin Maktoum Al Maktoum was briefly forced from office by his cousin, Mani bin Rashid Al Maktoum, and only reinstated with the help of the British. Then a band of his cousins, jealous of the oil concession money which insulated Saeed from the worst effects of recession, tried to murder him and might have succeeded but for a show of Bedouin support. Next they demanded money to leave him alone. Finally they formed an alliance with local merchants who pressed for a democratic committee with rights of veto over the ruler to solve the town's problems.

At first Sheikh Saeed capitulated and allowed cousin Hasher bin Rashid Al Maktoum to set up a consultative committee with authority to raise taxes. Saeed was appointed president. But as the balance of power shifted and the opposition demanded that the ruler should donate seven-eighths of his income to the public purse, he stayed away from meetings.

By March 1939, as the nations of Europe teetered on the brink of war, armed confrontation divided the town. On the south bank of the creek Sheikh Saeed clung to power, while on the northern bank rebels occupied the Customs House and other key locations. Keeping the two sides apart were snipers on rooftops who would fire at each other across the water.

Which posed a problem – because Sheikh Saeed's eldest son, Rashid, was due to marry Sheikha Latifa bint Hamdan Al Nahyan, the daughter of a former ruler of Abu Dhabi who had sought sanctuary in Dubai following the murder of her father, and bride and bridegroom lived on opposite sides of the divide. Sheikh Rashid lived with his father on the Shindagha waterfront: Sheikha Latifa lived with her mother in rebel-held Deira. Happily, however, a temporary truce was agreed which allowed the bridegroom and his band of Bedouin warriors safe passage across the creek.

For Sheikh Rashid it was too good an opportunity to miss ...

The Bedouin were armed with rifles – to fire celebratory shots, as was customary at weddings – and on their way to the place of festivities near Sheikha Latifa's home they seized vantage points and stormed the Customs House. Among the first to die were cousin Hasher and his son. Caught off guard at least eight other ring-leaders were killed and many more, including cousin Mani, were forced to flee for their lives. Of those who were captured many had one eye put out and were required to pay a fee to retain the other.

While oral history relates that there were still sufficient rifle rounds left over to celebrate the wedding, which went ahead as planned with music, dancing and a feast of *mansaf* (a traditional Bedouin dish of rice overlain with lamb cooked in sheep's yoghurt and flavoured with pine-nuts), the pre-nuptial massacre has largely been air-brushed from written accounts of the Maktoums and the rise of Dubai. The British Political Resident in the Trucial States set the precedent when filing his official report of the day's events. The committee had grown 'unpopular,' he wrote for a broadcast by the BBC, and was therefore 'dissolved.'

Seventy-one years on, as Sheikh Rashid's son steers Dubai through the worst economic crisis since the 1930s, there is no public dissent or democratic challenge. Nor, as news filters through of Dubai World's debt restructuring plan and the 'replacement' of board members at its Nakheel subsidiary, is there any suggestion of blood on the carpet – or so local newspapers would have us believe.

A movement for democratic reform in the UAE in the wake of the Arab Spring was nipped in the bud when five leading Emirati activists were arrested.

89. A STORY OF THE WIND
Abu Dhabi, 3 April 2010

*The men are the wool of the tribe but
the women are the ones who weave the pattern*
- Arabic proverb

At the end of the day a group of men huddle round the fire in the mouth of a 'house of hair' – the nomads' name for a traditionally-woven tent – talking and drinking coffee under a star-spangled sky until, embers dying and voices falling silent, each wraps himself in a blanket and lies down to sleep.

For a while all is still ... then the wind suddenly changes and starts to blow into the mouth of the tent, whereupon the leader of the group claps his hands to alert the women, who are sleeping behind a screen in a segregated part of the tent. So the women crawl from their beds, put up the wall on the side from which the wind is now blowing, and take it down on the sheltered side. Meanwhile the men remain ensconced in their blankets and their dreams.

The story takes us back to 1940s Transjordan. It comes from *Arabian Destiny*, the autobiography of the late Edward Henderson, successively distinguished soldier, oil pioneer and Gulf diplomat, and was brought to mind by a series of meetings last week at which I advised some police colleagues of the need to revise their project plans.

First I spoke to a lieutenant.

"The plans need to be amended," I advised, pointing out areas for improvement, whereupon he suggested another meeting.

On the second occasion the lieutenant was accompanied by a major.

"The plans need to be amended," I advised, pointing out areas for improvement, whereupon they suggested another meeting.

On the third occasion the lieutenant and the major were accompanied by a captain and a veiled woman.

"The plans need to be amended," I advised, pointing out areas for improvement.

For an hour or more we discussed each plan in turn after which the three officers – all male – conversed at length in Arabic and spoke to their colleague … then, as suddenly as the wind changed during that far-off night in the desert, the men departed, leaving the woman to the drudgery of revision.

90. TOURIST TRAP
Dubai, 5 April 2010

When you enter a town, swear by its gods
- Arabic proverb

Prospective visitors to Dubai will be delighted to learn that the observation deck in the world's tallest building has re-opened for business.

Within days of the inauguration of the Burj Khalifa in a blaze of fireworks earlier this year there was acute embarrassment when an elevator to the observation deck on the 124th floor suddenly stopped working. Fourteen people were trapped for over an hour when a lift became stuck between two floors.

Happily the double-deck elevator was soon restored to service, carrying up to twenty-eight people at a rate of some ten metres a second to the 'At The Top' public viewing area – which, bizarre as it may seem, is not actually at the top. At 440 metres above ground, it's only a little over half way up the 828 metre-high tower. But with floor to ceiling glass all round, an open-air platform and high-power digital telescopes, At The Top offers visitors an expansive view of the city – dust permitting.

Some four weeks after service resumed, however, there was alarm when a loud bang was heard and witnesses saw what they described as smoke or dust coming from one of the elevator shafts. On this occasion at least sixty people were stranded on the deck and many began to cry as calm gave way to panic. Another dozen or so were trapped inside the lift. Visits were immediately suspended for maintenance to be carried out, necessitated, so it was said, by the unexpectedly high volume of footfall during the first month of opening – and the Burj remained closed until yesterday's unheralded re-opening.

But some visitors may be deterred by another front page news story today. An appeal by a British couple against conviction for public indecency has failed and both will serve a month in jail followed by deportation. Their crime? Kissing in public. They were also fined Dh1,000 (£166) each for consuming liquor. The British press must be having a field-day.

Charges were brought after an Emirati woman complained that she saw the couple kissing on the lips in a restaurant in a popular tourist area of Dubai. The defendants said they had merely greeted each other with a peck on the cheek and there was a suggestion that the complainant had made inconsistent statements to police and prosecutors.

It's the latest in a string of high profile cases in which Britons have been charged with indecency and liquor consumption in Dubai. Most notorious of all were the drunken couple arrested on Jumeirah beach in 2008 after ignoring a police warning to curb their behaviour. More recently a drunken woman who made an allegation of rape against a hotel waiter was herself charged with having sex out of marriage after admitting the offence with her fiancé in the privacy of their room. Only when a marriage certificate was produced was the case dropped – though charges of consuming liquor were still pursued.

For nationals Islam prescribes a code of sobriety and decorum – although it's not uncommon to see men in Arab dress drinking beer in bars and restaurants. In the light of Dubai's public kiss some people are suggesting that the UAE requires a public decency law to clarify unacceptable behaviour for Western residents and tourists. Sharjah has long prohibited men from wearing shorts or walking bare-chested in public, while women are not permitted to expose backs or stomachs, wear tight or transparent clothing or skirts that are considered too short. In Abu Dhabi signs outside some malls prohibit shoppers from 'overt displays of affection.' The question is, where to draw the line? Should a kiss be allowed on the cheek but forbidden on the lips? And what of holding hands?

As tourism develops rubbing points will grow. Dubai promotes itself as one of the great shopping cities of the world, Sharjah markets itself as a cultural hub, Abu Dhabi plans to become a great cultural destination, and luxury housing developments and beach resorts point to the ambitions of the smaller emirates. Meanwhile many hotels turn a blind eye to unmarried couples sharing rooms, bars allow customers to drink liquor without a licence, and restaurants entertain diners with near naked samba dancers. Even the government's official on-line travel centre seeks to lure visitors to the UAE with the promise of clubs and discos, salsa and belly-dancing, and well do I remember the apple-scented evening of our induction dinner at which a latter-day Scheherazade welcomed us to the exotic world of the *Arabian Nights*.

If cultures clash, no wonder. Just as dust obscures the view from the 'top' of the Burj, so ambivalence and ambiguity cloud rules of public decency, risking offence to the nation's Muslims and creating traps for unwary tourists.

91. BIRDS OF LIGHT
Abu Dhabi, 8 April 2010

God has omitted women from his mercy
- Arabic proverb

By speaking out against a hard-line cleric from Saudi Arabia who issued a fatwa demanding death for anyone who opposes gender segregation, a Saudi housewife shocked the Arab world and won a place in the final of the popular *Millions Poet* competition.

I have seen evil from the eyes
Of the subversive fatwas
In a time when what is lawful
Is confused with what is not lawful.
When I unveil the truth
A monster appears from his hiding place;
Barbaric in thinking and action,
Angry and blind;
Wearing death as a dress
And covering it with a belt.
He speaks from an official,
Powerful platform,
Terrorising people
And preying on everyone seeking peace.
The voice of courage ran away
And the truth is cornered and silent,
When self-interest prevented one
From speaking the truth.

Hissa Hilal's denunciation was made in a qualifying round of the annual television poetry contest in Abu Dhabi to an audience of tens of millions from across the Middle East. While many people applauded, others condemned her; some even issued death threats on the internet.

But just as deafening silence inspires, so threats make her more determined.

'Arab society has the thoughts I have and the feelings I have,' she says, 'But nobody wants to talk about it.'

This is hardly surprising given the fate of Nadia Anjuman, whose verses so provoked her husband, who claimed she had disgraced the family, that he beat her to death. Her offence? To break the silence on oppression suffered by women in Afghanistan:

> *I am caged in this corner*
> *Full of melancholy and sorrow ...*
>
> *My wings are closed*
> *And I cannot fly ...*
>
> *I am an Afghan woman*
> *And I must wail.*

In pre-Islamic societies women were traded as commodities. The Quran, however, exhorts respect for women and rights to property, work and wealth. Yet Muslims are instructed that 'men have authority over women because God has made the one superior to the other.' No wonder Nadia Anjuman felt caged. 'Bedouin housewives, say they, are for the labour of the household and to be under discipline,' wrote Charles Doughty, and Bertram Thomas observed that men would treat women 'as an inferior, a chattel.' Despite huge advances in education and employment, many Muslim women still feel caged.

Born in a tent of Bedouin parents, Mrs Hilal could not come from a more traditional background. A love of poetry, however, has turned her into a voice for change. As a child she would write in secret and hide her poems under her bed. Now, through the popular medium of poetry, she rages against the discrimination and injustice faced by Muslim women, for example segregation which denies women opportunities in employment reserved for men.

> *I join the birds of light in a battle of enlightenment*
> *We want to rise with a world that is fighting its ignorance.*

Last night, covered from head to toe, she followed in the footsteps of Aydah Al Aarawi Al Jahani who last year attracted huge support when she became the first woman to reach a final of *Millions Poet*. While each had to contend with cultural traditions which dictate that women should not write poetry, nor speak in public or travel without the consent of their male guardians, both were fortunate in having the support of husbands who risked hostility, ridicule and shame to accompany them to the competition.

As happened last year, all talk beforehand was of a woman winning. In the event Mrs Hilal got the highest score from the studio panel, which counts for 60% of the total points, but lost the audience vote, which makes up the remaining 40%.

And the fact that the overall winner was again a male poet and Mrs Hilal was placed only third is, some would say, proof itself of the very discrimination against which she rails.

To overcome strict rules about gender segregation at work an Egyptian Islamic university professor came up with a novel idea based on the convention that children who share a woman's breast-milk are related. Since men and women who are related can be in the same room together, the professor suggested that women could overcome the rule that prevents them being alone in an office with men who are not of their immediate family – and which therefore prevents them from working alongside male strangers – if they were to breast-feed their male co-workers. He subsequently issued a fatwa saying that a woman who breast-fed a male colleague five times would be allowed to appear unveiled in the same room as him. It was later withdrawn: not because it was considered wrong – but because it attracted bad publicity for the university.

92. COLD COMFORT
Ajman, 10 April 2010

They have sowed the seed of the word
'tomorrow' and it has not germinated
- Arabic proverb

On a warm spring morning a cooling breeze from a rare functioning wind-tower is more refreshing than any modern air-conditioning system.

The idea of constructing towers to catch and funnel wind into domestic buildings is said to have been imported to the UAE during the growth of international relations occasioned by the rise of the pearl trade in the late nineteenth century. Soon they became a common feature of architecture in the expanding coastal communities of the Gulf – and still are, though only as decoration. Today's downdraught comes in the fort in Ajman, once home to the ruling Al Nuaimi family, subsequently a police station, and now a museum full of delightful insights into traditional life in the smallest, and one of the poorest, of the emirates.

In scenes from childhood we learn that girls would play games which mimicked their mothers' household chores until they reached maturity or married, the latter happening any time from the age of twelve, while boys would continue to play games of challenge and competition long after they had ceased to be children. In a barber shop in a souk a shaven-headed mannequin examines his bleeding scalp in a tin mirror. Blood and pain were part of everyday life. In other reconstructions a young boy cries after circumcision, a recumbent man grimaces with pain as a healer treads on his stomach, and another is held down while irons are heated to cauterize a tumour in his abdomen. And if hot pokers failed to do the trick, Islam might offer a cure. To ward off evil we are told Quranic charms would be worn, while to combat illness religious leaders would use ink made from saffron to write verses from the Quran on the surface of a plate, which would then be rinsed in rose-water – so producing a physic for drinking or embrocation for pouring on the body.

In the grounds of the fort a collection of old boats recalls the hardships of the pearl fishers and the city's historic dependency on the sea. Growth and development have now brought new dependencies. With wind-towers redundant demand for electrical air-conditioning exceeds supply. For almost two years many new buildings stood finished but vacant as Ajman Municipality and the Federal Electricity and Water Authority argued about which of them was responsible for providing water and electricity. Power cuts are not unusual and some residents have to make do with saline tap water. Such problems are not unique to Ajman nor the UAE; most countries in the Gulf face shortages. Looking ahead there's talk of a regional electricity grid fuelled by natural gas. The UAE is already investing in civil nuclear power and Ajman plans – or leastways, planned – to build a multi-million pound coal-fired power station by 2012. Meanwhile private generators have been installed in some buildings in the city and people are repeatedly urged to minimise consumption.

The contract for Ajman's new power station was signed in 2008 when the local real estate market was riding high on the coat-tails of rising prices in Dubai. Rumour has it that construction has now been delayed by the economic downturn. Property values in Ajman doubled in six months and thousands of projects were launched as the market peaked. In a frenzy of activity, as the government allowed freehold sales with the option of residency visas, developers snapped up land and often immediately sold it on at a profit, while speculators thrived trading villas and apartments off-plan. Subsequent recession has left many developers bankrupt, on the run or in prison, and investors are now counting their losses.

At the height of the boom the main trunk road linking Dubai and the cities of the northern emirates looked set to become a major commercial and residential corridor. In Ajman, where the municipality sold parcels of land to developers and marketing magicians spun dreams with threads of gold, the area bordering Emirates Road became known as New Ajman. Over nine hundred towers were planned in a dozen or more compounds. Today – it's a wasteland.

A broken hoarding advertises Escape where we are asked to 'visualise beautiful nestled villas among green paddocks, sand dunes and horse trails.' Two years after its launch under the patronage of the Crown Prince of Ajman only the sand dunes can be seen – and they've been there all along. Next al Meera Village: fifty residential buildings of traditional design, hotel apartments, a shopping mall, parks and gardens, fountains, restaurants and coffee shops. They should have been finished two years ago; today the site is furnished with roads, street lights, even decorative palms – but the only buildings are two or three concrete skeletons. Further on is Marmooka City, owned by the Sheikh of Ajman, a luxury development of over two hundred towers crowned by Manara Ajman, the emirate's tallest building – or so was the plan before the market collapsed; the project has since been reduced to a mere tenth of its original size. Nearby there's Ajman Uptown, described as 'the first (and long awaited) Villa and Townhouse Development that allows 100% Freehold Ownership with the inclusion of Residential Visa's (sic) for the owner and their family' – still awaited. Park View, 'designed to emerge as the lifestyle capital of Ajman' – yet to emerge. The Boulevard, 'distinguished by groundbreaking partnerships with renown architects, designers and artists' – where so far the only work to have been done is to break the ground. Green City, 'the largest single Villa development in Ajman' – still without a single villa. The list goes on …

Only on one site is there much to be seen. Billed as 'the World's largest single-phased development' and owned and managed by a real estate company headed by the ruler's youngest son, Emirates City will have almost one hundred residential and commercial towers, several luxury hotels, a shopping mall and mosque set among 'scenic lakes and beautiful green parks' – if all goes according to plan. But with completion delayed investors cling to hope on an internet forum. Many seek to swap or sell. Most are desperate for progress reports.

'I bought two flats in Rose Tower but I am not living in the UAE. Can anyone give me an update? Are they still working on the constructions?'

This plea comes from Mohamed, one of thousands of purchasers from over a hundred countries seduced by fanciful descriptions and computer-generated images of homes which, according to the developer's website, were scheduled for completion this year.

So how does the Rose Tower measure up to its promotional billing as the 'epitome of success and grandeur of living' and 'outstanding representation of the bounty of nature and aesthetic functionality?' Today I went to have a look.

As most of the towers in Emirates City have not progressed beyond their foundations and work on more than a dozen has not even started, Mohamed can take comfort from news that the Rose Tower is already three storeys high – albeit only a tenth of its intended height – and from the fact that I saw a crane move above the site this morning, which suggests that construction continues.

But since it's unlikely there will be enough electricity to service the building until Ajman's new power station comes on stream, which is a receding prospect – cold comfort at best.

Six months later I returned to Emirates City to check on progress at the

Rose Tower. As before it was three storeys high but this time the crane was still.

93. THE TERMINAL
Abu Dhabi, 24 April 2010

Going away is your decision: coming back won't be
- Arabic proverb

As a plume of volcanic ash drifts across northern Europe and airports shut down, thousands of travellers find themselves stranded far from home.

While most sit tight and enjoy a few extra days at their holiday destination, a former employee of Mubadala, a government-owned development company in Abu Dhabi, decides to break his return from Malaysia to Switzerland with two or three days' stop-over in the UAE. A golden opportunity, he thinks, to catch up with former colleagues and friends.

But his visit quickly turns into a nightmare.

At the airport immigration desk the computer says 'No!' Why? Because he is listed as a runaway after failing to cancel his residency visa on departure from the country three years ago.

Although a residency visa automatically lapses if the holder if absent from the country for more than six months, an employer may register someone they sponsor as absent without leave if a visa is not officially cancelled on resignation or departure. Employers do this to avoid any liability should an employee leave them and subsequently be discovered to have left debts behind or be working illegally. To avoid the possibility of confusion an employer will normally issue a 'No Objection Certificate' granting the employee permission to leave their post. In our case no such certificate was issued and the former Mubadala employee, who had no plans to work in the UAE again, failed to cancel his visa in the knowledge that it would be cancelled automatically in the fullness of time. And when, many months later, Mubadala was alerted to the fact that his visa had lapsed, they chose to play safe and register him as an absconder.

After an exchange of questions and answers with immigration officials at the arrivals desk there is a further exchange of the very same questions and answers with a more senior official, who then consults with an even more senior colleague – and the best that can be agreed is that a No Objection Certificate should be sought retrospectively from Mubadala. But since it is already evening, any such approach has to wait until next day – and our former Mubadala employee remains stuck in transit all night.

His plight brings to mind a Stephen Spielberg film, *The Terminal*, in which the arrival of an Eastern European traveller at JFK Airport coincides with the demise of his country in war – so invalidating his passport and preventing his entry to the USA. Inspiration for the film is said to have come from the autobiography of an Iranian refugee called Mehran Karimi Nasseri who became trapped in terminal one of Charles de Gaulle Airport in 1988 after losing his passport and refugee credentials – and therefore the legal documentation to either enter or leave France. Although the fog of bureaucracy eventually lifted, Mr Nasseri chose to make the terminal his home – and remained there for eighteen years.

At Abu Dhabi Airport one night turns into two as rescue plans unfold at Mubadala headquarters. First a No Objection Certificate has to be drafted … then approved … then signed … all of which require the right level of authority within the company. Meanwhile, denied access to his luggage and shivering in the air-conditioned chill of the terminal, our visitor seeks sanctuary in the airport hotel only to find it full with other Europe-bound victims of Iceland's Eyjafjallajokull volcano. So he considers buying a jumper from a shop in the airport mall – but stocks are limited to a fashion house from France and at 600 euros he resigns himself to shivering instead.

While his experience rather pales in comparison with that of Mr Nasseri in Paris, release comes not a moment too soon when on the third day, still waiting for the certificate from Mubadala, flying restrictions are lifted and he is allowed to board a flight home.

Two days later, recuperating from the ordeal in Switzerland, he receives the long awaited telephone call from Mubadala advising him that he is free to enter the UAE.

I understand it may be a while before he risks it again – and if he does, that he'll take the precaution of carrying some warm clothing in hand luggage.

Bureaucratic inflexibility proved fatal in October 2010 when an Indian housemaid died after being stranded for five days at Muscat Airport. Forty year old Beebi Lumada lost her passport at Doha while en route from Oman to Chennai. On being returned to Muscat she languished in a transit lounge where her plight was ignored by both her sponsor and the Indian Embassy. She was allowed entry to the country only after she suffered cardiac arrest and died on her way to hospital.

94. HOSTAGES TO FORTUNE
Abu Dhabi, 1 May 2010

The slave must be content with the joys of his master
- Arabic proverb

In a plot worthy of the late novelist Dick Francis an owner and a jockey were recently jailed in Abu Dhabi for cheating in a camel race.

They were convicted of using an illegal device to spur their camel with an electric shock in a race at al Ain last December. To picture how they did it you need to know that a jockey doesn't actually ride in races here but operates a robot mounted on the camel's back. In this case the device was hidden inside the mechanical jockey and operated remotely.

Robot jockeys were introduced as a result of international criticism of the widespread use of child jockeys in Gulf camel racing. Human rights organisations claimed that children as young as four were bought from poor parents overseas and maltreated as slaves in racing stables. The jockeys would be attached to the saddle by the seat of their pants – literally so, by Velcro – and carry radio receivers strapped to their chests so that owners could bellow 'Ya Allah!' (For God's sake, hurry!) from the sidelines. In the light of concerns for their health and safety the practice was banned in the UAE in 2002, and in 2005 the government funded a Dh37 million (£6m) programme with the United Nations Children's Fund (UNICEF) to repatriate and compensate some 1,700 child jockeys.

This week, as the programme draws to a close, a UNICEF goodwill ambassador spoke of its success during a visit to the UAE. As an example he described how he had recently met a former child jockey who is now living with his mother in Mauritania and excelling at school. His encouraging comments come at a time when human rights in the region are again under scrutiny. Navi Pillay, the United Nations High Commissioner for Human Rights, has just completed a ten day tour of the six Gulf Cooperation Council (GCC) countries: Saudi Arabia, Bahrain, Qatar, Kuwait, Oman and the UAE. While acknowledging progress, particularly in relation to the conditions in which labourers live and work, efforts to combat human trafficking, and educational and employment opportunities for women, she spoke of residual concerns, particularly the plight of housemaids.

'All too often many migrants to this and other regions experience discrimination, abuse, exploitation and other human rights violations,' she said, 'The situation of migrant domestic workers is of particular concern because their isolation in private homes makes them even more vulnerable.'

The recent case of Baina Mokalam, a twenty-seven year old Filipina, illustrates the risks. She arrived in the UAE in 2007, sponsored by an Egyptian family in Ras al Khaimah. In three years, she claims, she was not allowed to leave the house, never received any salary, and was denied any contact with her family. The abuse came to light when a neighbour heard her cries as her head was banged against the wall by her employer. While this may be an extreme example, the frequency of newspaper reports of runaway maids suggests that abuse is rife, whether by employers or unscrupulous recruitment agencies.

Few Emirati families do without a housemaid; some are said to have a maid for every child. Many expatriate families also employ maids to cook, clean and look after children. A study by the Abu Dhabi Chamber of Commerce and Industry in 2007 found that there were 268,000 domestic workers in the UAE – about 5% of the population – mainly from Indonesia and the Philippines. No wonder there is concern that local children, entrusted to the care of non-Arabic speaking foreigners, are losing touch with their language, culture and traditions.

The exploitation and abuse of housemaids in the UAE captured the attention of the world in the mid-1990s when a Filipina maid from al Ain was sentenced to death for killing her Emirati employer whom she alleged had raped her. Although the death sentence was waived on appeal, she had to pay $40,000 in blood money to the relatives of her victim, serve one year's imprisonment and suffer a hundred lashes. Since then the government has introduced legislation to provide greater protection and the number of disputes recorded between domestic workers and their employers is said to have fallen.

But the experience of Baina Mokalam would suggest that more needs to be done. Although a mandatory standard employment contract was introduced in 2007, it does not guarantee a minimum wage, maximum hours of work, overtime or entitlement to a weekly day of rest. Similarly, although sponsorship rules have been relaxed to allow maids to switch employers, they can only do so provided they have a No Objection Certificate from their employer – which only serves to underline their dependency. And what about spot checks in the workplace? The government of the Philippines is lobbying for a basic minimum wage of $400 a month and more stringent regulation of recruitment, while in a recent report, *Slow Reform – Protection of Migrant Domestic Workers in Asia and the Middle East,* the independent Human Rights Watch calls for more protection, particularly in respect of pay, hours of work, rest days and accommodation, as well as simpler procedures for complaints and redress.

Until then many maids will run away. The lucky ones will be cared for in shelters and given help to return home; others may find themselves forced into prostitution. A little over a week ago, in a co-ordinated operation across Qatar, Saudi Arabia and the UAE, 574 domestic workers were repatriated to the Philippines. Of these sixty-eight were flown from Abu Dhabi. In a ceremony of welcome in Manila a band played while President Gloria Arroya shook each returned worker by the hand.

'All I want to do now is to see my three year old daughter,' a bewildered April Balanse told reporters, 'I haven't seen her for fourteen months and I have some catching up to do.'

We are told that she left the Philippines to be a sales assistant in Abu Dhabi only to find herself working as a maid.

'I worked seven days a week and received no pay,' she explained, 'I just reached a point when I had had enough.'

Cynics say the timing of the repatriation programme, coming less than three weeks before national elections, is a political ploy to win the votes of overseas workers and their families – and given the reputation of Mrs Arroya's government for corruption they may well be right. Almost 48,000 Filipinos who have registered in the UAE have from today until 10 May to cast their votes and several election candidates have been courting support by funding runaway maids to return home. Meanwhile in the Philippines concern is being voiced that the new automated voting system, due to be used for the first time in over 80,000 polling stations, could fall prey to manipulation.

Besides an end to political violence and corruption, what most migrant workers would like to see from the candidates is not a free ticket home but jobs in the Philippines to negate any further need to work away.

But even without contributions from Baina, April and many others who went unpaid, overseas Filipino workers sent home more than Dh62 billion (£10bn) last year – almost 11% of the country's gross national product – suggesting that they will remain hostages to fortune whoever wins the election.

In September 2011 a twenty-six year old Bangladeshi maid appeared in court in Dubai charged with slicing off the penis of her seventy-seven year old Emirati sponsor with a razor. According to the maid the man had threatened to evict her unless she submitted to his sexual demands. She admitted guilt, explaining that she had acted to protect her honour, and was sentenced to one year's imprisonment. Her allegation that she was raped by the Emirati could not be proved.

95. THE SHEIKH'S NEW CAR
Abu Dhabi, 6 June 2010

Imitation is blind praise
- Arabic proverb

A story is told by Edward Henderson, onetime oil pioneer and later British Political Officer in Abu Dhabi, of the gift of a motor car to a sheikh in the early days of oil exploration in the emirates.

The presentation was made by the oil company by which he was then employed and was intended as a 'thank you' to the sheikh for allowing the company to prospect within his territory. While the car was very fine and had been specially shipped to the emirate, Henderson professed to qualms about its suitability: although serviceable on the hard salt flats of the town, there was not a single yard of tarmac and the vehicle was ill-equipped to handle loose sand. Nevertheless the sheikh, who did not own a car, was delighted.

Some time later Henderson received a visit from the sheikh and was surprised to see him driving a battered Chevrolet pick-up, a vehicle much favoured in desert terrain, so he asked what had happened to the car.

'I sold it,' replied the sheikh, 'And bought two of these.'

It's a lesson which reverberates still.

In post-Zayed Abu Dhabi the Crown Prince has a vision for change. His inspiration is said to come from tenth century Cordoba in Muslim-ruled Spain, the supreme expression of Arab cultural, economic and scientific achievement, in which multiple faiths co-existed peacefully, merchants traded with places as distant as China, and scholars gathered to study the largest collection of books in the world.

In seeking similar acknowledgement and acclaim for the up and coming capital of the UAE, Sheikh Mohammed bin Zayed has enlisted expatriate support. Consultants have set out an agenda for change which requires collaborative contributions from all sectors of government to promote social, cultural and economic development. At its heart is a shift from dependency on oil to knowledge, enterprise, culture and tourism. Key social themes include freedom and justice, safety and security, national health, skills and employability. While a master plan provides a framework for the development of the infrastructure – a new financial district, environmental city, cultural zone, roads, bridges, railways, etc – each government entity is required to define its own specific role in a programme of strategic priorities, targets and performance measures and to provide quarterly progress reports.

But government expectations are crafted in ideas and language which betray their Western origin – and what may be appropriate for organisations in the West, where there is a tendency to delegation, individualism, openness, competition and improvement may not be suitable in a highly secretive, rule-oriented society in which authority is centralised, responsibility collective, risk avoided and change resisted.

In a recent newspaper interview the Deputy General Commander of Abu Dhabi Police was asked whether he intended to improve openness in line with the government's agenda for public accountability and transparency.

'Why not?' he answered, 'But not now, in the future. It will come, it needs time.'

Which may explain why, as I struggle to engender a Western style of performance management and accountability in an unreceptive Arab culture, I get a sinking feeling – not unlike that which comes of car wheels spinning in soft sand.

96. THE WRITING ON THE WALL
Ras al Khaimah, 11 June 2010

Walls are the notebooks of fools
- Arabic proverb

Someone has scrawled 'Sweet Home' above the door of a house in the old coastal village of Jazirat al Hamra, some 25 kilometres south-west of the city of Ras al Khaimah, to which another hand has added, 'Get well soon!'

As well they might: because Jazirat al Hamra was abandoned some four decades ago and many of the buildings are now in an advanced state of decay.

Yet its ruins hold a special place in the hearts of local Emiratis. Not for their antiquity – although the site is said to have been occupied since the sixteenth century or even earlier, most of the buildings are little more than fifty years old – but for the fondness people retain for the traditional way of life that disappeared following unification and subsequent modernisation subsidised by oil money from Abu Dhabi.

Historically the people who lived here subsisted by combining pearling in the Gulf with date cultivation in the spring-watered mountains of Khatt. But when the world market for luxury goods crashed in 1929 the Sheikh of Ras al Khaimah gave them money to buy wood and tools for converting their pearling vessels to fishing and trading dhows. Fishing and boat-building provided the villagers with a life-line until the development of new houses with modern amenities elsewhere started an exodus after unification in the 1970s.

Dozens of houses and public buildings remain: mostly single-storey, though some have wind-towers or large-windowed upper chambers designed to catch a cooling breeze from the sea. There are also several mosques (one with an unusual conical minaret), a school, a jail, and a couple of defensive towers – which are all that remain of a fort. The oldest structures are made of coral and gypsum once topped with palm roofs now mostly rotted away; the source of the coral, which is said to have been harvested from the two Tumb islands lost to an Iranian invasion in 1971, adds to the poignancy of their neglect. Others of sand bricks encrusted with sea shells date to the 1950s and early '60s. The youngest, constructed of concrete blocks, were built in the late 1960s.

At first many of the former residents would regularly return to keep an eye on their homes and spin ghostly tales of guardian *jinn* – genies or spirits created, according to the Quran, of smokeless fire – to keep any squatters away. Isolation also helped. For centuries the village was cut off from the mainland each day at high tide. The story goes it was attacked by the Portuguese and the sand became stained with the blood of the slain – hence its name, which translates as Red Island. Much more recently a tarmac road was laid across the causeway, the tidal flats on either side were claimed for a new town, and some three or four years ago gangs of labourers began to arrive in search of cheap accommodation on the fringe of the abandoned village. This morning the electrical buzz of air-conditioning, blare of music from radios, piles of rubbish and sun-baked clothes draped on lines and trees, all point to continued occupation. And as the time for Friday prayer approaches, the stillness is broken as men emerge from hidden interiors and make their way to the mosque in the new town.

So the emirates' best preserved pre-oil village is no longer suspended in time: it has become a ramshackle labour camp which threatens to spread beyond the periphery and encroach upon the old quarter. Judging by the abundant graffiti it's also a popular trysting place for lovers. Such indignities pale, however, compared to the iniquities which could lie in store for a prime beach-front development site.

Two narrow flights of stairs take me to the top of one of the towers from where, wilting in the torrid mid-day heat, I have a glimpse of the future. The beach on which generations of fishermen used to haul their boats already lies buried under thousands of huge boulders gathered to underpin construction of ten leaf-shaped islands which will extend seven kilometres out to sea. There are also plans for a new coastal resort of some 4,000 apartments and villas embellished not only with the usual gardens, fountains and cascades but also a harbour, Arabian theme park and ecological wetland. On the landward side the finishing touches are being put to the imposing Palace Hotel in al Hamra's village of wind-towered houses, resort hotel, mall, marina, golf course and yachting club, while further north rise the snowy peaks of Ice Land, billed as the Middle East's largest water park, complete with its resident colony of giant plastic penguins.

As to whether there's a place at the heart of these construction projects for a cluster of old buildings which year by year crumble and decay – whether conserved, restored or transformed into a heritage park – only time will tell.

Meanwhile Red Island's mouldering houses and overgrown courtyards are in demand as a film set for horror movies – so the more mouldering and overgrown the better. One of the most recent productions, *The Curse of the Devil*, which premiered at this year's Gulf Film Festival in Dubai, carries eerie echoes of old tales of the village's resident ghosts, featuring powerful *jinn* who can make people disappear.

If only its real guardian spirits were as potent.

97. ELEPHANTS BREATHING FIRE
Sharjah, 26 June 2010

A journey of a thousand miles starts with one step
- Arabic proverb

On a hot and humid morning you find me in the Old Cars Museum in Sharjah, basking in a refrigerated atmosphere thick with the aroma of oil and polish.

Almost a hundred vehicles are on show, among them some gems: a rare 1930s Auburn boattail Sportster with wing-like fenders; a low slung Riley roadster from the 1950s; a monstrous 1959 Buick Electra with grinning chrome grille and delta-wing fins; a Dodge fire engine and a Cadillac ambulance – both custom-built in red; and a Ford Model T, which transports us back to the start of mass production and the dawn of popular motoring.

Easily overlooked among these classics of automobile history is a battered, bent and rusty 1950s Series 2 Land Rover. Abandoned by the departing British in 1971, Abdullah Al Shawi's former taxi has no pretensions to comfort, let alone luxury; certainly no air-conditioning. But this more than any other vehicle in the collection explains the Emiratis' love affair with the motor car. For Abdullah and his Bedouin community living in the desert the old military Land Rover brought undreamed access and opportunity. No longer were Sharjah and Dubai beyond easy reach. Food became more readily available, diets more varied. And for the first time women were able to leave their *barasti* huts and goat-hair tents and give birth in new hospitals in the cities. In almost forty years Abdullah reckons he drove it 1,000,000 kilometres (625,000 miles) – the equivalent of twenty-five times round the equator – and in so doing witnessed, in his words, 'the change of our country from a desert to an oasis.'

The first car in the Trucial States was imported to Ras al Khaimah in 1928 by the Native Agent of the British Political Resident, and a notice in the museum tells of the gift of a car from the King of Saudi Arabia to the ruler of Sharjah in the late 1930s. At first, of course, there were no roads and in his *Seven Pillars* Lawrence wrote of the 'style and art of sand-driving, which got them safely over the better ground and rushed them at speed over soft places ... leaping from ridge to ridge of the dunes and swaying dangerously around their curves.' In the emirates early driving was mainly confined to *sabkah* and beaches at low tide.

In contrast to their father, Abdullah's twelve children exchange their cars for new and better ones every year. For many Emiratis one is not enough and families often own a variety of models for different purposes and occasions. A Toyota Land Cruiser to take the family out ... a Nissan Patrol for venturing into the desert ... a Mercedes Benz, Lexus or BMW for every day ... a Rolls or Bentley to impress ... a Porsche or Lamborghini for fun. Cars are now the object of a passion once reserved for horses and camels, and just as ancient Arab poets would venerate a favourite mount by investing it with the qualities of beauty, speed and courage exhibited by other animals, so an early twentieth century Kuwaiti poet, Zain Al Aabedin ibn Baqer, was moved to compare one of the first motor cars to arrive in the Gulf states to an 'elephant exhaling fire.' For Lawrence's Arabs, who 'loved the new toys,' they were the 'sons and daughters of trains.'

But smoky metaphors may not stand the test of time. Abu Dhabi has recently entered into partnership with an American company to produce environmentally friendly cars. Government investors have acquired a 12% stake in the motor manufacturers Tesla – makers of high performance electric cars – as part of its programme for diversifying the emirate's oil-centric economy. So far Tesla has only produced one model: a premium $109,000 Roadster with lithium-ion batteries, a top speed of 125 mph, a range of over 240 miles, and the capability of accelerating 0-60 mph in less than 4 seconds. But more cars are planned. A $50,000 electric sports saloon is to be launched in 2012 and an entry level model is in the pipeline.

A hundred years ago Henry Ford revolutionised car ownership in America with financial backing from Horace and John Dodge. Ford designed the Model T and the Dodge brothers supplied the engines and chassis parts, while assembly-line production – from start to finish in 93 minutes – reduced production costs so making the vehicle more affordable, albeit limiting the choice of colour to black.

The electric car industry may now be on the verge of a similar breakthrough. As President Obama seeks to reduce carbon emissions and domestic dependency on imported oil, he is offering tax incentives to achieve his target of putting a million electric and plug-in hybrid cars on America's highways by 2015. Tax incentives also exist in the EU, and in Britain the last government promised a purchase grant of £5,000 which, if not since rescinded in measures to address the budget deficit, will follow the launch of the new Nissan electric Leaf. In the Middle East, on the other hand, where fuel is cheap and electricity supplies often precarious, Nissan is promoting a new petrol-driven four-wheel-drive Patrol but has no plans to market the Leaf.

While it may be going too far to say that Abu Dhabi's joint ventures with Tesla herald the end of the conventional combustion engine, the investment of Middle Eastern oil money in electrical car technology could well signal a seismic shift in the politics of oil.

Almost 5,000 advance deposits have already been paid for Tesla's new Model S, which is due to roll off its Californian production line in 2012. This 'game-changing' electric saloon, which has a top speed of 140mph, will be offered with three battery range options – 160, 230 and 300 miles – and cost about £45,000. There are also plans for a Model S-based Model X sports utility vehicle. Production of the trail-blazing Roadster, sales of which have reached some 75% of their 2,500 target, is to be gradually phased out.

98. WISHING ON A STAR
Abu Dhabi, 30 June, 2010

As soon as they are told to save water everyone begins to drink
- Arabic proverb

A new hotel in Dubai is having trouble with its bidets – or rather, the lack of them. The Sofitel Dubai Jumeirah Beach Hotel needs a bidet in each of its 438 bathrooms to qualify for the coveted 5-star rating.

The Amwaj Rotana Hotel, another recent addition to Jumeirah Beach, has a similar problem. Of its 301 guest rooms, just 21 have bathtubs – the rest only showers. Today's *National* explains that 4 and 5-star hotels require 100% baths under Abu Dhabi and Dubai's classification, whereas 50% is sufficient for 3-star establishments.

On the same page of the newspaper another article reminds us that the rapidly developing UAE has one of the highest levels of water consumption per capita in the world – 550 litres per person per day, enough to fill a couple of bathtubs to the brim – despite having one of the lowest levels of natural groundwater supply. More than 90% of current demand is met by desalination, which is slowly poisoning the Gulf and set to increase. Meanwhile, although more than three-quarters is swallowed by agriculture and greening the desert, the government has been broadcasting advertisements on the radio urging us to save water by fitting flow controls to domestic taps and turning the water off when we brush our teeth.

But where's the incentive to conserve, particularly during the hot sticky summer, when most people pay next to nothing for water and for the rest it's entirely free? Here water is treated as though it's as plentiful as oil – and as demand continues to increase in line with new development the problem is becoming acute.

Natural reserves are now so depleted that the National Centre for Meteorology and Seismology has accelerated its programme for generating rain-bearing clouds. Earlier this month half a millimetre of rain was produced after a light aeroplane released a mixture of potassium chloride, sodium chloride and magnesium into clouds over Abu Dhabi's eastern region. In the right conditions the salts attract moisture which coalesces into droplets that become so heavy as to fall as rain.

Not everyone is convinced that 'cloud seeding' is a good idea. The soil and groundwater here are saline enough without more salt falling as rain. Then there's the unpredictability of it. Two years ago an artificially triggered thunderstorm caused chaos in Abu Dhabi and Dubai – and no little consternation among weather forecasters. Yet the government remains confident that controlled cloud-seeding may be an effective way of recharging underground aquifers and intends to recruit a fourth pilot and build a new base for its two sprinkler planes at al Ain.

Perhaps reducing the greening programme, encouraging consumers to shower instead of taking baths and charging them a realistic water rate are other options it ought to consider.

In 2011 the Dubai Department of Tourism revised its hotel star rating system. Now the emirate's 20,000 5-star hotels can have a gold or platinum label added provided they meet certain standards of luxury above and beyond those of a normal 5-star establishment. These include a series of different nightly gifts with the turn-down service and complimentary poolside refreshments. To qualify for the platinum rating full-size (as opposed to miniature) shampoo and toiletries must be offered from a globally recognised luxury brand. It would appear there are no marks for environmental good practice.

99. THE MOUNTAIN
al Ain, 9 July 2010

However high you raise your castle to the sky
you will be buried down in the earth
- Arabic proverb

It has been described as the greatest driving road in the world. At less than 12 kilometres (7.5 miles) from one end to the other the thrill may seem brief. But double the distance and add over 1,200 metres of ascent – and descent – through a succession of tight hairpin bends and you certainly have an experience to remember. All too memorable for some judging by the many scuff marks on the low concrete wall which is all that stands between the highway and the abyss.

The huge limestone mass of Jebel Hafeet rises abruptly some 1,300 metres from the flat desert floor south of al Ain in the Buraimi Oasis. Sir Wilfred Thesiger, the great explorer of Arabia's Empty Quarter, likened its appearance to a hog's back. He spent a week on the mountain in the late 1940s when hunting the Arabian tahr – a now endangered relative of the wild goat (its Latin name, *Hemitragus*, means half-goat) – at which time it was accessible only on foot, and even then only by scrambling. Now a three-lane road takes tourists straight to the top where a cup of sweet tea can be had at a cafe to restore energy after the walk from the car. For the adventurous there's the Mercure Hotel to be explored. Besides restaurants, bars and a swimming pool this 5-star eyrie boasts a hanging garden in the public atrium and vertiginous views over an expansive sea of sand. Nor are guests likely to be disturbed by neighbours. The only other residence on the mountain is a palace belonging to a sheikh – rumour has it, the President himself – who visits only occasionally.

Yet for some the thrill of the ascent is let down by the bleak outlook from the viewing platform set below the bare jagged peaks of the summit. People have suggested that a garden should be added with a play area for children. For others a traditional Arabian souk would enliven the place. The feeling of desolation at the top is perhaps compounded by verdant scenes in the foothills to the north where a lush pleasure garden has been created with a boating lake, pools for swimming, and channels of hot spring water which gush from deep underground.

The writer Roderic Owen, who doubled as court poet to Sheikh Shakhbut of Abu Dhabi, described a very different scene when he accompanied the sheikh to Buraimi for a meeting with the Sultan of Oman in 1955. He wrote of seeing a mountain which he likened to a whale stranded in the middle of nowhere. As they approached, however, he noticed that the stunted trees and shrubs they passed grew taller and greener the closer they got to it, suggesting that the mountain might be a secret source of water.

'Hidypok!' said Sheikh Shakhbut suddenly, 'Boydebloyn!'

At first Owen had no idea what he meant – then it dawned on him that Shakhbut was referring to places he remembered from a visit he had made to Europe. The Jebel foothills were more like the Bois de Bologne, they agreed, than Hyde Park.

Little do those who resort to Sheikh Shakhbut's Bois de Bologne today know that they picnic, boat and bathe in the vicinity of an early Bronze Age cemetery; the name of the mountain – the root of which may be the Arabic word *hafata*, which means perished or dead – is perhaps a clue. Some 5,000 years ago people with links to the early civilisations of Mesopotamia subsisted around the lower slopes. While no evidence has been found of the houses in which they lived, the dead were entombed in cairns of stones which endure to this day – to the east of the mountain at least; those on the northern side have succumbed to modern development. More than five hundred multiple burial cairns can still be traced on the pediment and gravel-strewn plain to the east, a small cluster of which have been restored to show the different stages of construction, culminating in a beehive shape similar to others found in the region. But no signs point the way for tourists. Nor is there a road: just wheel tracks across eight kilometres of sand.

The balance between preserving the emirate's heritage and promoting development and tourism will become even more challenging if Abu Dhabi Authority for Culture and Heritage achieves its wish for al Ain to be listed as a UNESCO world heritage site. The 'Garden City of the UAE' is currently named on the tentative list for its traditionally *aflaj*-watered date plantations, the renovated mud-brick forts and watchtowers built to protect them, and some remnants of human habitation dating as far back as the late Stone Age. Abu Dhabi's second city also occupies a special place in Emirati hearts for its association with Sheikh Zayed with whom Wilfred Thesiger stayed for almost a month after completing his second crossing of the Empty Quarter in 1948.

Even before the most exciting driving road in the world opened access to Jebel Hafeet in the 1980s, Thesiger was disillusioned by Abu Dhabi's oil-funded modernisation. Now there's a master plan for road, rail and residential development in al Ain to accommodate the emirate's fast growing population. There's also talk of building a ski resort on the hog's back with artificial snow, hotels, theme parks, houses, a golf course and shopping mall.

While visitors to the mountain may be delighted at such a prospect, others will turn in their graves.

The Arabian tahr is now protected on the Jebel Hafeet. Critically endangered, it's estimated there are only two thousand left in the wild, most of which live in the Wadi Sareen Reserve south of Muscat in Oman. There are thought to be just thirty left in the UAE.

In 2011 al Ain was added to the list of UNESCO world heritage sites.

100. AN ARAB TRAGEDY
Ras al Khaimah, 17 July 2010

Man is like a palm on the beach: moving with the wind of life
- Arabic proverb

At ninety-two years old Sheikh Saqr bin Mohammed Al Qasimi is the oldest ruler in the world – but probably not for much longer: confined to hospital, he's said to be dying, and when the inevitable happens the stage appears set for an uncertain succession.

Sheikh Saqr seized control of Ras al Khaimah from his uncle sixty-two years ago and is the last surviving member of the founding fathers who bound themselves in federation 'to promote a better life, more enduring stability and a higher international status for the Emirates and their people.' But look for him in the official photograph of signatories to union on 2 December 1971 and you'll search in vain. Abu Dhabi, Dubai, Sharjah, Fujairah, Umm al Qawain and Ajman are all represented – but not Ras al Khaimah: because at the last minute Sheikh Saqr decided to plot his own course independently of the others.

For the roots of his reluctance to cede autonomy we must turn to history. The Qawasim (plural of Qasimi) are relative newcomers to the lower Gulf. They arrived from the coast of Persia in the early eighteenth century and established themselves in Sharjah and Ras al Khaimah. From pearl fishing and sea trade they soon became wealthier and more powerful than the indigenous Bani Yas tribes of Abu Dhabi and Dubai. But all changed when they came up against the British after Arab 'pirates' began conducting *ghazu* raids on British merchant ships in the Gulf. Rightly or wrongly the Qawasim got the blame and in 1819, after earlier inconclusive attempts, a fleet of British warships led by the flagship *Liverpool* bombarded the ports of Ras al Khaimah and Sharjah and destroyed the Qawasim's hold on power. Ras al Khaimah and Sharjah subsequently split, and by forcing truces on all the coastal emirates, the British ensured maritime peace and security until 1971.

When the British government announced its intention to withdraw protection from the Trucial States, Sheikh Saqr was reluctant to commit himself to a federation dominated by the tribal leaders of Abu Dhabi and

Dubai. Instead, in the hope of independent recognition, he offered Ras al Khaimah to the US navy as a Cold War base to strike at the Soviet Union. His dream of independence was sustained by oil: huge reserves under Ras al Khaimah's territorial waters, or so he was led to believe.

Another reason to spurn his neighbours' overtures came from Iran's invasion of the two small but strategically important Tumb islands that had been occupied by the Qawasim since their Persian days, and a third Gulf island, Abu Musa, belonging to Sharjah. The invasion came just hours before the British formally withdrew protection, so underlining the UAE's potential isolation and vulnerability. Before committing himself Sheikh Saqr wanted to be satisfied that the new federation would actively lobby for the return of the islands. Meanwhile the Trucial States' erstwhile protector not only stood by and watched but actively sought to bolster the Shah of Iran by offering to sell him hundreds of Chieftain tanks.

All things considered, it's little wonder Sheikh Saqr held a grudge against the British which was only assuaged when the latest reincarnation of *HMS Liverpool* made a goodwill visit to Ras al Khaimah in the late 1990s and honoured the ruler with a 21-gun salute.

Sheikh Saqr's flirtation with independence proved short-lived. In February 1972, after his offer to the Americans was rejected and test-drilling revealed that the promised oil reserves were commercially unviable, Ras al Khaimah became the seventh member of the UAE. Even then, despite a generous subsidy from Abu Dhabi and equal political standing with Sharjah, Sheikh Saqr remained alert to other opportunities. Having failed to woo American recognition for independence, he twice offered Ras al Khaimah's port to the Soviet government, and during the First Gulf War he approached Iraq with an offer of airbases within striking distance of Iran – each time without success.

As the UAE approaches its 39th anniversary the founding vision for federal coordination and common purpose remains only partly fulfilled. Given historical antipathies union was never going to be easy. Now there's a danger that the growing economic gulf between the emirates, laid bare by global recession, could rekindle centrifugal instincts.

Look no further than rumours that Ras al Khaimah is in league with Iran.

So says Sheikh Saqr's eldest son, Sheikh Khalid, who was Crown Prince and deputy ruler to his father (and still styles himself as such) from 1958 until replaced in 2003 by his half-brother, Sheikh Saud, now *de facto* ruler and heir presumptive. Sheikh Khalid's removal, three months after he led a demonstration against the American-led invasion of Iraq in which US flags were allegedly burnt, sparked several days of street protests. Federal tanks were deployed and soldiers fired machine-guns over the heads of the crowd to restore order. Ever since he has lived in exile from where he pursues an international campaign to de-stabilise the current regime and promote his own case for succession.

'It's a rogue state,' he says of his father's emirate.

If Sheikh Khalid is to be believed, the port once offered in turn to the US and Soviet navies is now leased by the Iranians to allow them to circumvent international sanctions. He also cites a foiled plot by an al Qaeda cell in Ras al Khaimah to blow up the world's tallest building in Dubai.

UAE government sources deny the allegations, insisting they should be seen in the context of a family dispute. But cynics will recall the scheming sheikh of Sharjah, another of the Qasimi clan, who did not, according to gossip, lose the island of Abu Musa to an Iranian invasion in 1971 but sold it to them for an annuity of $3 million, prompting a coup in which he was murdered by his brother two months later.

In the latest twist there are whispers that Sheikh Saqr is not dying but already dead, the formal announcement being a question of timing.

As the curtain falls on our tragic protagonist I am at a loss to know how to conclude: is it the end of the final act, or simply the prelude to the closing scene?

In August 2010 the Central Bank of the UAE ordered local banks to declare any money sent to Iran to help it differentiate between legitimate and illicit trade and thereby assist in the enforcement of UN sanctions. Of Sheikh Saqr, there was no news until the announcement of his death on 27 October 2010. Although Sheikh Khalid proclaimed himself ruler on the internet, he appears to have had little support and the UAE government moved quickly to endorse Sheikh Saud as successor. At eighty-four Queen Elizabeth 11 became the oldest ruler in the world. Eighty-two year old King Bhumibol of Thailand, who ascended the throne six years before Queen Elizabeth and two years before Sheikh Saqr, remains the world's longest serving head of state.

101. CAT AND MOUSE
Abu Dhabi, 20 July 2010

A fool has his answer on the tip of his tongue
- Arabic proverb

Woe betide anyone who leaves their car unattended for too long on the streets of Abu Dhabi. A British expatriate used to park his cherished 1964 Series One E-Type Jaguar under a plastic cover in a space right outside his house – until he returned home one evening to find it missing.

A gang of thieves? No. Officials from Abu Dhabi Municipality assumed that the vehicle had been abandoned and therefore arranged for it to be towed away. No message was left and it took several telephone calls to the police and municipality before the owner traced it to a pound outside the city. Even then he had to pay a fine of Dh270 (£45) to secure its release.

When the frustrated owner asked the municipality to explain the towing rule he was simply told that they could remove any car that was parked on one of their streets. 'What if I go on vacation?' he asked. 'Tough,' was the gist of the reply.

He's the victim of a crackdown to remove abandoned vehicles from the city's congested streets. In the last nine months the municipality has removed 2,268 vehicles – compared to 1,595 during the whole of last year. More fortunate owners get a warning notice first advising that their vehicle will be towed away unless cleaned and moved in the next 24 hours.

To fool the inspectors the owner of the E-Type now resorts to a game of cat and mouse, regularly moving his car to different locations. Meanwhile a public relations representative of the municipality offers this advice:

'I just give my building watchman Dh200 (£33) to wash it every day.'

Which would be fine if washing cars on the street did not happen to be illegal.

102. IN THE HEAT OF THE NIGHT
Sharjah, 23 July 2010

God sends adversities and consolations together
- Arabic proverb

A few weeks ago, while travelling in the northern emirates, I called into a cafe with a book in my hand.

"*When The Lights Went Out,*" observed a waitress glancing at the title, "What's that about?"

"It's about power cuts in the UK," I replied.

"Ah," she said, "Just like Sharjah."

Following repeated blackouts earlier this year and throughout last summer the long-suffering people of Sharjah are now enduring another round of intermittent electricity cuts – or power outages as officials prefer to call them. The outages began in the city's industrial districts last weekend and by mid-week had spread to residential areas. No advance warning was given and over the last couple of days 150,000 residents have been without electricity for up to eight hours at a time.

Any faith in Sharjah's Electricity and Water Authority is fast evaporating as daily temperatures consistently exceed 40C and humidity climbs to 70% – day and night. SEWA (an unfortunate, albeit apt, acronym if ever there was) is simply incapable of meeting demand and people are growing more and more impatient for long overdue improvements to infrastructure and supply.

'Sleepless, furious in Sharjah,' was one newspaper headline above tales of blackouts and powerless high-rise lifts, leaking fridges and idle air-conditioning systems. In the sweltering heat of the night many people have been seeking sanctuary in hospital waiting rooms, moving into hotels or sleeping in their cars. In the blinding heat of day many banks, supermarkets and doctors' surgeries have stayed closed. At least one labourer has died from heat stroke and two motorists were killed when their vehicle crashed in an area where neither streetlamps nor traffic lights were functioning.

Yet SEWA has remained largely silent – perhaps they, too, have closed their doors against the heat – leaving the director-general of the local Chamber of Commerce and Industry to make a public statement.

'The Sharjah government is doing everything to solve the problem,' he said reassuringly, before adding, 'This is summer time and these things are expected.'

Meanwhile some of his members have been doing a roaring trade. Although hotels affected by power cuts have lost occupancy, others have been enjoying a surge. Sellers of electricity generators and portable lights have done particularly well. One man sold a month's worth of rechargeable lights in three days, while petrol stations have spoken of increased demand as people abandon their homes and cruise the streets in air-conditioned comfort.

But one new business is unlikely to find many new customers in Sharjah. Just days after the government announced a 13% rise in the price of road fuel the Dubai-based international business conglomerate Al Yousef has bought the American electric car manufacturer Phoenix Motors. Electric vehicles are clearly all the rage. Only last month Abu Dhabi investors increased their stake in the American electric sports car makers Tesla.

Now Phoenix plans to launch the first battery-powered sports utility truck in the UAE. There's a suggestion it may even manufacture them here if government incentives similar to those in the US are made available. The company claims that the 2-ton truck has a range of about 160 kilometres (100 miles) and can be charged at home in five hours or just ten minutes at a public recharging station.

In Sharjah it may take rather longer.

103. THE DOGS OF WAR
Abu Dhabi, 27 July 2010

A thousand friends can't undo the harm of one enemy
- Arabic proverb

Invasion by a deadly enemy has prompted fighting talk at this year's national date festival.

Rhynchophorus ferrugineus – more commonly known as the red palm weevil – infiltrated the emirates in the mid-1980s. The miniature beetle hails from tropical Asia and kills palms by boring into their trunks and laying up to three hundred and fifty eggs at a time. When the eggs hatch the young lavae feed on soft tissue, forming cavities which weaken and destroy trees. Often the first a farmer knows of an infestation is when a tree starts to fall down.

In Abu Dhabi the forces of law and order have been drafted in to protect al Ain's precious date plantations. After months of training and secret trials a team of police dogs more used to sniffing for firearms, explosives and drugs has been deployed to root out infested trees so that insecticide can be inserted to kill the weevils. Six German shepherds have been sniffing out eighty to ninety trees a day at distances up to 100 metres.

The government is also experimenting with pheromone traps to lure weevils to a watery death in buckets half-buried in the sand. A single trap can draw weevils from a hundred trees.

If a reminder is required of what's at stake we need look no further than last week's annual date festival at Liwa which celebrated the historical importance of the fruit in Emirati culture. In Doughty's 'land of dearth and hunger' dates were a staple of the Bedouin diet; even their stones, when ground, had a use as animal fodder. Although subsistence has long since been banished by oil, some 3,000 date farmers entered produce at this year's event, which concluded yesterday after eight days of competition attended by an estimated 75,000 visitors. The recently established Farmers' Services Centre, a government advisory body tasked with reforming agricultural practices, held talks on such themes as water resource management, marketing and integrated pest control. To encourage responsible agriculture entries are no longer judged simply by the fruit submitted at the competition but by farm visits and inspections for hygiene, irrigation and pest control.

Neither sniffer dogs nor pheromone traps will solve the problem alone. Government officials have adopted the language of war and talk of 'fighting' and waging 'a campaign.' With not only the national heritage but their livelihoods at risk, farmers are the Home Guard. They are being asked to root out dead and damaged trees, clean irrigation tanks and plant new trees further apart. But the odds are still heavily stacked in the weevils' favour. Some 5% of the country's 42 million trees are already thought to be infected.

While the UAE accepts that it has to look beyond oil, a future without date palms is unthinkable.

104. STITCHES IN TIME
Abu Dhabi, 1 August 2010

Old silk is better than new wool
- Arabic proverb

In 1883 an Anglican missionary called Henry Lansdell was presented with a horse and bridle by the Emir of Bukhara and a saddlecloth which he described as 'the handsomest I have ever seen ... of crimson velvet, embroidered with gold and silver thread and silk of various colours.'

A photograph of the cloth can be seen in Lansdell's monumental travelogue, *Russian Central Asia*, in which the author poses in embroidered trousers and a full suit of chain mail, also gifts from the emir.

A saddlecloth similar to that depicted is among more than two hundred items currently on show at an exhibition of Islamic embroidery at the Emirates Palace in Abu Dhabi. In a journey that takes us from the mountains and valleys of Pakistan to the Atlantic coast of Morocco exhibits have been arranged to contrast nomadic and urban traditions. So the highly elaborate Bukharan saddlecloth can be compared with coarser, but no less beautiful, examples decked with floral and talismanic scorpion images made by the pastoral tribes of Central Asia as they migrated between summer and winter pastures.

Islamic in this context is cultural rather than religious. So, although the interpretation of Islamic law discourages the depiction of human and animal form as potentially idolatrous, the image of a celebrated thirteenth century princess appears on a silk tapestry (*suzani*) from the Iranian city of Rasht, while a couple of cotton yurt hangings (*ilgich*) produced by a notorious marauding tribe of the steppes feature matchstick men on matchstick horses. Most of the embroideries, however, have abstract patterns, whether the circles, squares and polygons which predominate in urban art or the colourful animal, insect and floral designs produced by the nomadic tribes. Nor are patterns and materials the only distinctions. We learn that the rugs, blankets and *ilgich* of the nomads served to demonstrate the technical skill and imagination of their creators, each the handiwork of just one woman for her dowry, whereas in urban centres women often worked communally on a single piece, young and old together, as did groups of men, for commercial gain.

While articles can be enjoyed for their beauty, art and craftsmanship alone, they also reveal obscure customs, secrets and superstitions. The excess fabric of a Pashtun dress from Pakistan evokes the wealth of its owner, the long sleeves allowing the hands to be concealed out of politeness … from the Central Asian steppes a child's bib (an *elek*) is embroidered with lucky symbols to protect its young wearer from evil spirits … in the beautiful Swat Valley, now all too familiar as a battleground between Pakistan government forces and the Taliban, there is a fondness for the colour red … from the hat-wearing Turkmen of Central Asia we learn that a man's soul lies under his hat – or rather two hats, it being customary to wear an embroidered skullcap beneath the traditional tall sheepskin … stretch marks in the embroidered centre disc of a leather picnic rug betray another use as a blanket for a camel … from Tetuan in Morocco there are veils made specially to cover mirrors during a honeymoon and so ward off the evil eye … a dense geometric cross-stitch characteristic of Fez is thought to have been introduced to the Moroccan capital by Turkish women captured by Barbary pirates and sold into slavery … the heavier stitches on the lower third of a silk curtain from Rabat are indicative of a door drape between the harem and inner courtyard of a typical Moroccan house, weighted to prevent it being lifted by a breeze and exposing the secret world within.

At the end of my tour I cannot help but compare the rich heritage of Islamic embroidery with the simple woven textiles traditional across much of Arabia. Using wool from camels, goats and sheep and dyes from desert plants, Bedouin women would weave clothes, blankets, rugs, cushion covers, even the black tents in which they lived. Of the quality of their wool, Doughty wrote:

'It is little worth, that which is shipped to Europe from Syria hardly serving for carpet weaving.'

And when the women compared his woollen garments with their own they thought he was wearing silk.

So we find in *Arabian Sands*, the account of his travels among the tribes of modern day Yemen, Saudi Arabia, Oman and the UAE, that Sir Wilfred Thesiger wrote not of fine silk but coarse desert fibre. Not for him a richly embroidered saddlecloth for the camel which carried him across the Empty Quarter to the ruler's fort in 'the small dilapidated town' of Abu Dhabi in 1948 – but a rug and a blanket topped by a ragged black sheepskin which doubled as bedding at night.

Today replicas of Thesiger's saddlery are on display at an exhibition of photographs of his travels at al Jahili Fort in al Ain. And while rug, blanket and sheepskin may lack the lustre of the embroideries of the Silk Roads of Asia, yet we may stand and wonder: if not at art or beauty, at Bedouin life and derring-do.

The traditional Bedouin art of weaving is now being revived in Abu Dhabi's western desert with the help of a government scheme for enterprise development. Women are being taught how to stitch their thick cloth with modern sewing machines to produce purses, pencil cases, bags and laptop cases for the tourist market.

105. HARRY POTTER AND THE GARDEN OF PARADISE
Yemen, 6-9 August 2010

Always walk proudly in the land of your fathers
- Arabic proverb

A story is told of God visiting the Earth to see the places of His creation. But all the cities of the world are unfamiliar save one.

'Ah, San'a,' He says, 'This is as I remember.'

San'a is a city of tall houses and perhaps even taller stories. A square fortified palace belonging to the kings of Saba (or Sheba, into whose domain San'a was absorbed in prehistory) is mentioned in a third century inscription. Four bronze lion heads, one at each corner of a lofty parapet, would roar when the wind blew. Some said the building was so high that its lights were visible some 1,200 kilometres (750 miles) away in Medina.

But San'a was already old when the legendary tower was built. Tradition says that the city was founded by Shem, a son of Noah, who was guided to the spot by a bird, and that the mountains that encircle it flew from Sinai in shock when Moses asked to look upon the face of God. Set on a plateau over 8,000 feet above sea level, its name in ancient Arabic is thought to mean 'well fortified' – as it needed to be, with the rival (and ultimately ascendant) Sabaean kingdom centred on the city of Marib to the east.

For centuries San'a and Marib dominated the main caravan routes for spices, frankincense and myrrh from the Arabian south to the pre-Christian Roman Empire in the north. While San'a controlled passage through the mountains, Marib governed the road across the fertile plain between the mountains and the empty Sands of the interior – the route perhaps taken by the biblical Queen of Sheba when she visited King Solomon with gifts of spice, gold and precious stones. Watered by a huge dam, the famous orchards and plantations of Marib – known also in Arabic as *Jannah*, which means Garden Paradise – were described as 'the garden of God implanted on Earth.' The Greeks dubbed the area *Eudaimon Arabia* (Fortunate or Happy Arabia, better known in its Roman form as *Arabia Felix*) and the indomitable Alexander is said to have had covetous designs until death intervened. For the elder Pliny Marib was 'the diadem on the brow of the universe.' Artefacts in the National Museum testify to a sophisticated sun and moon-worshipping civilisation with close links to the classical world of the Mediterranean – until the collapse of the incense market associated with the decline of paganism and the rise of new monotheistic religions.

"Over there are the houses and synagogue of the Jews," says Saudi, my driver and guide, pointing to a cluster of stone ruins in an abandoned hilltop village outside San'a, "And over there are the houses of the Muslims."

Muslims and Jews co-existed here peacefully for centuries. From the time that the Romans destroyed the principal Jewish temple of worship in Jerusalem until the founding of the modern state of Israel in 1948, Jews were welcomed in Yemen while persecuted elsewhere. Little more than sixty years ago as many as 75,000 still lived here. Now there are fewer than 300. For a brief time Judaism was even the official religion of San'a – until the conquering Ethiopian allies of the Christian emperors of Byzantium sought to establish the city as a place of Christian pilgrimage in the sixth century to rival the pagan shrine at Mecca.

A large hole in the ground in a quiet corner of the city is now all that marks the site of a pre-Islamic cathedral around which wondrous tales were spun to create an aura of religious mystery. There is a story that Jesus was miraculously transported to San'a from the Garden of Gethsemane on the night of his betrayal and here spent time in prayer before being returned to Jerusalem for his arrest and crucifixion. Another relates how he prayed on the very spot on which the cathedral came to be built during his wanderings in the wilderness. But Mecca triumphed over both Judaism and Christianity: no longer as a pagan shrine but as the spiritual home of Islam which swept across the whole of Arabia in the seventh century and spread into the old empires of Byzantium and Persia too. So the cathedral was pulled down, some say at the behest of the Prophet himself, and its stones incorporated in new mosques. Today there are over a hundred mosques in San'a from which five times a day a divine dissonance erupts as the muezzins chant the faithful to prayer.

While a similar fate probably befell the old fortified palace of the kings of Saba, the square tower became the blueprint for an architectural form which endures to this day. Most houses within the walls of the old city (now a UNESCO world heritage site) are at least five storeys high, constructed of stone at their base and often of mud-brick above. Many are hundreds of years old. Traditionally animals were stabled at the bottom and a sitting room – a *majraf*, which derives from the Arabic word *faraja*, meaning dispelling grief and anxiety – often features at the top. For the most part windows consist of small circles or fanlights, the oldest once filled with translucent alabaster but now with stained glass, while doors are often framed and walls embellished with decorative friezes of gypsum. To my untrained eye old and new are largely indistinguishable.

An exhibition in the National Museum reinforces the notion that San'a is suspended in time. Apart from the modern roof-top water tanks, electricity cables and satellite dishes, the townscape of the old city appears little changed from images in a collection of photographs taken by the German traveller Hermann Burchardt over a hundred years ago. Nor is this sense of timelessness restricted to architecture. When Burchardt had his luggage seized by customs officials in the southern city of Hota he sought an audience with the local ruler whom he found in his *majlis* with some forty others. The sultan was very friendly and immediately gave orders for the luggage to be released. But Burchardt noted that coffee was not served: instead bundles of *qat* were laid out which, he observed, 'were chewed with great eagerness' – as they had been for centuries, and still are today.

In the noisy labyrinth of narrow, traffic-congested streets, while women wander in search of gifts and treats for Ramadan, men pore over freshly-harvested bundles of the leafy green stimulant, weighing provenance, cost and quality. It's legal, ubiquitous and said to induce a sense of stillness which dispenses with the need for travel. By early afternoon calm descends as men huddle on the ground, their cheeks bulging as if about to burst. Others indulge as they go about their business. Saudi munches as he takes me on a drive through the countryside.

Legend tells that the narcotic qualities of qat were first revealed by some goats. A goatherd is said to have noticed that his animals became more relaxed and contented after chewing it. An estimated 80% of Yemeni men and 45% of women habitually indulge (it's not said how many goats), about a third of agricultural land is given over to growing it, and some families spend more than half their meagre income buying it.

"It's bad," says Saudi, over and over, "Very, very bad" – alluding not to the effect of qat on local driving standards (though well he might) but to the impact of cultivation on the nation's critically depleted water resources – yet he never passes a day without it.

In the qat groves beyond the sprawling suburbs of the new city we stop at the towering Bayt al-Hajar Palace, once the rural retreat of North Yemen's pre-republican rulers, which is perched precipitously on top of a large outcrop of rock. Here more old photographs are on display and the image of a bustling souk taken in 1944 evokes the sights, sounds and smells of my wanderings in the old city in the morning.

"Welcome," say half a dozen Yemeni students on vacation from Aden when they hear I am from the UK – and we pose for a photograph together.

How odd, I muse, as we shake hands and exchange pleasantries: my earliest conscious memory of Yemen is of the British being driven out of Aden in 1967 – yet now I encounter not simply affection for Britain but nostalgia. A four-litre Jaguar 'belonging to Queen Elizabeth of England' and used on the occasion of a state visit is on display in the Military Museum in San'a, albeit stripped of useful parts, and her portrait is said to still hang in the British-built Crescent Hotel overlooking the harbour in Aden.

Elsewhere an elderly man kisses my hand, a visitor from the south buys me a glass of mint tea, and two qat chewers offer to share their precious stash. Women, some veiled in black but for their eyes, others wrapped in colourful *sitarahs*, are also keen to engage – which is unthinkable in the UAE.

"Where did you learn to speak English so well?" I ask one.

"From songs and films," she replies.

Celine Dion is a favourite singer ... *Titanic* a favourite film.

There's a warmth, curiosity and openness more akin to neighbouring Africa perhaps than to the more traditional countries of Arabia. Yet here, where a garden paradise once bloomed in the desert, lie the roots of many of the indigenous people of the modern day UAE. Tradition has it that the ancient ancestors of the Bani Yas tribes of Abu Dhabi and Dubai were forced to migrate from Marib when the dam burst in the sixth century. Some accounts say that holes were gnawed through the 620 metre-long wall by a giant rat with teeth of iron. The more prosaic suggest that it was overwhelmed by a build-up of sediment carried from the mountains by torrential rain. Whatever the cause, the irrigation system failed and the people of Marib dispersed to others parts of the peninsula. And some 1,400 years later the President of the UAE donated $150 million to the construction of a new dam at Marib from his modern garden paradise in Abu Dhabi – so acknowledging his common heritage with the people of Yemen whom he described as 'brothers of the same family.'

But from the mountains above the 'Rock Palace' I can only gaze towards Marib. Though little more than a 160 kilometres (100 miles) away, the road is too dangerous to travel, as is the country at large, and foreign visitors are thin on the ground.

"You are my first customer for five months," says a lone souvenir vendor – somewhat presumptuously before I even enter his steel cabin.

He looks vaguely familiar. The spectacles ring a bell – the haircut, too.

"What's your name?" I ask.

"Harry Potter," he replies, throwing open the door of his cave of treasures.

As I look for a magic lamp to buy he wraps a turban round my head and a *futah* (sarong) around my waist about which he fastens a gold-embroidered belt fitted with a *jambia* – a curved dagger unchanged in style from one I saw tucked in the belt of a 2,600 year old statue in the National Museum.

"There!" he cries triumphantly, "You are a Yemeni."

Then, with second thoughts, he tucks the loose end of the turban around my face concealing all but the eyes and steps back admiringly.

"We call this the Bin Laden look," he says.

For Sheikh Zayed of Abu Dhabi the new Marib dam was more than simply an affirmation of his shared roots with the people of Yemen: it was also intended as symbol of continuing unity and vitality in the ancient heartland of Arabia. But unity has long been in short supply in these parts and the idea of vitality hardly squares with many Yemenis' qat-fuelled quest for inner stillness.

"It's bad," Saudi keeps repeating, "Very, very bad."

But when he stops the car to scatter his leftover leaves before a herd of grateful goats, his act takes on the quality of a sacrament – like a supplicant making an offering at the altar of his god.

Motivated by Islamic duty to help those in need and the belief that good fortune should be shared, Sheikh Zayed was among the world's most generous donors of foreign aid. His nickname was Zayed al Khair – Zayed of Good Deeds – and his example is still followed. In its brief lifetime the UAE has donated some Dh163 billion (£27bn). In 2009 it distributed Dh9 billion (£1.5bn) among ninety-two countries, which equated to 1% of GDP against a UN target of 0.7%. Current projects include the $100 million Sheikh Khalifa City for the poor which is being constructed on the outskirts of Cairo.

106. A PIECE OF THEATRE
Abu Dhabi, 30 August 2010

O God, do not trim a single custom from us
- Arabic proverb

You join me in the *majlis* of Sheikh Mohammed bin Zayed Al Nahyan, Crown Prince of Abu Dhabi, for an evening lecture on 'Diversity and the Future of Sustainable Transportation' – food for thought in the fasting month of Ramadan.

To conjure the scene imagine an immense room with tiers of soft seating all around, a vast carpeted space in the middle, overhead three large chandeliers suspended from a tented roof, and symbolic images of Sheikh Zayed and his family, with horses and falcons, camels and Bedouin encampments, hung on every wall.

The first hour is all commotion as the almost exclusively male guests, all in national dress, arrive and wander about the room greeting each other with lingering hand-shakes and Bedouin-style nose-kisses.

"It's like a piece of theatre," whispers my neighbour as we feast on dates and spiced coffee.

Some guests wave and offer a cheery 'Salaam alaykum' to all in the room, to which we chorus 'Alaykum assalaam' (And upon you be peace). One or two swagger, camel stick in hand. Others walk hand-in-hand after the custom of their desert ancestors. An elderly man is almost knocked to the floor when he is surrounded by a mob and bustled to a hastily-vacated space in their midst. Long lost friends? The chances are they saw each other only yesterday – this morning even. Meanwhile we duly jump up from our seats as our host and his sheikhly brothers glide through the pressing throng.

It's a modern variation on an ancient theme. Access to tribal leaders has long been a traditional right. Once any man was free to walk into a sheikh's *majlis*, enjoy his hospitality and petition him over any grievance or dispute. Although legal jurisdiction has now passed to the state, the *majlis* remains an important social interface between ruler and subjects.

The guest-speaker is Mr Carlos Ghosn, chairman and chief executive of Renault and Nissan.

"Ramadan is a time for reflection and introspection," he begins, "To think about the person you would like to be."

He takes us from the past, through the present to the future. We are told that Nissan's association with the emirate began in the 1950s with the launch of the still popular four-wheel-drive Patrol. He warns that emissions from conventional combustion engines are contributing to global warming and applauds the development of the world's first zero-carbon city at Masdar in Abu Dhabi.

"We think there are a lot of possibilities for collaboration," he says in a thinly-disguised bid for business.

He predicts that 10% of new cars in ten years' time will be electric – which is a cue to talk about the imminent launch of the battery-powered Nissan Leaf in the United States, Japan and Europe. And he concludes by suggesting that electric vehicles could be commercially successful in the Middle East if governments were to lend support.

"Vision without action becomes a dream," he says, "And action without vision just passes the time."

One might think that the prospect of an electrical future for the automobile industry would prompt some unease from an audience sustained by oil – but no. Nor should it: after all, if Mr Ghosn is right, 90% of new cars in ten years' time will still run on fossil fuels – and emerging markets in India and China will more than make up demand.

As to whether any his audience will take heed and change their oily habits remains to be seen. Reality is this evening's ritual gathering of a sheikh and his followers is less about embracing change than preserving tradition.

107. JOURNEY'S ECHO
Abu Dhabi, 1 September 2010

If a gazelle falls ill do not send the lion to diagnose the complaint
- Arabic proverb

Yesterday President Obama withdrew US combat troops from Iraq, so bringing to an end more than seven years' foreign occupation; some 50,000 American soldiers will remain to the end of 2010 to advise and assist their Iraqi hosts.

A cause for celebration? It would be nice to think so. But even if Prime Minister Nouri Al Maliki's claim that Iraq is now 'a sovereign and independent country' capable of defending itself is true, people here are wondering why the Americans ever ventured there in the first place. To destroy Saddam Hussein's weapons of mass destruction? To liberate Iraq from his tyranny? Well, no weapons of mass destruction were found and although Saddam has been removed the replacement government remains fragile, corruption is rife, basic services are inadequate and sectarian violence persists. Meanwhile more than 100,000 Iraqi civilians and almost 5,000 American and British military personnel have been killed. Countless more have been injured and maimed.

And even if people here were inclined to celebrate, they would now probably think twice – because yesterday George W. Bush's partner in the invasion, Tony Blair, in a ghostly echo of 2003, called upon the world to be prepared to continue the war against weapons of mass destruction – this time in Iran.

'It is wholly unacceptable for Iran to have a nuclear weapon capability,' he said, 'And I think we have got to be prepared to confront them, if necessary militarily.'

Mr Blair was speaking in a television interview with the BBC to mark the publication of his memoirs – *A Journey* – in which he justifies the war in Iraq and defends his decision to join in the invasion.

The interview was pre-recorded. As Special Envoy of the Diplomatic Quartet charged with mediating peace across the Middle East, Mr Blair is currently in Washington for the opening of peace talks between Israel and the Palestinians: an occasion which engenders little cause for hope in the UAE and none for celebration.

108. THE SLEEPER IN THE SAND
Fujairah, 8 September 2010

Burial is the way to honour the dead
- Arabic proverb

In a quiet corner of Fujairah, encircled by mountains and the sea, is the grave of a British airman who was killed on active service during the Second World War.

Sergeant William (Billy) Donnelly of the Royal Air Force Volunteer Reserve died when his Wellington bomber crashed near Dhadnah on St. Valentine's Day in 1943. He was a navigator in the Middle East Command who helped to deliver aircraft to operational units. The Wellington had set off from RAF Sharjah at nine o'clock that morning bound for Gwadar in Pakistan. On board were four crewmen and one passenger. But about half an hour into the journey the pilot spotted an oil leak from the casing of the port engine and immediately turned back. Minutes later, however, the propeller on the port side flew off and he was forced to make an emergency landing on the coast near Dhadnah. One eye witness, then a young boy mending fishing nets, now an elder of the village, has described how the plane approached from over the sea, clipped some date palms and bounced along the ground in a cloud of dust.

Billy, aged 31, was the only fatality. He was buried nearby among the ancestors of the fishermen who witnessed the crash – but because his grave was later washed away and could not be located he was listed as 'missing' on the British War Memorial at al Alamein in Egypt. Nor was the crash site remembered – except in stories passed down by the fishermen of Dhadnah. And it was only very recently, after research by two local historians, that the location of the crash was confirmed which then allowed the site of the cemetery to be traced.

Curiously, although British and an occasional visitor to relatives in Britain, Billy hailed from Peru. His father, originally from Ireland, had emigrated from Manchester and established a successful shipping business in the southern port of Mollendo. As to what prompted his only son to join the Allied cause we can only surmise. Perhaps it was as W. B. Yeats wrote of his Irish airman, Major Robert Gregory, who died fighting for the British in the Royal Air Corps during the First World War:

> *Nor law, nor duty bade me fight,*
> *Nor public men, nor cheering crowds,*
> *A lonely impulse of delight*
> *Drove to this tumult in the clouds.*

Yeats was so moved by Major Gregory's death that he wrote four poems to his memory. For almost seven decades little more than oral tradition kept Billy's sacrifice alive. But earlier this year a marble stone inscribed with his name was placed at the approximate site of his resting place, a gift from the ruler of Fujairah, Sheikh Hamad bin Mohammed Al Sharqi, whose father had been among those who went to help the survivors – and just in the nick of time, because before his arrival some local opportunists had started to plunder the wreckage.

'He, and the crash in which he died, are part of our history,' said Sheikh Hamad in an official statement, and he promised that the story would be preserved in a special exhibition at the national museum in Fujairah.

So if ever Billy was restless in his unmarked grave, he may now sleep more easily; and with the mountains and the sea evoking the Andes and Pacific of the city of his birth, he may even feel at home.

109. REPUTATIONS
Abu Dhabi, 11 September 2010

A good name is the fruit of life
- Arabic proverb

"Who is your favourite Pakistani cricketer?" asks Mohammed, from his seat in the barber shop beside mine.

Oh, dear! I can hardly say Salman Butt, the captain – or rather, former captain – of the current test team in England. But his is the only name I know – and I only know it because I recently read in the paper that he has been suspended by the International Cricket Council following the launch of a police investigation into match fixing.

Mohammed is from Pakistan, as are the barbers and two other customers waiting their turn. All have a passion for cricket and feel shamed by the scandal involving members of their national team.

"Ninety-eight per cent – no, ninety-nine per cent of Pakistani people like cricket," says one of his waiting friends.

"We play every weekend in a parking lot in the evening," explains the other, "Twelve overs. Soft, not hard ball."

I've seen them – or rather, thousands like them – every Friday, for most their one day off a week, up and down the emirates in parks, on beaches and wasteland, wherever they can find space, using makeshift wickets and wearing T-shirts, baseball caps and jeans. Mohammed and his friends mostly play against other Pakistanis but occasionally against teams of Indians or Sri Lankans. They dismiss nationality as irrelevant: love of cricket, they would have it, is all that counts. And they assume that everyone from the birthplace of cricket shares their passion. So not only is my personal credibility at stake – but the reputation of the entire nation. Both barbers pause, cut-throat razors in hand, waiting for my answer …

Today is no ordinary day and Mohammed has been at pains to defend his countrymen.

"In the media we are portrayed as terrorists making bombs," he says, "But most of us believe in humanity. We do not support terrorism."

His face beamed when I said I am from England.

"Very nice people," he observed, "Very nice country. Lots of history."

Mohammed has never visited the UK. His impressions come from newspapers and television and relatives and friends who live there.

He is less enthusiastic about the United States, however, and I am curious to know what he considers to be difference between the English and the Americans.

"They have no respect," he replies, "We do. You do. They do not."

Hardly a surprising view, perhaps, given the fuss over proposals to build an Islamic cultural centre and mosque near the former site of the twin towers of the World Trade Centre in New York and the threat by a Christian pastor in Florida to publicly burn two hundred copies of the Quran later today.

On this most sensitive of anniversaries we are both glad of the opportunity to distance ourselves from extremism and talk instead about cricket.

"Imran Khan," I reply, "He's my favourite Pakistani cricketer."

It turns out to be a good choice. Although Imran's professional cricketing days are long over, he is still very popular in Pakistan and has recently been active raising money for the victims of the country's devastating floods.

So my credibility remains intact and England's reputation, too.

If only America played test cricket.

110. A CLOUD ON THE HORIZON
Abu Dhabi, 17 September 2010

The cure for high prices is abstinence
- Arabic proverb

Extraordinary as it may seem, petrol in the UAE is sold to consumers at less than cost price, although probably not for much longer.

The price of fuel is fixed by the government. At the start of the year a litre of petrol cost from Dh1.26 (21p) to Dh1.48 (25p) according to the grade. After increases of Dh0.15 in April and Dh0.20 in July it now costs from Dh1.61 (27p) to Dh1.83 (31p) a litre. But that's still less than cost price. Although the government makes up some of the difference in subsidies, any gap has to be met by the quartet of government-owned fuel distributors.

Yesterday, after some petrol stations in Dubai ran dry, we were led to believe that the Dubai-based distributor Emirates General Petroleum Corporation (Emarat) was cutting back on supplies because it could no longer sustain huge losses on its sales. Emarat denies any such suggestion. A statement today assures us that it was a technical problem which has now been resolved. But every litre of petrol that Emarat sells costs the company about Dh0.40 (7p) – and if, as it claims, it sells some five million litres a day, it's losing more than Dh14 million (£2.3m) on sales every week.

The Emirates Petroleum Products Company (Eppco) and Emirates National Oil Company (Enoc), which, like Emarat, buy petrol on the open market, sustain similar losses and, with a break even point of about Dh2.19 (37p) a litre, they are lobbying for a pump price of at least Dh2.50 (42p). On the other hand Abu Dhabi's National Oil Company (Adnoc), which refines its own crude and can therefore supply retail outlets more cheaply, is loath to see customers upset by another price rise.

In the longer term the government wants to phase out subsidies and liberalise the market. But wary of the impact that higher fuel prices would have on inflation, let alone on the mood of consumers, it is reluctant to raise prices too quickly. Having already had to contend with price increases averaging 26% this year, motorists are incensed at rumours of another rise of about Dh0.20 (3p) a litre this month or next – but that's still far short of what Emarat, Eppco and Enoc want to see.

In a symbolic, although ultimately futile protest, some Emirati and expatriate motorists in Dubai boycotted petrol stations on the day that prices went up in April. Anger is further fuelled by the fact that petrol is already more expensive here than in any other country in the region. In Saudi Arabia a litre costs the equivalent of just Dh0.70 (12p). Smuggling petrol across the Oman and Saudi borders is now said to be getting out of hand. In a recent newspaper article a tanker driver admitted to making as many as a dozen return trips a week to Oman where petrol can be bought for about half the price.

Given the long-term unsustainability of subsidies – subsidising energy and water currently costs Abu Dhabi and Dubai £4.1 billion and £1 billion a year respectively – and the UAE's eagerness to demonstrate sound economic and environmental governance to the rest of the world, the question is not *will* the price of petrol go up again but *when?*

For consumers the prospect of another price rise is like a dark cloud on the horizon – but, as with rain in the desert, it may be no bad thing.

In April 2011 fuel shortages were again reported in Dubai. Petrol stations said that tanker deliveries had fallen behind schedule. In May it was the turn of motorists in Sharjah. This time petrol stations blamed 'maintenance work' though little refurbishment or technical upgrading was in evidence. Long queues were subsequently observed at Enoc and Eppco stations up and down the northern emirates. In June Sharjah was particularly hard hit and the government gave the petrol companies seventy-two hours to resume normal service or be shut down. As the deadline passed at mid-

day on 24 June, the government carried out its threat and ordered some thirty petrol stations to close. Meanwhile, in Abu Dhabi, the Crown Prince ordered Adnoc to increase its petrol production to ensure demand could be met. The pump price has not been increased since July 2009 and petrol companies still operate at a loss.

111. THE EIGHTH EMIRATE
Abu Dhabi, 18 September 2010

If the camel once gets his nose in the tent, his body will soon follow
- Arabic proverb

On the front page of today's *National* newspaper there's a photograph of Sheikh Khalifa bin Zayed, ruler of Abu Dhabi and President of the UAE, being greeted by family and friends at al Ain airport. He has been away for three months recovering from illness in Switzerland and returns looking a good deal fitter.

Medical treatment is a common reason for Emiratis to travel abroad – which probably says as much about national health in the UAE as it does about the state of its national health service. Only last week one hospital in Bangkok disclosed that it takes more than 10,000 patients from the UAE every year – though that may change: because the disclosure was made as it discharged ten Emiratis mid-treatment after bills amounting to Dh20 million (£3.3m) remained unpaid by their sponsoring authorities.

But most Emiratis travel to escape the heat and humidity of summer and to indulge their passion for shopping. Whole families decamp: brothers and sisters, parents and grandparents, children and grandchildren, aunts, uncles and cousins – all taking along their maids. For many London is a favourite destination – as another article in the same newspaper reveals. Under the headline 'UK points finger and fines at bad UAE drivers' we are told that visitors from the UAE owe more than Dh1.9 million (£316,000) to Westminster Council and Transport for London, of which Dh1.6 million (£266,000) has been written off as uncollectable. That leaves Dh322,177 (£53,000) being pursued in respect of unpaid parking tickets and congestion charge.

The problem is not only attributable to Emiratis, of course. In fact the emirates are responsible for a mere 8% of total fines incurred in Westminster by drivers from overseas. That means America, Europe, Russia and elsewhere are responsible for 92% – or £3.7 million. But it's a problem popularly associated with the oil-rich Middle East after videos recently posted on YouTube showed a £1.2 million Koenigsegg CCXR and matching blue £350,000 Lamborghini Murcielago, both belonging to members of the Qatari royal family, clamped outside the front of Harrods – which the family happens to own.

Over 20,000 Emiratis visited Britain last year – from royal sheikhs with multi-million pound investments to ordinary tourists who arrive with two or three suitcases and take home twice as many filled with presents. Others come to study at universities or seek medical help in Harley Street. And while transport authorities may be losing patience with foreigners who flout London's traffic laws, they would do well to reflect on the huge contribution that the UAE makes to the UK economy.

Where, for example, would British horse-racing be if there was no investment from Dubai? Inside information suggests that Newmarket would collapse without Sheikh Mohammed. As to whether English football won or lost by Sheikh Mansour's £200 million purchase of Manchester City may be more open to question – but there is no doubt it has made Manchester City fans very happy (and Abu Dhabi a household name in the UK). And what of Abu Dhabi's help during the current recession when Sheikh Mansour joined with investors from Qatar in a lucrative £7 billion bail-out of Barclays Bank? This year alone Abu Dhabi has invested £125 million for a 15% share in Gatwick airport and completed a £165 million extension to ExCel London, the international exhibition and conference centre in Docklands which was bought by the Abu Dhabi National Exhibitions Company for Dh2.3 billion (£380m) two years ago. And over the next ten years the British Museum's partnership with the Sheikh Zayed National Museum in Abu Dhabi will bring not only kudos to Britain but multi-million pound funding for art in the UK at a time of severe domestic constraint.

Nor is traffic only one-way. BP and Shell have worked with Abu Dhabi for more than seventy years and Rolls-Royce turbines have powered the emirate's oil production since 1973. UK expertise helped to build the Sheikh Zayed Grand Mosque, the Dubai Metro and the UAE's golden dune-shaped Expo pavilion in Shanghai. Critical health care is being provided by the Imperial College London Diabetes Centre in Abu Dhabi and the government acknowledges the vital role of its 100,000 British residents in the development of the country.

The British ambassador in Abu Dhabi has spoken of London as the 'eighth emirate' of the UAE – a sentiment David Cameron is clearly keen to nurture. For neither sunshine nor sand brought him here in June on his first overseas trip after becoming prime minister. Following Gordon Brown's visit two years ago Abu Dhabi took a 20% share in the London Array – the world's largest offshore wind farm. Hoping for similar munificence Mr Cameron has set up a special task force to boost British trade with the emirates (Britain's 13th largest export market) from an annual £7.5 billion to £12 billion by 2015. He also wants to encourage UAE investment in UK government bonds. To oil the wheels and cement goodwill, the Queen and Prince Philip have accepted an invitation to visit the UAE in November.

Against the millions and billions of UAE oil money helping the UK economy, £316,000 in unpaid congestion charge and parking tickets rather pales.

And if it's any consolation, with Dubai owed more than Dh100 million (£16.6m) in unpaid motoring penalties and Abu Dhabi offering 50% discount as an incentive to drivers to settle their outstanding fines quickly, Emiratis on holiday in London are simply behaving as they do at home.

During her state visit in November 2010 the Queen unveiled a plaque to mark the start of the construction of the Sheikh Zayed National Museum in Abu Dhabi. It was her second visit to the UAE. On the first occasion she opened the World Trade Centre in Dubai and inspected the new UAE University in al Ain. In Bygone Heat: Travels of an Idealist in the Middle East, C.W.R. Long recalled her arrival at al Ain airport in February 1979. As her Andover taxied towards the red carpet where Sheikh Zayed was waiting to greet her, some of the sheikh's retinue began tapping on drums and Zayed started skipping in time to the beat. When Her Majesty descended the steps she was invited to join in. 'Sadly,' wrote Long, 'She declined.'

112. THE TEST OF TIME
Abu Dhabi, 29 September 2010

Squeeze the past like a sponge,
smell the present like a rose, and send a kiss to the future
- Arabic proverb

'How can contemporary art, that is, art produced in the present time, be defined, when the present is a continuing series of unfurling new developments?'

This is the question which confronts visitors at an exhibition of seventy-two contemporary works of art from the private collection of the American art dealer, Larry Gagosian, at Abu Dhabi's temporary gallery on Saadiyat Island.

The title of the exhibition – RSTW – is taken from the initials of the surnames of the six artists from America whose work is featured: Rauschenberg, Ruscha, Serra, Twombly, Warhol and Wool. Their names were chosen from the end of the alphabetical index of Mr Gagosian's catalogue rather than the beginning to mimic the direction in which Arabic is read – from right to left – and to reflect the east-west movement which created modern America and culminated in the post-Second World War flowering of art illustrated here. The parallel is not only neat but symbolic: for it alludes to Abu Dhabi's own creative journey from desert obscurity to global capital – integral to which is a plan to transform a barren island into an international centre for art that challenges convention and 'redefines contemporary aesthetics.'

Such is the vision: a cultural theme park – and there's an award-winning interactive display, with scale models, photographs and film, to show what it will look like.

'Saadiyat Island is positioned to become an international destination of desire,' a notice tells us, 'A flagship for Abu Dhabi and a treasure of the world.'

In the meantime the exhibition space at Manarat al Saadiyat is a lone oasis in a sea of sand and construction. Yet there could be no better backdrop for Richard Serra's lead and steel sculptures. When his monumental *Tilted Arc*, a tilted steel plate 120 feet long and 12 feet high, was erected in Federal Plaza in New York in 1981, it so upset residents – 'an eyesore' is how some described it – that it was eventually demolished, despite protests from the artist.

'I don't think it is a function of art to be pleasing,' he said.

Here, whether they please or not, Serra's industrial sculptures certainly blend in, so much so that one of my companions this evening mistakes an exhibit for a piece of building material and causes alarm with a touch.

"Give me a landscape with water, a horse and some trees any day," he grumbles, revealing a rather more conservative taste for his native Constable.

I'm inclined to agree – but just as any water in the desert will do, so any culture is better than none.

While most visitors will appreciate Ed Ruscha's painting of a robin, if not those of his amphetamines, Christopher Wool's graffiti-inspired abstracts may prove more challenging. And although local sensibilities will be tested by a naked figure in one of Robert Rauschenberg's giant collages, the fusion of poetry and acrylic in Cy Twombly's huge floral paintings may resonate in a society which makes television stars of poets. To a red rose Twombly addresses this beautiful fragment of Rilke:

> *Rose*
> *Flower of all flowers, petal over petal*
> *Do you feel our own palpable pleasure?*

Of all the artists whose work is on show, however, none will be more eagerly anticipated than Andy Warhol. Visitors will linger over his famous pop art portraits of Marilyn Monroe, Mao Zedong and Elvis Presley, though they may hurry by his images of death, destruction and the electric chair. And even those who profess not to understand art may catch a fleeting echo from his pencil sketch of a Roll of Dollar Bills. After all:

'Pop is for everyone,' he said.

But Warhol's presence takes us back to the question posed at the start of the exhibition. Ruscha, Serra, Twombly and Wool are still producing work. Rauschenberg died two years ago. But for how much longer can Warhol's work be considered contemporary when he has been dead for almost a quarter of a century – and Monroe, Mao and Presley are but dust and history?

Only time will tell.

Cy Twombly died in July 2011, aged eighty-three. Describing his work he once said, 'It's more like I'm having an experience than making a picture.' Of acclaim, he told the New York Times, 'I couldn't care less.'

113. SNOW UPON THE DESERT'S DUSKY FACE
Ras al Khaimah, 30 September, 2010

A monkey in his mother's eye is a gazelle
- Arabic proverb

Imagine, if you can, a piece of ice from the Antarctic breaking free and being carried thousands of miles by ocean currents into the Arabian Gulf and washing up on the shores of the UAE – complete with igloos, snow and a colony of emperor penguins.

Should you have trouble conjuring such a scene you have only to visit the new water park near the old fishing village of Jazirat al Hamra in Ras al Khaimah. Ice Land was officially opened last night in a ceremony attended by the ruling family as befits the emirate's much delayed flagship theme park. A photograph in today's *National* newspaper shows Sheikh Saud bin Saqr Al Qasimi, Crown Prince and de facto ruler, seated among other male VIPs, all dressed in white *kandouras* and *ghutras* and being cooled by two large electric fans.

Inspired by global warming, Ice Land is the first phase of WOW RAK – a $100 million theme park complex designed to establish Ras al Khaimah on the world's tourist itinerary. With reduced demand for stone and cement for construction from its mountains, dwindling natural water supplies for its date gardens, and diminishing stocks of fish to sustain its fishing fleet, Ras al Khaimah could do with a boost – and it's surely no coincidence that the opening of the water park was preceded by the resumption of passenger services from Ras al Khaimah International Airport which had been suspended on account of the recession.

Official statistics show that 542,000 tourists visited Ras al Khaimah in 2009, up 130% on the previous year. But why should a water park attract more visitors? After all there's one just along the coast in Umm al Quwain, at least two in Dubai, and another will soon sit alongside Abu Dhabi's Ferrari World theme park. The answer is – Ice Land is no ordinary water park:

'When you enter you have the ambience of Antarctica,' a public relations officer is reported as saying, 'Everything is white, everything is snowy.'

Among the main attractions are the Penguin Falls (at 37 metres high and 165 metres wide, the largest man-made waterfall in the world) and Penguin Bay with its rain dance pool (an outdoor disco), plastic Coral Isle (where swimmers can snorkel among REAL fish) and Aqua Games (a blue Astroturf football field where paddling players are showered with water).

When the gates were opened last night free of charge many expatriate visitors gave Ice Land their endorsement. For some it was the closest they had ever come to seeing snow. Others warned that the cost might be prohibitive. A day ticket for a child is Dh175 (£29), for an adult it costs Dh225 (£37) – and that's without a fast food feast and fizzy drinks from Platter 'pick n go.' For the environment the cost will be greater still. With its own power and desalination plants to keep the water flowing in sub-tropical heat, Ice Land is set to add to the UAE's environmental footprint – which is already the largest in the world.

While the idea that a colony of penguins should set up home in Ras al Khaimah may stretch the imagination, we would do well to remember that Antarctica has not always been covered by ice. Fossils of plants and animals from 40 million years ago evince a moist, temperate climate when global temperatures were much warmer than now. Similarly the UAE has not always been *sabkah*, mountains and sand. Eight million years ago there were rivers and lakes, grassland and swamp, with crocodiles, giraffe and rhino.

The absurdity of Ice Land is not the message – after all, most of the country's population and infrastructure are thought to be at risk as climates change and sea levels rise – but the medium. By presenting global warming as a theme for fun and celebration Ras al Khaimah has subverted the message and quite literally lost the plot.

From across the centuries comes Omar Khayyam's siren warning:

> *The Worldly Hope men set their Hearts upon*
> *Turns Ashes – or it prospers; and anon,*
> *Like Snow upon the Desert's dusky Face*
> *Lighting an Hour or two – is gone.*

114. IN THE FOOTSTEPS OF IBN BATTUTA
Dubai, 1 October 2010

Who lives sees much. Who travels sees more.
                        - Arabic proverb

In 1325 a young lawyer left his home in Tangier with no more in mind than a pilgrimage to Mecca but then just kept on going – for almost thirty years: criss-crossing the entire length and breadth of the Islamic world and sailing beyond to China.

Sheikh Abu Abdullah Mohammed ibn Battuta was driven to travel by faith in the virtue of learning from experience.

'Seek knowledge,' said the Prophet, 'Even as far as China.'

As far as we know no notes were taken or book intended. He travelled for travel's sake and the account he left behind was dictated from memory many years later. His contemporaries in Morocco were so sceptical about his stories that they branded him 'a liar' and for centuries his *Rihla* – literally journey or travelogue – was largely ignored and forgotten. Only in the last 150 years or so has the story of his travels become widely known – probably nowhere more so than in Dubai.

At Ibn Battuta Mall we can follow in his footsteps. Six themed courts reflect some of the regions he explored – Andalusia, Tunisia, Egypt, Persia, India and China – each with its characteristic style and architecture. In Egypt, for example, there are walls and columns decorated with colourful hieroglyphics and resplendent images of gods, kings and queens, while in Persia there's a great dome inlaid with Islamic mosaics. From end to end the courts extend for almost a mile, so providing an opportunity for visitors to undertake a journey of their own. This morning two Pakistani oilmen have travelled all the way from Ruwais in Abu Dhabi's western region – some three hours away by bus – to spend their day off in the mall. After meeting by the elephant clock in India we greet one another like long lost friends when paths cross again beside the fountain of lions in Andalusia – just as inter-continental travellers in the real world would do. For many, of course, this *is* the real world: for all around, in a scene that evokes Ibn Battuta's fourteenth century observations about Mongol women in the gold and perfume souks of Tabriz, people are indulging in the nation's favourite pastime – shopping.

'They were buying huge quantities and were trying to outdo one another,' he said, which could well describe the scene in some of the upmarket emporia here today.

In China a life-size junk, stranded on rocks and holed in each side, serves to illustrate the trials he endured. Not only was he shipwrecked and nearly drowned but robbed and imprisoned. As well as the usual hazards to health he also had to contend with starvation, thirst and the Black Death. In Dehli he feared for his life after incurring the displeasure of the sultan whom he described as being 'too free in shedding blood … Every day there are brought to the audience hall hundreds of people, chained, pinioned and fettered, and (they) are executed … tortured, or … beaten.' All this and much more (although nothing of his many wives and slave girls) we are told in an interactive display in Egypt Court: for Ibn Battuta Mall is not simply about entertainment, whether the 275-plus retail outlets, 21-screen cinema, varied cuisine or quirky architecture – but education and enlightenment.

Marketing gurus have even invented a word for it: *edutainment*. So between visiting shops we can learn not only about Ibn Battuta but Arab culture, science, engineering and innovation. In Andalusia we can look to the sky and see Abbas bin Firnas from ninth century Cordoba who, at the age of seventy, built a glider and became the first man to fly – albeit briefly, for he crashed and damaged his back. In Egypt the mapping of the heavens is explained with the aid of a reproduction 'observational armillary sphere,' while in India there is a model of Al Jazari's intricate twelfth century hydraulic clock with drums, cymbals and trumpets which, beaten, clashed and blown, would chime the passing hours at the court of the King of Anatolia.

While there are plenty of reviewers on the internet who enjoyed their edutainment experience – 'breath-taking,' 'beautiful,' 'charming' and 'special' are the cream of their comments – others 'were bored with it,' thought it 'ordinary' or said 'I will never go back.' At one extreme it is 'not just a mall but a museum.' At the other the shops are 'a huge let down.' And somewhere in between – 'it is very long and narrow so if you have to go to opposite ends it is a bit of a pain.'

The cynic within inevitably looks to find fault. Yes, there are architectural anomalies. The fountain of lions at the Alhambra Palace, inspiration for the lion fountain in Andalusia Court, postdates Ibn Battuta's visit to Granada. Nor would he have stood before the elephant clock which was never more than a concept in Al Jazari's thirteenth century *Book of Knowledge of Ingenious Mechanical Devices*. There are thematic oddities, too. In China Court much is made of the fifteenth century voyages of discovery of Admiral Zheng He, whose only connection with Ibn Battuta is that he was also a travelling Muslim. And it's only natural to ask, 'Why Dubai?' – where he never set foot. But it's not as though Ibn Battuta's own account is free of contradictions, inconsistencies and fiction, and, given that almost a million people visit every month, the mall has probably done more to raise public awareness about his travels than any museum, film or book.

But the most compelling defence of the largest themed mall in the world can be gleaned from the traveller himself. For he loved local markets – his memoir is full of references to the price of food and goods and rates of exchange – and what was he doing in conjuring images like the sultan's triumphal parade in Delhi, in which catapults fitted to the backs of elephants fired gold and silver coins into a scrambling crowd, if not pioneering the art of edutainment?

115. THE LOST WORLD
Oman, 8 October 2010

If you hear that a mountain has moved, believe;
but if you hear that a man has changed his character, believe it not
- Arabic proverb

From below it looks just like the rest of the Hajar mountain range: bare slopes and bare jagged peaks, albeit at over 2,500 metres much higher than most. But for centuries travellers have been lured here by romantic tales of verdant gardens and orchards dripping with oranges and apricots, peaches, walnuts and pomegranates. The only clue lies in the name: *el Jabal el Akhdar* – the Green Mountain.

Stories of forests and fruit trees so tantalised Sir Wilfred Thesiger that he risked his life to see them for himself. It happened towards the end of his last Arabian expedition in 1949/50 at which time political control of Oman was divided between the sultan in Muscat and an imam elected by tribal leaders in the interior. But Imam Mohammed not only refused to allow a Christian to visit the mountain but threatened to have him killed if he came near. So one of Thesiger's guides suggested that he should by-pass the imam and make a direct approach to Sheikh Sulieman bin Himyar, the self-styled Lord of the Jabal Akhdar. The sheikh was happy enough to sanction a visit but only if Thesiger agreed to persuade the British government to support him in a personal bid for independence. It was too much to ask so Thesiger turned back, but only when the sheikh guaranteed safe passage until he was beyond the imam's reach.

Now anyone can go where the great explorer was denied provided they have a four-wheel-drive vehicle. Whereas in his day the ascent involved a gruelling climb up steep rubble-strewn tracks by donkey at best, today a tarmac road runs all the way up. Yet we may still feel intrepid because police officers check that drivers are licensed and vehicles are capable – especially of handling the descent. For dangers are real: as a crushed car and the bloated corpse of a donkey testify this morning.

For some 20 kilometres the climb is relentless and even at slow speed tyres screech on tight bends. Throughout the landscape is as desolate as the plain below. The only noticeable difference is the temperature which quickly drops – so that by the time a broad plateau is reached some 2,000 metres above sea level the air is all of 10C cooler. But still the mountain belies its name: there's barely a shrub, let alone a verdant forest, to be seen.

A pile of scrap on a ledge beside the road takes us back half a century. Within a few years of Thesiger's retreat civil war broke out between Sultan Said and the imam's successor over territorial sovereignty and oil rights. Sheikh Sulieman joined forces with Imam Ghalib and after the towns of Ibri, Bahla, Rustaq and Nizwa fell to the sultan's forces the Jabal Akhdar became the last seat of resistance. So impregnable was the mountain that in 1957 the sultan asked Britain for help. At first RAF Shakletons were sent to bomb the rebels into submission while leaving the villages intact. Then Venom fighters were ordered to attack with rocket and machine-gun fire – also to no avail. Finally, in 1958/59, a squadron of the SAS was deployed, whereupon the insurgency was quickly brought to an end.

The scrap beside the road is all that remains of a Venom that failed to return to its base at RAF Sharjah in 1958. One version has it that the pilot misjudged a dive. In another rebels claim to have shot him down. Official records merely state that Flight Lieutenant Owen Wilkinson died. In the immediate aftermath he was buried by local villagers under stones near the crash site. After the war, in compliance with restrictions on non-Muslim burial, the British authorities went to remove him to the Christian cemetery in Muscat. But local people said no: they wanted him to stay: so he was formally reinterred in a grave close by. The wreckage from his aircraft is all that marks the site.

There's no sign to say what it is: no epitaph to the deceased: no information to relate the story. Nothing but curiosity tempts tourists from their cars as they wander in search of the elusive forests and fruit trees.

Round a bend and without warning appears the first sight of greenery. It's enough to prompt a gasp. Instantly the name of the mountain makes sense: for on precipitous terraces built into the side of a deep canyon is the luxuriant foliage of row upon row of spring-watered vegetable gardens and fruit groves.

"The best view is from over there," says an Omani tour guide called Saleh, pointing to the top of a rocky cliff, "The Princess of Wales once had a picnic there. I have had a picnic there many times but still it is called Diana's Point, not Saleh's Point."

Opposite Diana's Point small houses cling to the mountainside above terraced farms overhanging a near-vertical drop into the wadi below. It's a scene that epitomises traditional life here. But modern times impinge. After the end of the war the Omani army came to stay – it's still encamped here today – and as oil money from the sultan's treasury began to filter through to new social welfare projects people abandoned their primitive huts in the wadis for modern houses on the plateau.

Meanwhile Thesiger wrote *Arabian Sands*, an account of his travels across the Empty Quarter, in which he lamented the imminent demise of traditional Bedouin life in the wake of the discovery of oil. But it was the modernisation of Oman under the unifying rule of Sultan Qaboos that allowed Thesiger to succeed where he had earlier failed. The opportunity came when he returned to the country in 1977 for a reunion with two of his Bedouin guides. Together they climbed the Jabal Akhdar – 'the unattainable goal of my last journey in Arabia' – only to find a military airfield at the top with helicopters and jet planes. For Thesiger it provoked disillusion and resentment – not least because rather than trek up the mountain, as he insisted, his companions would have preferred to accept the offer of a lift in a helicopter.

So I shudder to think what he would make of it now. In the last decade the new road has brought parties of holiday-makers and the principal settlement on the plateau has all the amenities of a town on the plain. Yet visitors are drawn to the ghosts of the past and in the Wadi Bani Habib tourists linger to take photographs of a deserted village set among fruitful orchards and gardens.

"The village has been here for two hundred years," explains a man selling fruit, "But forty years ago the people moved to a new village."

As I feast on a pomegranate as large as a grapefruit I follow his gaze towards a cluster of large villas on the edge of the plateau above. Old and new are within a stone's throw of each other but separated by a deep gorge – and world's apart in time.

After climbing the Jabal Akhdar in 1977 Thesiger went on to the youthful UAE where he found the capital 'an Arabian Nightmare, the final disillusionment.' Towards the end of his life, however, he wrote that he had become reconciled to Arabia's oil-fuelled progress, and after returning to Abu Dhabi for an exhibition of his photographs in 1990 he described it as 'an impressive modern city, made pleasant in this barren land by avenues of trees and green lawns.'

Somehow I doubt he would be as sanguine today as contractors race to open more hotels, roads and the Ferrari World theme park before visitors descend for next month's Formula One Grand Prix.

"We don't want to be like Abu Dhabi and Dubai," says Saleh during a break from guiding tourists round the green terraces of the Jabal Akhdar, "When I was in Dubai I saw no Emiratis. They were hiding behind dark glass in their cars. They have become strangers in their own country."

But there's already one hotel on the mountain and at least two more are planned ...

Perhaps romantics should stick to reading *Arabian Sands*.

116. A BURJ-EYE VIEW
Dubai, 22 October 2010

Looking upward tires the neck
- Arabic proverb

Relief, if not excitement, is growing in Abu Dhabi at the imminent completion of a new sea crossing which is being compared to San Francisco's Golden Gate and the Sydney Harbour Bridge.

The Sheikh Zayed Bridge will be able to carry up to 1,600 vehicles at any one time between the island capital and its desert hinterland, so relieving pressure on two neighbouring bridges which often become gridlocked during the morning rush. For commuters the sooner it opens the better. But the unique undulating design of its frame, intended to evoke shifting sands, has made construction an engineering nightmare. Work began in 2003 and even now authorities seem unwilling to name the day when it will be open to traffic.

Meanwhile, in Dubai, work started and finished on the world's tallest building using ground-breaking techniques to pump concrete uphill and overcome wind stress at high altitude. Excavation for the foundations of the Burj Khalifa began in January 2004 and the 828 metre-high tower, set among lakes and fountains beside the world's largest shopping mall, was officially opened in January this year. It has already won three international awards for architecture and engineering and currently holds over a dozen world records, including tallest extant structure, tallest ever structure, tallest free-standing structure, building with the most floors, highest swimming pool and fastest elevator. It also has the highest outdoor observation platform, which is where I'm off to now.

"Will we be higher than the sky?" asks a young companion after passing a sign which reads, 'Prepare to enter the record books.'

It certainly seems so in the darkened elevator when images of space suddenly flash on window-like screens.

"Stupendous!" she says.

In less than a minute we are 'At The Top,' that is to say – on the panoramic observation deck on the 124th floor. At 452 metres above ground At The Top is not, as you may recall, actually at the top: it's only just over half way up. But it *feels* like the top. Little of the tapering structure above is visible from the platform other than as a long shadow cast on the ground like a huge pointer on a sundial and even at this height it towers over every other tall building around.

When fully occupied the 160-storey Burj could be home to 35,000 people. But for now most of the population seem to be commuters – more specifically, visitors to At The Top. Of the 900 apartments only just over 100 are currently occupied despite a 40% discount on rents. Some people are blaming high service charges, others the outlook – or rather, the lack of it. While signs below boast of views of over ninety kilometres, dust restricts visibility to barely half that distance this afternoon.

Not to worry. Digital telescopes mounted around the deck allow things to be seen not only as they are but as they would look on a clear day. By pressing other buttons it's also possible to conjure the same view by night and as it was in years gone by. So I point a telescope at the 149 metre-high World Trade Centre, now almost lost among a cluster of taller buildings in the heart of the commercial district, and see it as it was some thirty years ago when it was the tallest building in the Middle East – isolated and alone in desert. Switching my gaze to the 7-star Burj al Arab Hotel, which floats like a great sailing ship on its artificial island in the Gulf, I see nothing but waves rolling towards a sandy shore.

But no lens is required to see the future. The Sheikh Zayed Bridge is being built to last a hundred years and will be judged by its capacity to ease traffic flow long after its wavy architecture dims in the public imagination. For the Burj, on the other hand, it's a question of how long it can hang on to its status as the world's tallest building. Just as Dubai seized the record from Taiwan, so others are gathering in the wings. There's already a kilometre-high tower under construction in Kuwait. Another is planned in Saudi Arabia. Rumour has it that Abu Dhabi intends to build one, too. Everyone is watching to see how high others dare go.

The story goes that Sheikh Mohammed was unimpressed with the original plans for the Burj when he learnt that Taipei 101 would remain the world's tallest building. So the developers went away and came up with a new design that just pipped Taiwan's giant tower. Still the sheikh was not happy and he insisted that they build a lot taller – which they did.

But when will 'taller' ever be tall enough?

The architects of the Burj Khalifa have been contracted to design the Kingdom Tower in Jeddah. Word is it will be 173m taller than the Burj. Abu Dhabi's new bridge was officially opened on 25 November 2010.

117. THE END OF THE ROAD
Liwa, 27 October 2010

*The fortunes of the Arabs who wear sandals
have been eaten by the Arabs who wear slippers*
- Arabic proverb

I am listening to the car radio when news of catastrophic floods in Thailand is suddenly drowned by an imam chanting verses from the Quran.

It's a sign that a sheikh has died and soon comes the announcement of the death of Sheikh Saqr bin Mohammed Al Qasimi of Ras al Khaimah. At ninety-two (officially – in the absence of written records, no one is quite certain) he was oldest ruler in the world and last of the generation of leaders who oversaw the transformation of the medieval Trucial States into the modern United Arab Emirates.

If perspective on his life is required it comes from my journey this morning, the last as my adventure here draws to a close. By camel it used to take ten days to traverse the salt flats and sand dunes south of Abu Dhabi to reach the oasis of Liwa on the northern edge of the largest sand desert in the world – a week if pushed. Even when cars first arrived, which was before there were roads, it would take a couple of days. This morning it takes me a couple of hours.

When Sheikh Saqr became ruler in 1948 no European had ever visited the historic homeland of the Bani Yas tribes at Liwa where the story of Abu Dhabi began. The first to do so was Sir Wilfred Thesiger who, before setting out to cross the Rub al Khali in the winter of 1946/47, heard beguiling tales of palm groves, wells and villages extending for two days' camel ride beyond the vast emptiness of the Sands.

It was the prospect of finding plentiful food and water there which sustained him as rations dwindled on that first trek across the Empty Quarter. But when he reached a well on the edge of Liwa he learnt that the tribes of Abu Dhabi were at war with the tribes of Dubai. More worryingly there was a marauding band of Saudi tax-collectors in the area who would not have taken kindly to the presence of a Christian had he been discovered. So Thesiger laid low while some of his Bedouin guides went in search of fresh provisions.

For three days he subsisted on a handful or two of roasted maize. At night he would dream of food. He had asked for flour, sugar, tea, coffee, butter, dates, and rice if possible. Above all he craved a goat for a stew. But the people of Liwa proved 'an unfriendly lot' and the search party returned with only a little wheat and some poor quality dates.

Days later their luck appeared to change when one of the Bedouin caught a hare. Another produced some onions and spices and made some bread and all sat round in the vast emptiness of the desert while the hare was stewing. Sampling the soup they decided to let it simmer a little longer. Having eaten meat just once in the last month the delay only served to whet their appetite. It was then that three Arabs appeared out of nowhere. Hospitality demanded that guests should be offered food first so the hare and bread were set before them – which meant that Thesiger and his companions had to make do with sand-coated dates. Many years later, his hunger long assuaged, the story of the hare became a favourite anecdote.

No such hardships face the traveller in Liwa today. The dun-coloured walls of *Qasr al Sarab* – the Mirage Palace, a luxury resort which 'blends cultural passion with desert tranquillity' – rise from the Sands like an enchanted castle in a tale from the *Arabian Nights*. A valet parks my car while a doorman shows me inside, where a receptionist calls to a concierge who guides me to the panelled library where pictures of bearded men in traditional Arab dress hang like ancestral portraits. There a waitress welcomes me and returns with a pot of tea.

"How many staff do you have?" I ask from the depths of a sumptuous armchair.

"Over three hundred," she replies, "From more than twenty countries."

"And how many guests?"

"Last night less than thirty."

After tea, as I linger over displays of Bedouin paraphernalia, another member of staff sidles up.

"We had a sunset wedding here recently," she tells me, "The couple came from Switzerland. It was very romantic."

Romance is standard fare at the Mirage Palace. Old maps and journals left behind by fictitious travellers transport us to the pioneering days of Arabian exploration and serve to remind that voyaging in the desert was once only possible because of the tradition that rendered every home a temporary sanctuary and all visitors the guests of God.

Beyond the hotel lie the hollows and dunes where Thesiger waited in vain for his goat stew. He came this way again during his second crossing the following year, shortly after fifty-two local tribesmen had been killed by a raiding party from Dubai. On that occasion he hurried on to Abu Dhabi, which he reached in seven days, and it was not until the end of 1948 that he finally got to explore Liwa.

'It was a pleasant journey,' he recalled, 'The sands were like a garden.'

Less happily he found a trail of footprints which turned out to be the tracks of a slave caravan bound for Saudi Arabia where money from oil was fuelling demand and driving up prices. His concern was not for the slaves, however, but for the impact of oil money on the traditional life of the Bedouin whom he feared would become 'a parasitic proletariat squatting around oil-fields in the fly-blown squalor of shanty towns.'

By then prospecting fees were also boosting the depressed economies of the Trucial sheikhdoms, which had never recovered from the demise of the natural pearl market. In Ras al Khaimah Sheikh Saqr used oil money to restore the traditional *aflaj* irrigation system, introduce national education and build the first hospital. Across the emirates traditional remedies were banished by modern medicine, classes were no longer held under the shade of a tree, camels were superseded by motor vehicles, and *barasti* huts and hair tents were gradually abandoned for concrete houses with mod cons.

But oil also made the emirates vulnerable to predatory neighbours and so proved the major driver for union in 1971/72. Now, as the UAE approaches its 39th anniversary, it enjoys stability and prosperity to a degree unrivalled in the modern Middle East. While the tribes may not always agree, they no longer raid and kill each other; the economy may depend on cheap Asian labour but slavery has been abolished; and Western infidels are not only tolerated but welcomed.

From the Mirage Palace I continue through the oasis – two days' camel ride reduced to one hour's car drive – to mountainous drifts on the edge of the Empty Quarter which covers an area more than twice the size of the UK. At the end of a tarmac road lies the largest dune of all: the 278 metre *Tal Moreeb* – the Hill of Fear, a playground for weekenders from Abu Dhabi and Dubai and the epitome of all that Thesiger scorned. For him it was not the goal that mattered but the way – and the more difficult and challenging the better.

In the emirates, however, the goal is everything – whether it is to have the tallest or most inclined towers in the world, race Formula One cars, build the first zero carbon city, open a Louvre and a Guggenheim, conjure romance, snow and water in the desert, or host the Olympic Games – and the way, paved with petrodollars, is short.

Abandoning my vehicle I trudge up the soft 'dun-red' slope of a 'high-heaped' dune and turn my back on the modern world. On such a ridge, 'hard by the foe's marches,' did the pre-Islamic poet Lebid stand guard over his tribe

> *... till the red sun dipped hand-like in obscurity,*
> *till the night lay curtained, shrouding our weaknesses.*

The view from my summit is unchanged since his day: a sea of sand, its wave crests gilded by the sinking sun, its deep folds cast in shadow. Time slumbers ... or so it seems. Reality is the Empty Quarter today is as illusory as the Mirage Palace. Just over the horizon (and undefined border) is Saudi Arabia's vast Shaybah oil development, source of some of the world's highest grade crude, and right beneath my feet is a huge reservoir of 'sour' (sulphur-rich) gas.

When up and running the Shah gas field is expected to produce one billion cubic feet of sour gas a day which, once processed, will be used to fuel power stations and desalination plants to sustain the UAE's domestic growth. Meanwhile sand hills are being levelled, roads constructed, wells sunk, gathering systems built, pipelines laid ... which may be why the

Liwa Sands, although nominated in a global competition to identify the seven natural wonders of the world, have not joined the Amazon Rainforest and twenty-seven other candidates on the new7wonders of nature shortlist.

Thesiger used to say that he came here 'only just in time.' In the UAE they say the best is yet to come – *Inshallah*.

EPILOGUE
UK, September 2011

O God, spare us the winds of change
- Arabic proverb

Some weeks after my return to the UK my attention was drawn to a photograph in a Sunday newspaper of two British golfers taken during an international competition at a desert island resort. They were standing on a carpet of green. Behind them waves were breaking on a long receding shore on which a wooden sailing dhow could be seen being pushed out to sea by men in traditional Gulf dress. On the strand a man in a pristine white *kandoura* and *ghutra* was waving them off. It was a glimpse of old Arabia. Only a caption in Arabic-style calligraphy exposed it as an advertising image on a hoarding carefully positioned behind the tee:

> Abu Dhabi: travellers welcome

Yachts and jet-skis may well have lurked behind.

As popular unrest sweeps across the Arab world and superannuated leaders struggle to maintain their precarious authority with force, bribery or promises of future reform, the UAE has remained a rare haven for tourists in the Middle East. But a country with strong regional ties in which so many people have family and friends caught up in turmoil at home cannot be untouched by events elsewhere.

As a humanitarian crisis unfolded in Libya the UAE was a leading voice within the Gulf Cooperation Council (GCC) in calling for the League of Arab States to persuade the international community to intervene. The Arab League duly supported a United Nations Security Council resolution to impose a no-fly zone. Arab backing at the Security Council's emergency night-time meeting on 17 March 2011 proved crucial to the adoption of the resolution; the UAE itself promised to send twenty-four aircraft to enforce the no-fly zone. Meanwhile trouble was brewing in Bahrain and when the Sunni royal family, challenged by the majority Shiite population, called upon fellow members of the GCC to help quell street protests, the Sunni-led UAE dispatched paramilitary assistance.

Western observers were perplexed. How could the UAE pledge military support for the popular movement against Muammar Gaddafi in Libya yet deploy riot-trained police officers to suppress pro-democracy protests in Manama? In the face of Western criticism the UAE reacted by reneging on its night-time promise to the United Nations Security Council to send military aircraft to support the UN operation. A former commander-in-chief of the UAE air force was quoted in newspapers as saying they would send only humanitarian aid.

From a distant corner of Charles Doughty's Arabia comes an ancient echo:

Promises made in the night be not binding by daylight.

But just as the Bedouin who broke their promise to lend Doughty a camel eventually relented after seeing him struggle, so the UAE's Minister of Foreign Affairs later announced that they would, after all, send aircraft to enforce the no-fly zone – though only twelve, not twenty-four.

Since then calls for change to the UAE's limited electoral system in line with its constitution's stated aim of 'progressing by steps towards a comprehensive, representative, democratic regime' have led to the arrest of five Emirati activists. In the wake of the Arab Spring some 160 academics and intellectuals signed a petition seeking comprehensive democratic reform of the consultative Federal National Council.

'Calling for a parliament with legislative powers was probably a demand too far,' said a Gulf expert from the London School of Economics.

Indeed. Nor did it help when their leading spokesman, Ahmed Mansour, caused offence during a television interview when he described subsidies handed out by the Crown Prince of Abu Dhabi as bribes. He was subsequently arrested for possessing alcohol.

'We're not used to this kind of confrontation between leadership and society,' observed one local commentator.

You would probably have to turn the clock back to the Buraimi crisis of the 1950s to find the last significant challenge. On that occasion two families from Abu Dhabi sided with Saudi Arabia when the kingdom laid claim to the oasis and sent an occupying force which was eventually driven out. In the aftermath Edward Henderson witnessed the moment when the two leaders of these families were taken to see Sheikh Zayed, who was then the ruler's representative in the region. He described how the two men approached bare-headed on their knees, whereupon Zayed helped them to their feet, forgave them and sent them home.

Mr Mansour and four others are not so fortunate. They have been charged with a string of offences including threatening the security of the state, opposing the government system and insulting members of the ruling families.

There is a mantra in Abu Dhabi about change.

'It needs time,' say the men. 'It takes time,' is how a woman phrased it.

To Western tourists, seeing luxury resorts where until recently there was only sand, this may seem paradoxical. But the soul of the nation remains rooted in the world of the desert and the dhow – whereas hotels and golf courses are simply veneer.

BIBLIOGRAPHY

Memoirs and Travelogues

Burton, Richard *A Secret Pilgrimage to Mecca and Medina*

Doughty, Chares Montagu *Travels in Arabia Deserta*

Henderson, Edward *Arabian Destiny: The Complete Autobiography*

Heude, William *A Voyage up the Persian Gulf: and a Journey overland from India to England in 1817*

Izzard, Molly *The Gulf: Arabia's Western Approaches*

Lansdell, Henry *Russian Central Asia*

Lawrence, T. E. *Seven Pillars of Wisdom*

Long, C. W. R. *Bygone Heat: Travels of an Idealist in the Middle East*

Morris, Jan *Sultan in Oman*

Owen, Roderic *The Golden Bubble: Arabian Gulf Documentary*

Phillips, Wendell *Qataban and Sheba: Exploring Ancient Kingdoms on the Biblical Spice Routes of Arabia*

Phillips, Wendell *Unknown Oman*

Raban, Jonathan *Arabia through the Looking Glass*

Severin, Tim *The Sindbad Voyage*

Thesiger, Wilfred *Arabian Sands*

Thomas, Bertram *Arabia Felix: Across the Empty Quarter of Arabia*

Ward, Philip *Travels in Oman*

History, Biographies and Context

Abdulla, Adnan K. and Al Naboodah, Hassan M. (editors) *On the Folklore and Oral History of the United Arab Emirates and Arab Gulf Countries*

Abdullah, Muhammad Morsy *The United Arab Emirates: A Modern History*

Al Fahim, Mohammed *Rags to Riches: A Story of Abu Dhabi*

Al Mansoori, Dr. Ahmed K. A. *The Distinctive Arab Heritage: A Study of Society, Culture and Sport in the UAE*

Armstrong, Karen *Islam: A Short History*

Armstrong, Karen *Muhammad: A Biography of the Prophet*

Asher, Michael *Thesiger: A Biography*

Brent, Peter *Far Arabia: Explorers of the Myth*

Coll, Steve *The Bin Ladens: Oil, Terrorism and the Secret Saudi World*

Davidson, Christopher M. *Abu Dhabi: Oil and Beyond*

Dawood, N. J. (translator) *The Koran*

Emirates Center for Strategic Studies and Research *With United Strength: H. H. Shaikh Zayid bin Sultan Al Nahyan: The Leader and the Nation*

Emirates Heritage Club *Zayed: A Photographic Journey*

Heard-Bey, Frauke *From Trucial States to United Arab Emirates: A Society in Transition*

Hellyer, Peter and Ziolkowski, Dr Michele (editors) *Emirates Heritage*

Volume Two: Proceedings of the 2nd Annual Symposium on Recent Archaeological Discoveries in the Emirates and of the Symposium on the History of the Emirates, Al Ain 2004

Hourani, George *Arab Seafaring*

Howarth, David *The Desert King: A Life of Ibn Saud*

Kay, Shirley *Enchanting Oman*

Kay, Shirley *A Portrait of Ras al Khaimah*

Krane, Jim *Dubai: The Story of the World's Fastest City*

Lewcock, Ronald *The Old Walled City of Sana*

Mackintosh-Smith, Tim *The Hall of a Thousand Columns: Hindustan to Malabar with Ibn Battutah*

Maitra, Dr Jayanti, and Al Hajji, Afra *Qasr Al Hosn: The History of the Rulers of Abu Dhabi 1793-1966*

McKinnon, Michael *Arabia: Sand, Sea, Sky*.

Potts, Daniel; Al Naboodah, Hasan; Hellyer, Peter (editors) *Archaeology of the United Arab Emirates: Proceedings of the First International Conference on the Archaeology of the UAE*

Searight, Sarah, and Taylor, Jane *Yemen: Land and People*

Simmons, James C. *Passionate Pilgrims: English Travellers to the World of the Desert Arabs*

Taylor, Andrew *God's Fugitive: The Life of C. M. Doughty*

English-language Arab Newspapers

Arab News, Saudi Arabia
Gulf News, Dubai

Khaleej Times, Dubai
The National, Abu Dhabi.

INDEX

(Numbers refer to chapters – not pages)

Abbas bib Firnas *114*
Abbas, President Mahmoud *72*
Abu Dhabi *Introduction, 1, 2, 3, 4, 5, 6, 7, 8, 9, 10, 11, 12, 13, 14, 15, 16, 17, 24, 25, 26, 27, 28, 29, 30, 31, 33, 34, 35, 36, 37, 38, 39, 40, 41, 43, 45, 46, 48, 50, 51, 52, 56, 57, 58, 59, 61, 62, 63, 64, 65, 66, 68, 69, 70, 72, 73, 74, 81, 84, 86, 89, 91, 93, 94, 95, 98, 101, 103, 104, 106, 107, 109, 110, 111, 112, 117, Epilogue*
Abu Dhabi Authority for Culture and Heritage (ADACH) *26, 30, 53, 68, 99*
Abu Dhabi Cultural Foundation *8, 12, 13, 48*
Abu Dhabi Grand Prix *5, 70, 72, 73, 115*
Abu Dhabi Guggenheim *5, 34, 65, 70, 73, 117*
Abu Dhabi Louvre *5, 34, 51, 65, 70, 73, 117*
Abu Dhabi Municipality *101*
Abu Dhabi National Exhibitions Company (ADNEC) *2, 9, 43, 68, 111*
Abu Dhabi National Oil Company (Adnoc) *77, 110*
Abu Dhabi Police/policing *1, 6, 7, 8, 23, 29, 31, 34, 45, 50, 69, 84, 89, 95, 103*
Abu Musa *43, 100*
Abu Ubayda bin Al Qasim *85*
Ajman *Introduction, 25, 53, 86, 92, 100*
al Ain, Abu Dhabi *2, 3, 17, 18, 19, 22, 23, 42, 52, 53, 63, 64, 67, 68, 75, 76, 82, 94, 98, 99, 103, 104, 111*
al Ain Palace Museum *23*
Al Bassam, Sulayman *48*
al Fahidi Fort, Dubai *75*
al Hamra Village, Ras al Khaimah *96*
Al Jahani, Aydah Al Aarawi *40, 46, 91*
al Jahili Fort, al Ain *42, 53, 104*
Al Jazari *114*
al Mahatta airport/RAF Sharjah *Introduction, 55, 108, 115*

Al Maktoum, Hasher bin Rashid *88*
Al Maktoum, Sheikh Hamdan bin Mohammed *19, 74*
Al Maktoum, Sheikh Majid bin Mohammed *19, 47*
Al Maktoum, Mani bin Rashid *88*
Al Maktoum, Sheikh Mohammed bin Rashid *Introduction, 6, 19, 33, 35, 43, 49, 60, 74, 75, 79, 111, 116*
Al Maktoum, Sheikh Rashid bin Saeed *42, 75, 79, 88*
Al Maktoum, Sheikh Saeed bin Maktoum *42, 88*
Al Mu'alla family, Umm al Qawain *87*
Al Nahyan, Sheikh Diyab bin Isa *2*
Al Nahyan, Hamad bin Hamdan (Rainbow Sheikh) *67*
Al Nahyan, Sheikh Isa bin Zayed *52*
Al Nahyan, Sheikh Khalifa bin Zayed bin Khalifa *48, 67*
Al Nahyan, Sheikh Khalifa bin Zayed bin Sultan *Introduction, 6, 13, 35, 49, 65, 79, 111, 116*
Al Nahyan, Sheikha Latifa bint Hamdan *88*
Al Nahyan, Sheikh Mohammed bin Zayed *6, 61, 70, 95, 106*
Al Nahyan, Sheikh Shakhbut bin Diyab *2, 48*
Al Nahyan, Sheikh Shakhbut bin Sultan *31, 42, 48, 51, 64, 67, 85, 99*
Al Nahyan, Sheikh Zayed bin Khalifa (Zayed the First/Great) *48, 53*
Al Nahyan, Sheikh Zayed bin Sultan *Introduction, 4, 5, 6, 12, 16, 18, 22, 23, 25, 26, 31, 34, 36, 42, 43, 48, 51, 53, 64, 65, 67, 68, 74, 79, 83, 87, 99, 105, 106, 111, 116, Epilogue*
Al Nuaimi family, Ajman *92*
al Qaeda *76, 81, 100*
Al Qasimi, Sheikh Khalid bin Saqr *100*
Al Qasimi, Sheikh Saud bin Saqr *100, 113*
Al Qasimi, Sheikh Saqr bin Mohammed *100, 117*
Al Qasimi, Sheikh Sultan bin Mohammed *13, 80*
Al Qasimi, Sheikh Sultan bin Saqr *55*
Al Raha Beach Hotel, Abu Dhabi *17, 18*
Al Rumaithi, Mohammed Khaflan *56*
Al Sharqi, Sheikh Hamad bin Mohammed *108*
Al Shawi, Abdullah *97*
Al Zaidi, Muntazar *28*
Amwaj Rotana Hotel, Dubai *98*
Anjuman, Nadia *91*
Arabian/Persian Gulf *Introduction, 4, 17, 25, 42, 51, 54, 58, 71, 75, 77, 80, 83, 87, 113*

Arab League *Epilogue*
Arab Spring *34, 88, Epilogue*
Arafat, Yasser *26, 88*
Atlantis the Palm, Dubai *21, 25*
Baby Bling *47*
Bahla, Oman *85, 115*
Bahrain *Introduction, 25, 28, 32, 36, 42, 43, 58, 64, 74, 75, 77, 85, 94, Epilogue*
Bangladesh *3, 75*
Bani Yas tribal federation *2, 42, 48, 53, 72, 100, 105, 117*
Barrada, Yto *81*
Bathenay, Dominique *56*
Bin Laden family *81, 87*
Blair, Andrew *39*
Blair, Tony *107*
British Protectorate *3, 13, 25, 42, 43, 48, 49, 54, 55, 83, 87, 88, 97, 100*
Brown, Gordon *13, 111*
Buraimi Oasis *18, 43, 53, 64, 99, Epilogue*
Burchardt, Hermann *53, 105*
Burj al Arab, Dubai *73, 116*
Burj Dubai/Khalifa, Dubai *35, 79, 90, 116*
Burton, Sir Richard *18, 23*
Bush, George W. *28, 107*
Camels/dromedaries *Prologue, 13, 30, 32, 43, 44, 63, 68, 83, 84, 87, 97, 104, 106, 117*
Cameron, David *111*
Capital Gate *9*
Caracalla Dance Theatre *26*
Christianity *31, 76, 105*
Cleopatra *71*
Coffee *Prologue, 1, 49, 66, 71, 80, 85, 89, 105, 106, 117*
Cox, Sir Percy *18, 53*
Crosby, Bing *76*
Curzon, Lord George Nathaniel *13*
Dhadnah, Fujairah *108*
Das Island *67*
Dates *1, 14, 63, 65, 71, 85, 86, 87, 103, 106, 117*
Diabetes *Introduction, 74, 111*
Dibba *3, 77*

Dodge, Horace and John *97*
Donnelly, William (Billy) *108*
Doughty, Charles *Prologue, 1, 5, 32, 36, 37, 47, 59, 68, 74, 91, 103, 104, Epilogue*
Dubai *Introduction, 5, 6, 7, 10, 14, 15, 19, 20, 21, 25, 29, 31, 33, 34, 35, 36, 39, 41, 42, 43, 47, 49, 53, 55, 58, 59, 60, 61, 64, 68, 71, 72, 73, 74, 75, 76, 77, 78, 79, 80, 86, 88, 90, 92, 96, 97, 98, 100, 102, 105, 110, 111, 113, 114, 115, 116, 117*
Dubai World *60, 75, 79, 88*
Dubai World Trade Centre *74, 75, 111, 116*
East India Company *13, 54*
Ed Dur/Omana, Umm al Qawain *87*
Emirates Airlines *5, 75*
Emirates General Petroleum Corporation (Emarat) *110*
Emirates National Oil Company (Enoc) *110*
Emirates Petroleum Products Company (Eppco) *110*
Etihad Airways *5, 73, 82*
Emirates Palace *5, 8, 29, 65, 73, 104*
Etisalat *59, 62*
Falcons/falconry *2, 16, 26, 68, 106*
Ferrari World, Abu Dhabi *5, 113, 115*
Field of Dreams *73*
Ford, Henry *97*
Fujairah *Introduction, 25, 77, 78, 86, 100, 108*
Gaddafi, Colonel Muammar *87, Epilogue*
Gagosian, Larry *112*
Ghazu (raid) *Introduction, 13, 100*
Ghosn, Carlos *106*
Gilgamesh *71*
Great Gatsby, The *70*
Gulf Cooperation Council *36, 94, Epilogue*
Hajar mountains *18, 77, 78, 80, 85, 115*
Hamad Khalifah Bu Shihab *49*
Henderson, Edward *1, 64, 89, 95, Epilogue*
Heude, William *54*
Hilal, Hissa *91*
Houbara bustard *68*
Human Rights *94*
Ibn Battuta *85, 87, 114*

Ibn Battuta Mall, Dubai *114*
Ibn Majid, Ahmad *80*
Ibri, Oman *85*
Ice Land, Ras al Khaimah *96, 113*
Imperial Airways *55*
Imperial College London Diabetes Centre *74, 111*
India/Indians *Introduction, 3, 4, 31, 55, 71, 75, 80, 85, 87, 88, 93, 106, 109, 114*
Intercontinental Hotel, Abu Dhabi *45*
Intercontinental Hotel, al Ain *17*
International Renewable Energy Agency (Irena) *57*
Iran *4, 42, 43, 56, 58, 64, 75, 77, 78, 79, 81, 96, 100, 104, 107*
Iraq *28, 40, 48, 55, 58, 77, 79, 81, 100, 107*
Iraq Petroleum Company *75*
Islam *Introduction, 4, 18, 31, 44, 48, 55, 63, 65, 66, 68, 73, 76, 77, 80, 81, 85, 90, 91, 92, 104, 105, 109*
Islamic embroidery exhibition *104*
Israel *33, 37, 72, 81, 105, 107*
Japan *Introduction, 6, 64, 71, 89, 106*
Jazirat al Hamra, Ras al Khaimah *96, 113*
Jebel/Jebal Akhdar, Oman *115*
Jebel Hafeet/Hafit, Abu Dhabi *18, 99*
Jenkins, Simon *49, 74*
Jesus *31, 76, 105*
Jordan/Transjordan *19, 64, 81, 89*
Joyce, James *44*
Julfar, Ras al Khaimah *71, 80*
Khasab, Musandam *78*
Katanec, Srecko *56*
Khor Fakkan, Fujairah *77*
Khayyam, Omar *113*
Kuwait *32, 36, 71, 74, 77, 79, 94, 116*
Lansdell, Henry *104*
Lawrence, T. E. *Prologue, 1, 25, 33, 74, 97*
Lebanon *40, 48, 64, 81*
Lebid ibn Rabiah *6, 16, 117*
Lewis, John Frederick *44*
Light of Letseng (diamond) *15*
Liwa, Abu Dhabi, *2, 63, 117*

Lollia Paulina (wife of Emperor Caligula) *71*
London *26, 41, 73, 81, 111*
Madinat Zayed, Abu Dhabi *32*
Magan/Majan, Oman *85*
Manarat al Saadiyat, Abu Dhabi *73, 81, 112*
Manasir tribe *42, 72*
Manchester City Football Club *5, 35, 111*
Mandelson, Lord *49*
Marib, Yemen *105*
Mark Antony *71*
Masdar City, Abu Dhabi *36, 57, 106*
Maysun *23*
Mazyad Mall, Abu Dhabi *61*
Mecca *5, 23, 30, 48, 53, 83, 105, 114*
Medina *23, 46, 48, 105*
Melville, Herman *78*
Mesopotamia *71, 75, 77, 85, 87, 99*
McDonald's *14, 56*
Miles, Colonel Samuel Barrett *85*
Minogue, Kylie *21*
Millions Poet *40, 46, 91*
Mohammed bin Zayed City, Abu Dhabi *61*
Mohebi, Camelia *47*
Mondrian, Piet *65*
Morris, Jan *64*
Mubadala *93*
Muhammad, The Prophet *Introduction, 4, 32, 63, 66, 76, 77, 105, 114*
Musandam *78*
Muscat, Oman *85, 93, 99, 115*
Nakheel *35, 60, 75, 79, 88*
Nasser, President Jamal Abdel *81*
Nasseri, Mehran Karimi *93*
Natural Gas/Oil *Introduction, 1, 3, 5, 10, 12, 20, 34, 36, 42, 43, 48, 55, 57, 64, 67, 68, 73, 75, 77, 79, 81, 83, 85, 88, 92, 96, 97, 100, 106, 111, 115, 117*
Nejd, Saudi Arabia *18, 32, 53*
Nizwa, Oman *85, 115*
Nuclear Power *42, 43, 49, 77, 83, 92, 107*
Obaid, Salah *56*
Obama, President Barack Hussein *13, 37, 57, 81, 97, 107*

Obesity *56, 74*
Oil/Natural Gas *Introduction, 1, 3, 5, 10, 12, 20, 34, 36, 42, 43, 48, 55, 57, 64, 67, 68, 73, 75, 77, 79, 81, 83, 85, 88, 92, 96, 97, 100, 106, 111, 115, 117*
Okaz, Saudi Arabia *30*
Old Cars Museum, Sharjah *97*
Oman *3, 15, 18, 32, 36, 64, 74, 78, 80, 83, 85, 93, 94, 99, 104, 110, 115*
Omana/Ed Dur *87*
Oryx Hotel, Abu Dhabi *23*
Owen, Roderic *31, 99*
Ozturk, Ali *82*
Pakistan *27, 39, 55, 65, 75, 104, 108, 109*
Palestine/Palestinians *33, 34, 37, 48, 72, 81, 107*
Pearling *Introduction, 2, 53, 55, 64, 65, 71, 75, 87, 88, 92, 96, 100, 117*
Peridotite *15*
Periplus Maris Erythraei *87*
Persian Gulf/Arabian Gulf *Introduction, 4, 17, 25, 42, 51, 54, 58, 71, 75, 77, 80, 83, 87, 113*
Philippines/Filipinas/Filipino *3, 31, 77, 94*
Phillips, Wendell *8*
Phoenix Motors *102*
Pliny *71, 87, 105*
Qaboos bin Said, Sultan of Oman *78, 85, 115*
Qasr al Hosn/palace fort, Abu Dhabi *2, 12, 48, 64*
Qasr al Sarab, Abu Dhabi *117*
Qasr al Zabba/Sheba's Palace, Ras al Khaimah *80*
Qat *81, 105*
Qatar *13, 25, 28, 32, 42, 77, 83, 94, 111*
Qawasim tribal federation *78, 80, 100*
QE2 *60*
Queen Elizabeth the Second *26, 42, 68, 100, 105, 111*
Quran *Introduction, 3, 31, 65, 66, 71, 76, 91, 92, 96, 109, 117*
Ras al Khaimah *Introduction, 25, 34, 37, 43, 54, 71, 78, 80, 86, 87, 94, 96, 97, 100, 113, 117*
Rauschenberg, Robert *112*
Red palm weevil *103*
Regency Hotel, Abu Dhabi *11, 17*
Rilke, Rainer Maria *112*
Rotana Hotel, al Ain *76*
Ruscha, Ed *112*

Rustaq, Oman *115*
Saadiyat Island *5, 34, 65, 73, 81, 112*
Sadat, Anwar *81*
Said bin Taimur, Sultan of Oman *85, 99, 115*
Salim, Namira *27*
San'a *81, 105*
Sands Hotel, Abu Dhabi *11, 17*
Saudi Arabia *3, 13, 18, 28, 30, 32, 34, 36, 42, 43, 46, 47, 55, 56, 64, 67, 74, 77, 81, 83, 87, 91, 94, 97, 104, 110, 116, 117, Epilogue*
Semeih, Abu Dhabi *42*
Serra, Richard *112*
Seven Pillars of Wisdom *33, 74, 97*
Severin, Tim *85*
Shah gas field, Abu Dhabi *117*
Shakespeare *48*
Shanayl, Abu Dhabi *67*
Shankly, Bill *72*
Sharjah *Introduction, 3, 17, 25, 34, 36, 43, 44, 53, 55, 77, 80, 86, 87, 90, 97, 100, 102, 108, 110, 115*
Sharjah Electricity and Water Authority (SEWA) *102*
Sharp, Flight Lieutenant Mike *82*
Sheba/Queen of Sheba *80, 105*
Sheba's Palace, Ras al Khaimah *80*
Sheikh Zayed bin Sultan Al Nahyan Mosque *4, 85, 111*
Sheikh Zayed Bridge, Abu Dhabi *117*
Sheikh Zayed National Museum *111*
Shelley, Percy Bysshe *49*
Shihuh tribe *78*
Shindagha, Dubai *58, 60, 88*
Sila, Abu Dhabi *83*
Sofitel Dubai Jumeirah Beach Hotel *98*
Space tourism *72*
Sri Lanka *3, 75, 109*
St. Andrew's Church, Abu Dhabi *31*
Suetonius *71*
Superstition *92, 96, 104*
Surveillance *62*
Tarafa *30*
Telegraph Island, Musandam *78*

Tesla Motors *97, 102*
Thesiger, Sir Wilfred *3, 36, 42, 99, 104, 115, 117*
Thomas, Bertram *30, 59, 78, 84, 91*
Trucial States *Introduction, 13, 42, 43, 53, 64, 68, 88, 97, 100, 117*
Tumb islands *43, 96*
Twombly, Edwin Parker (Cy) *112*
Umm al-Nar civilisation *85*
Umm al Quwain *Introduction, 25, 53, 86, 87, 113*
United Nations Children's Fund (UNICEF) *94*
United Nations Educational Scientific and Cultural Organisation (UNESCO) *68, 85, 99, 105*
Vasco da Gama *80*
Vitellius, General *71*
Warhol, Andy *112*
Webb, David *82*
Wellsted, Lieutenant James *30*
Wilkinson, Flight Lieutenant Owen *115*
Wool, Christopher *112*
Yas Island *5, 72, 73*
Yas Marina Circuit *5, 70, 72*
Yeats, William Butler *68, 108*
Yemen *33, 75, 81, 104, 105*
Zain Al Aabedin ibn Baqer *97*
Zheng He, Admiral *114*
Ziad Hajeb bin Naheet *46*

Lightning Source UK Ltd.
Milton Keynes UK
UKOW031358230112

185899UK00005B/33/P